THE HEART OF THE COUNTRY

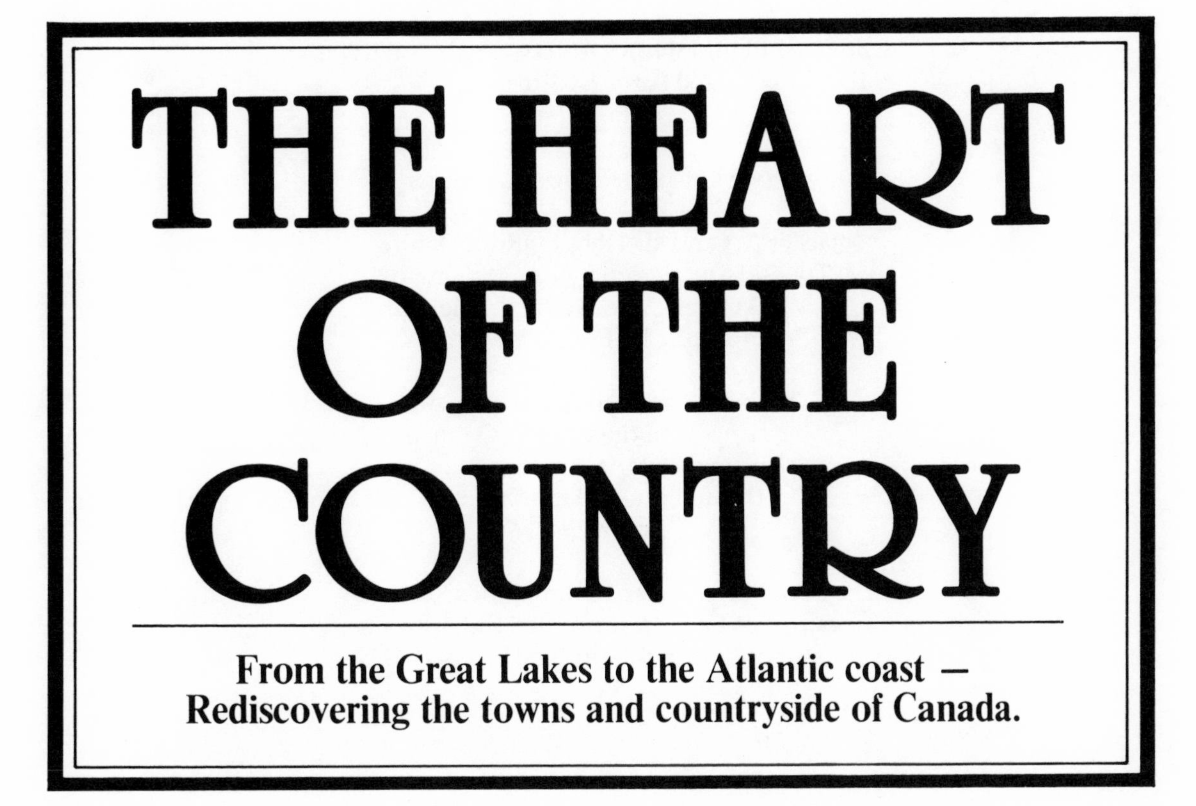

THE HEART OF THE COUNTRY

From the Great Lakes to the Atlantic coast —
Rediscovering the towns and countryside of Canada.

Fredric A. Dahms

DENEAU PUBLISHERS AND COMPANY LTD.
760 Bathurst Street
Toronto Ontario

Jacket Art and sketches by Ruth Dahms
Typeset and design by J.A. McLennan
Jacket design by Kathy Brayley
Photography by Fredric A. Dahms

This book has been published with
the support of the Canada Council
and the Ontario Arts Council
through their Block Grant
programs

The Social Sciences and Humanities Research
Council of Canada supported the research
upon which this volume is based

0-88879-182-8

This book is dedicated to my mother and father

EILEEN *and* ARTHUR

who provided an environment which stimulated

intellectual contemplation and instilled the love of country

reflected in the pages that follow

Table of Contents

Acknowledgements

A book such as this could not have been created without the dedication and assistance of many individuals. Andy McLennan was responsible for the excellent design and layout of the text, for artistic advice, and for drafting the maps. Ann Duffy and Nici Linnell were my enthusiastic and helpful research assistants during much of the preliminary field work and data analysis. The Social Sciences and Humanities Research Council of Canada financially supported the sabbatical during which I completed the writing. I am deeply indebted to them all for their assistance and encouragement.

My wife Ruth has been the principal artist and primary literary editor. She has laboured long and hard to convert my writing from "dry academic" to "interesting popular". She has also painted the watercolour for the cover, and has produced the pencil drawings which adorn the book. During our field work, she was my navigator, sometime driver, artistic advisor and companion. Without her dedication, talent and constant encouragement, this volume would not have been completed. My son John and daughter Tanya joined her in providing support and inspiration when it was needed. Ultimately, the errors and omissions are my own, but much that is interesting and successful is the result of the constant assistance and encouragement that I received from my wife and children.

Fredric A. Dahms
Guelph, Ontario

15 April 1988

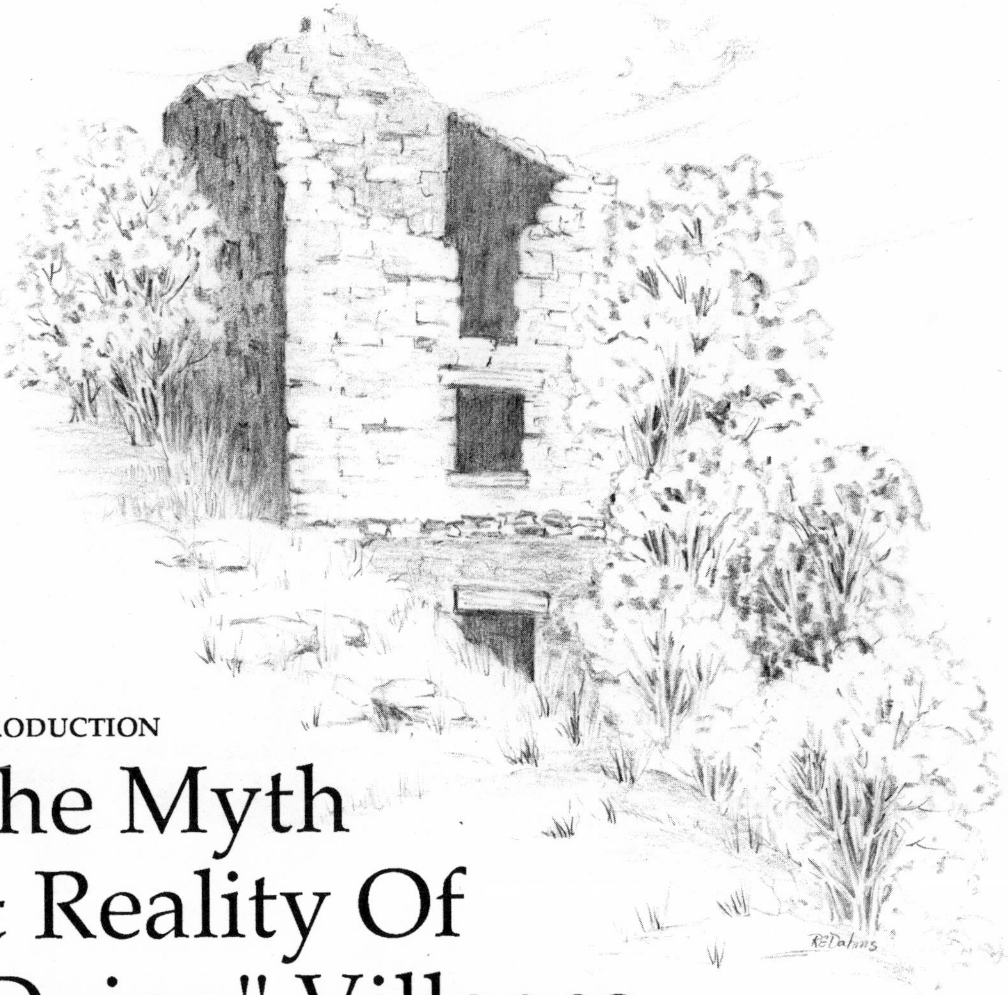

INTRODUCTION

The Myth & Reality Of "Dying" Villages

What has happened to Wroxeter, Duparquet, Oxford Mills and Berwick? Why do their centres seem so different from the main streets of my memories? And what has happened to the land between the towns and villages? Why are there no fences in the fields? Where did all the woodlots go? How do we account for suburban bungalows in the countryside? Who lives in Bayfield, Kensington and Parrsboro? Why has Labelle gained dramatically in population while Millville has lost? How do we explain the rapid growth in business enterprises in Mahone Bay and the decline in Brussels?

The old mill, general store, blacksmith shop and gracious churches often remain to remind us of their historic functions.
This restored blacksmith shop was discovered in Dashwood Ontario.

Why do some towns seem on the verge of death while neighbouring villages are burgeoning? Why are more than one third of the people in Lion's Head over 65? What has happened to revitalize the towns and villages that were supposed to be dying? And why is the government planning to close so many village post offices?

A traveller through rural Ontario, whatever the route and whatever the purpose -- whether hunched gripping the wide wheel of a tractor trailer or intensely manoeuvering the back roads in search of the perfect site for the perfect home -- cannot help but be struck by the profound and widespread changes occurring there. When hiking, trekking, skiing, or jogging through the countryside just for the pure pleasure of the experience, one senses major alterations in the character of rural life. These transformations and metamorphoses are apparent hard by our largest metropolitan centres as well as in the farthest reaches of Ontario. With variations that reflect local history, economy and physiography, the same is true in every other province in Canada.

The heritage of our traditional settlements continues to be preserved in their buildings which have changed little over time despite recent and dramatic modifications of their functions.
The main street of Fergus, Ontario displays the craftsmanship of the Scottish stone masons who constructed the buildings in the 1800s.

How can we explain the major population increases in some of our smallest settlements? Who lives there? Why do they live there and what does the future hold for these communities? Why are former rural concession roads now lined with bungalows, split levels and elaborate residential estates? These questions and others will be explored in the pages to follow.

Why should we be concerned with the transformation of the rural landscape and with the changing functions of towns, especially if we are city dwellers? We are all affected by such changes because everyone depends on evolving food production systems. And anyone who ventures beyond the city observes the changes in our towns and villages.

For some of us, the subject of our rural heritage has become more important as increasing leisure time has enabled us to visit and explore the countryside. This book will answer many of the questions about what we see and experience on our travels. For others, the dream of a retirement along a country road or in a quaint village holds great appeal. For those involved in the process of deciding where and when to migrate to the country, this book will provide useful information by describing and exploring many such places. Some people are simply interested in heritage, in architecture and in the character of our environment. Much that is fascinating lies just beyond our doorstep, in places we will visit together in this book.

The pleasure of travelling through the country is enhanced immeasurably by a knowledge of its roots, by an appreciation of the underlying soils and geology, and by some acquaintance with the plants. Our travels will take us through regions of varied history, differing land uses, distinctive cultures and dissimilar natural environments. Knowledge of a town's origin beside a millstream, its evolution as a trade centre or its transformation into a retirement centre can add depth and excitement to a trip into the countryside. In the pages that follow, we will examine all of these factors, providing examples in numerous settlements from Ontario to Newfoundland. The history and interpretation of settlements and events which may once have seemed commonplace will illuminate our journey. Whether we travel for relaxation, for the practical purpose of making a moving decision, or for the pure intellectual joy of discovery, our travels through the countryside will be enriched and enhanced by greater knowledge.

In the 1970s, those who studied demography told us that a majority of Canadians would live in Montreal, Toronto and Vancouver by the year 2000. But this has not happened. In fact, the most rapid population growth in some areas has been in the very villages, hamlets and towns that were supposed to die. Often it has occurred in areas classified by Statistics Canada as "Rural Non-farm" -- along rural roads and in clusters of houses at crossroads. In Ontario from 1971 to 1981, rural farm population decreased by some 23 percent, while rural non-farm population increased by over 30 percent. This was especially true in places near to major employment centres, in those having heritage architecture or local scenic amenities, and in settlements near lakes, hills and streams.

Elsewhere, many small and medium sized cities like Guelph, Kitchener and Kingston were gaining population while some of our old central cities in metropolitan areas were losing. Smaller, remote settlements like Bancroft have witnessed population increases of almost 40 percent since 1971, and a doubling of the number of local businesses. In contrast, the Toronto Census Metropolitan Area (CMA) gained about 7 percent from 1976 to 1981, while the City of Toronto lost 5.4 percent of its population in the same period. The city of Montreal has been a steady loser since 1971,

while its CMA population increased slightly.

Between 1981 and 1986, the City of Toronto City made small gains as did Vancouver, but the percentage increases did not match those in either smaller places or in the rural non-farm population. In fact, recent research indicates that much of the population increase in the CMAs of our largest cities has occurred in their outlying "rural" constituent areas such as Caledon Township, or in formerly quiet villages like Oak Ridges and Pickering.

This population turnaround has become so widespread in some parts of North America that it has been given a name -- it is now referred to as "demetropolitanization" in much of the academic literature. Until the 1960's, the major direction of migration in North America was from rural or non-metropolitan areas to urban or metropolitan cities. This was primarily the result of economic factors, since the young tended to leave farms and small town homes for jobs in the city while their parents aged in the town, village, or farm where they had lived all their lives. By the 1960's, rural population decline in North America had slowed and by the 1970's, a genuine rural-urban migration turnaround became evident in many areas. For the first time in recent history, many rural areas and small towns were growing from in-migration, while some major cities were losing population. While not always large in absolute numbers, even the addition of fifty or a hundred newcomers can make a profound difference to the character and functions of a village or hamlet of a few hundred souls.

Recently, a growing number have become retirement communities, commuter dormitories or amenity centres, sometimes inhabited by wealthy yuppies who compete with the locals for accommodation. Houses such as this are often available in a town or village for less than half their cost in a city.

After 1971, the elderly comprised a significant proportion of migrants from major urban areas, especially in small towns. Following historic trends, some continued to leave the isolation of their farms to retire in the local market town but, more recently, others abandoned the city for a more intimate, quieter and more attractive residential environment in a village or hamlet. Increasingly, former city dwellers have opted to reside permanently in their annual vacation resorts, or in planned retirement communities.

In Canada and the United States, a growing number of persons over 60 have moved from the cities to planned retirement communities in areas with warm, sunny climates, or to settlements near to ski hills, lakes, golf courses or woods. Those with different tastes and aspirations may have renovated an old mill or schoolhouse and created their own private country retreat. Where planning regulations allow, others have severed a few acres from a farm and built a retirement bungalow. In most cases, these new arrivals to small towns and the countryside have had greater financial resources than the local elderly. Such trends have all contributed to the change and revitalization now apparent in so many of our smallest communities. They have also given birth to new settlements where none existed before. Similar trends have appeared in Europe, the United Kingdom and the United States.

We have discovered that the strongest migration links are often among the smallest settlements. Migrants may be creatures of habit who prefer places similar to those where they used to live. They generally find suitable employment opportunities only in settlements with population totals close to those of the towns from which they have moved. Recent American and European studies have shown that migration for retirement is almost always inspired by the desire to live in a pleasant environment offering amenities and recreational opportunities, or in locales where one has contact with old friends. Canadian studies indicate that these trends are also important here, although there are some major regional variations in the magnitude and intensity of migration and population trends across the country.

Only by examining the past and contemporary character of our towns and villages can we completely appreciate the reasons for the recent changes in historic migration trends, and their im-

plications for the future of our settlement patterns. The history of our villages and hamlets is long and complex. Many have died, but others remain. Some have grown and prospered to become major cities, while others have languished. Recently, a growing number have been rejuvenated to become retirement communities, commuter dormitories, or "amenity" centres, sometimes inhabited by wealthy yuppies who compete with the locals for accommodation.

Contemporary literature also identifies "DINKS" (Double Income; No Kids) among the new residents. Affluent, young professionals who both want to work often compromise on a location in the country or in a small town, equidistant from each job. Others may open a boutique or craft shop while the spouse travels to the nearby city for employment. Sometimes those with one or possibly two children seek the tranquility and quality of life in the country. As we become more affluent and as technology enables us to live and work almost anywhere, such trends will intensify. Alvin Toffler predicted many such occurrences which have now become commonplace.

The heritage of our traditional settlements continues to be preserved in their buildings, which have changed little over time, despite recent and dramatic modifications of function. A former rural service centre may now be a major tourist attraction

A former rural service centre may now be a major tourist attraction or a quiet retirement centre. Most shops and restaurants on the main street of Bayfield, Ontario now cater to tourists and day visitors.

This abandoned home in a hamlet which has long since disappeared from all maps is a symbol of the popular notion of dying villages.

while another languishes, only slightly different from a hundred years ago. Its general store/post office remains the major social centre in the community and is often its only remaining raison d'être. For many of these settlements, the major function is no longer to supply goods and services to farmers nearby, but the old mill, general store, blacksmith shop and gracious churches often remain reminding us of the towns original purpose. New subdivisions may have sprung up, and a few modern stores may have appeared on the main street, but the historic environment tends to endure.

The countryside around our villages and hamlets has also been altered dramatically. Instead of hundred acre plots planted in mixed wheat, pasture and hay, with a few cattle, pigs and chickens, we now find vast fields surrounding gleaming silos and modern agribusiness establishments. The family farm is beginning to disappear. Woodlots have given way to rural residential estates. Gravel roads have been paved and are often lined by the elegant homes of hobby farmers or by the more modest abodes of commuters to the nearest city.

The look of the land is different, as cities invade the country and farming practices evolve. But in the country, as well as in the villages, remnants of the past remain. Converted schools have become residences; former churches are now restaurants; old mills are converted into trendy antique shops. Formerly abandoned farmhouses are now inhabited by young families or by the affluent elderly escaping from the city. Farm ponds have been stocked with trout or converted into swimming holes. Barns have been turned into flea markets or workshops. There is a constant evolution of function but a continuing occupation of old buildings. The built environment of the past carries on into the future.

In the north, the story sometimes differs. There, Indian Reservations may still be found, and vestiges of logging towns remain. In some places the original form of agriculture persists; in others, most traces have vanished. In many areas, tourism has replaced logging as forest fires have devastated this once profitable activity. Elsewhere, only scrub bush, abandoned log farmsteads, derelict mines and barren rock remain to remind us of a northern economy based upon mining and forestry. Numerous former logging or mining communities remain only as a memory or a name on a map, while others have acquired outfitters, restaurants, cabins and motels, catering to fishermen or hunters. Complexity and variety abound, even North of Superior.

"Small is beautiful", "escape to the country", "rural renaissance", "quality of life", and many other reasons are cited to explain recent migration to the countryside and population increases in villages near to major cities. In some areas such explanations suffice, but elsewhere the situation is more complex. Change is the culmination of trends that started years ago. Sometimes change is the result of decisions made by one man; at other times it is the product of chance, technology or fashion. Regardless of its origins, change has occurred and has visibly affected our hamlets, towns and villages.

If we are to understand the contemporary character, complexity and change that characterize today's Ville Marie, Neguac, Iron Bridge or Mahone Bay, we must look to the past. Fortunately, history is visibly preserved in the buildings or found in data and books that we may read. The former mills, general stores, houses, blacksmith shops, carriage factories and hotels generally remain, despite alterations to their architecture or functions. Their history and future prospects are both fascinating. By examining their well-preserved pasts andthrough careful planning and foresight, we can affect their futures.

We will explore their history together -- through visits to the places where it happened, through sketches, through photographs, through discussions with the people and through our reconstruction of long forgotten events. The searcher need only stop, look and talk; or, better yet, walk and explore to discover our legacy and our roots. We will do this together in the pages that follow. Just off the superhighway or beyond the bypass lies our rich historical, cultural and architectural heritage. To discover it yourself, follow the secondary roads and get off the main streets of the towns and villages. Follow Mill Street to see for yourself why a settlement was initially established. Explore the residential areas a block or two off the main street. Here you will discover the essence of our richly historic settlements.

Let us take a trip through the small towns and the woodlands of Eastern Canada. To explore the outports, fishing villages, heritage towns, or just the plain old rural service centres, is to discover the essence of our contemporary character. It is also to catch a glimpse of the future. And let us not forget the land between, where the farms, the landscape and the fabric of the forest have been changed and "improved". There we can still see some of the things that attracted our ancestors, and much that will fascinate our children.

When you leave the major highways, look carefully around, and dare to explore a little. Even fifty kilometers from Toronto, the world is new and fascinating. And that is where we'll start. Then we will head north and west through Ontario, then east through the old seigneurial settlements of Quebec to the lumber towns of New Brunswick, through the fishing and farm villages of Nova Scotia, and, finally, to the tranquil towns from another era on the red soil of Prince Edward Island. At times we will recreate the past and at others we will visit together in contemporary communities enjoying their attractions, seeking out their heritage and speculating on their futures.

We will examine the settlement of the land, trace the evolution of farming, and explore the exciting development of our hamlets, towns and villages. Our journey will take us to a long forgotten past, but it will also suggest what the future may hold for an increasing number of Canadians.

CHAPTER ONE

From The Pioneer Farm To The Village

THE BEGINNINGS

Long before the whites conquered the land, the native peoples had built their settlements, carved their trails and established their harbours. These conformed to the natural contours of the land and were adapted to the climate. What a contrast to the Europeans who followed! They invariably tried to alter the land and challenge the elements. This is the genesis of our settlement history: growing, then declining villages; prospering, then declining economies; struggle and hardship, sometimes leading to success but often to bitter disappointment and failure.

The Maritimes, Ontario and Quebec saw the earliest incursion of the whites, first as explorers, then as fishermen, later as traders in wood, fur and fish and, finally, as settlers.

They penetrated the river valleys, followed the coasts and set up their primitive villages wherever they found an inlet with access to the old country and a way into the interior. As time passed, some places like Halifax, Kingston and Quebec thrived; others, like Louisbourg, were, at one time important strategic centres and then declined; still others such as Kitchener-Waterloo and Markham have grown to recent prosperity. Often those established first or those with an aggressive local entrepreneur such as John Galt in Guelph became the largest in their county and remain so today. But most of these communities do not concern us here. We are interested in the hamlets, towns and villages; places which are no larger than 5000 even now, although they may have been more important in the past.

The true adventure, romance, diversity and complexity of Canadian settlements is most clearly seen in its smallest towns. Here a human scale enables us to discern the past and the future clearly; here we can appreciate individual lifestyles, and local idiosyncrasies and begin to understand why there is now a migration back to our smallest towns and villages.

The roots of "demetropolitanization" and the flight to the country are deep. They go far beyond the needs and wants of the yuppie generation or the commitment of many to "small is beautiful", although these too are ingredients. The lure, the charm, the growth of our smaller settlements lie in both physical and psychological needs. In our towns and villages we encounter a blend of current lifestyles, past history, and aspirations for the future. The realization of dreams for many is no longer found in Toronto or Montreal; they are in Iron Bridge, Cataract, Trout River, Ferme Neuve, Wroxeter, Athens, Mahone Bay or Millville; all unique, all small, all changing, and all with a story to tell about our past and our future.

The Land

Eastern North America offered secluded coves, vast estuaries, deep river harbours and forbidding cliffs. The climate was harsh and unfamiliar -- cold and snowy in the winter, sometimes scorchingly hot in the summer, often interminably rainy between the two. The land was rough and cruel, with precambrian wastes and scrub forests in Newfoundland, dense evergreens in the Maritimes and vast, barely penetrable forests of deciduous or coniferous trees in Ontario and Quebec.

Few open areas except for river terraces or granite uplands beckoned the settler into the interior. The earliest pioneers therefore hugged the coasts, the lake shores, and the banks of the rivers. The task of conquering the land fell to the missionaries, soldiers, administrators and entrepreneurs who led the way and firmly planted the seeds of the settlement system. They were followed later by the pioneers, the farmers, the road builders and the railways. When the permanent settlers arrived, farms were established to produce flour and meat and mills were built to saw the logs and later to grind the grain.

The road which led from exploration to saving souls, through military domination to agriculture and finally to commerce was long and eventful. Fortunately, much of this epic struggle remains in the fabric of our towns and villages, as symbols on outdated maps, or in books, and in the minds of those who chose small-town Canada in which to live.

The Earliest Permanent Settlements

By the 1600s, small groups of French and English were to be found along the coasts of Nova Scotia, while around the Bay of Fundy, Acadians farmed the land. Despite the fact that Quebec had been founded in 1608, and Port Royal in 1606, few people other than natives lived in permanent settlements in this new and hostile country. This was partially the result of British and French policies that were more concerned with establishing mercantile links than with planting permanent settlers on the land. Their major concern was with the exploitation of the forests, the fisheries and the fur trade.

Most of the first permanent places functioned as forts, ports, trading posts or administrative centres. Quebec, St.John's, Annapolis Royal, Kingston and Louisbourg were among them. Only later, as adventurers became businessmen and entrepreneurs saw the value of the wholesale trade, did interior crossroads such as Toronto, and much later, London and Winnipeg become supply depots and eventually, entrepôts. Meanwhile, forests along the coasts were denuded and fisherman came and went, while the British fought the French over the fisheries and trade routes.

Slowly, and then with a quickening pace, settlers followed where the traders and missionaries had led. Many were hoping to escape poverty in the old country by establishing farms. Others such as the Loyalists who settled around Kingston, Bath and Cobourg wanted to avoid the American Revolution, and still others were lured by groups which were selling land to turn a profit. In 1827, John Galt came to Guelph to establish his new settlement for the Canada Company, a group of British investors. It was used as a base from which to sell land from the company's Huron Tract which stretched west to Lake Huron. Galt's schemes were ultimately responsible for the clearing and development of much of the colony between Guelph and Goderich.

A number of years earlier in 1792, Lord Simcoe arrived as Lieutenant-Governor of Upper Canada and shortly thereafter established a plan for the colony. He was determined to move the capital from Newark (Niagara-on-the-Lake), where it was too close to the American threat, to London. Ultimately it was established at York (Toronto) instead. Simcoe settled garrisons of soldiers along the lake and laid out town plots for many new settlements, most of which did not develop until much later. He also made the plans for Yonge Street to run north to Georgian Bay from York, and laid out the route for Dundas Street to the west. His schemes stimulated settlement in Newmarket, Barrie and Penetanguishene along Yonge Street while London, Chatham and Woodstock ultimately derived benefit from the Dundas Street connection.

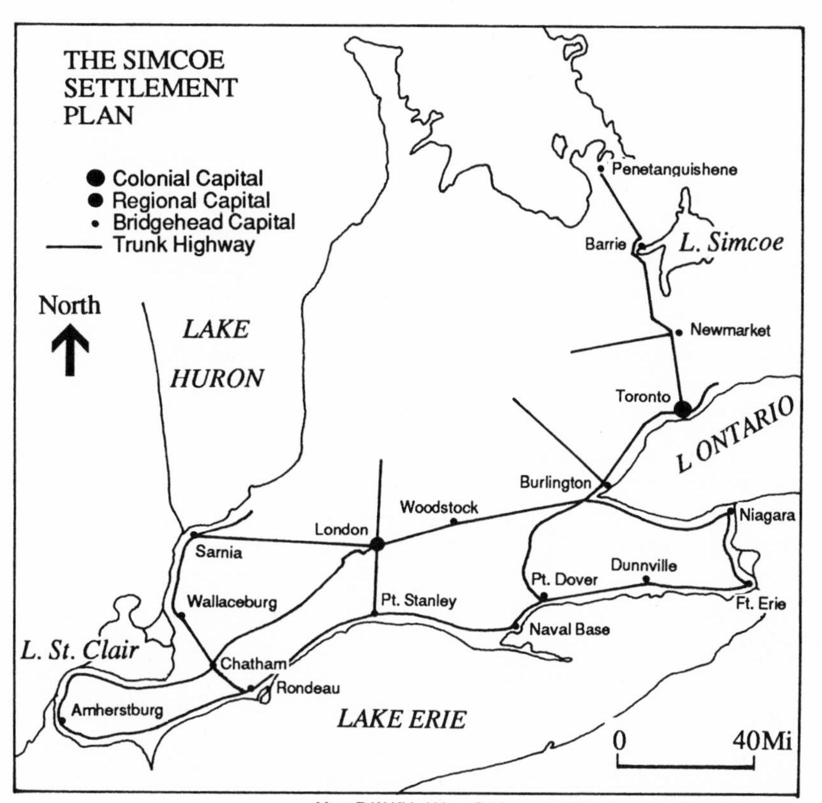

After: D.W.Kirk. Urban Settlements Of Southwestern Ontario In 1850.

Lord Simcoe formulated his plan for roads and military settlements in 1793. It has affected the development of Ontario ever since.

Some of Simcoe's policies delayed the populating of the land. He granted tracts to the church consisting of one seventh of every township, scattered about to provide a good selection of land. He also granted vast areas to friends and to retired officers. Such lots were dispensed in Newark, in York and throughout townships as they were surveyed. By 1824, almost 50 percent of the land granted in Upper Canada had gone to these privileged groups who often held their areas for speculation. The result was that parts of many townships were not settled and many roads were not cleared, since this was the responsibility of the settler. For a number of years this legacy of patronage slowed settlement and made life more difficult for those who obtained land near to the reserves. The effect of Simcoe's early plans, road building and patronage remains in many areas still today.

Some of the early, but ultimately less successful, settlements endure as they were in the beginning, bypassed by the progress that went to more fortunate communities. In these stagnant settlements we can still see the intentions of our ancestors, unspoiled by progress. Until a few years ago, Niagara-on-the-Lake was in this category, along with others such as Port Royal and Bayfield. A number of even smaller places like Alton and Elora changed little until recently. Others such as Shelburne and Bath are still almost living museums.

Where there has been rapid growth, the past has usually been obscured by newer buildings, modern roads and greater economic development. Places like Toronto, Kitchener and Montreal come to mind. It is the backwaters that preserve our heritage, and it is to these that many now wish to return. Unfortunately, the very charm that attracts people to these places bears within it the seeds of its own destruction. One of our challenges now is to preserve the relict features in bypassed places against their newfound attraction for the retired, the footloose, the tourist and the commuter.

SAWMILLS, GRISTMILLS & SETTLEMENTS

When permanent settlers finally became widely established in the late 1700s and 1800s, they faced dense forest, sometimes hostile Indians and a long cold winter. To compound the situation, surveys were often sloppy or incomplete, and the hapless pioneer had to find his land from a blaze mark on a tree. In many areas, roads were non-existent and most travellers followed the rivers and shore. Eventually, after they had discovered and occupied their allotment, settlers were required to clear and maintain half the road allowance across the front of their parcel.

Faced with dense bush, few im-

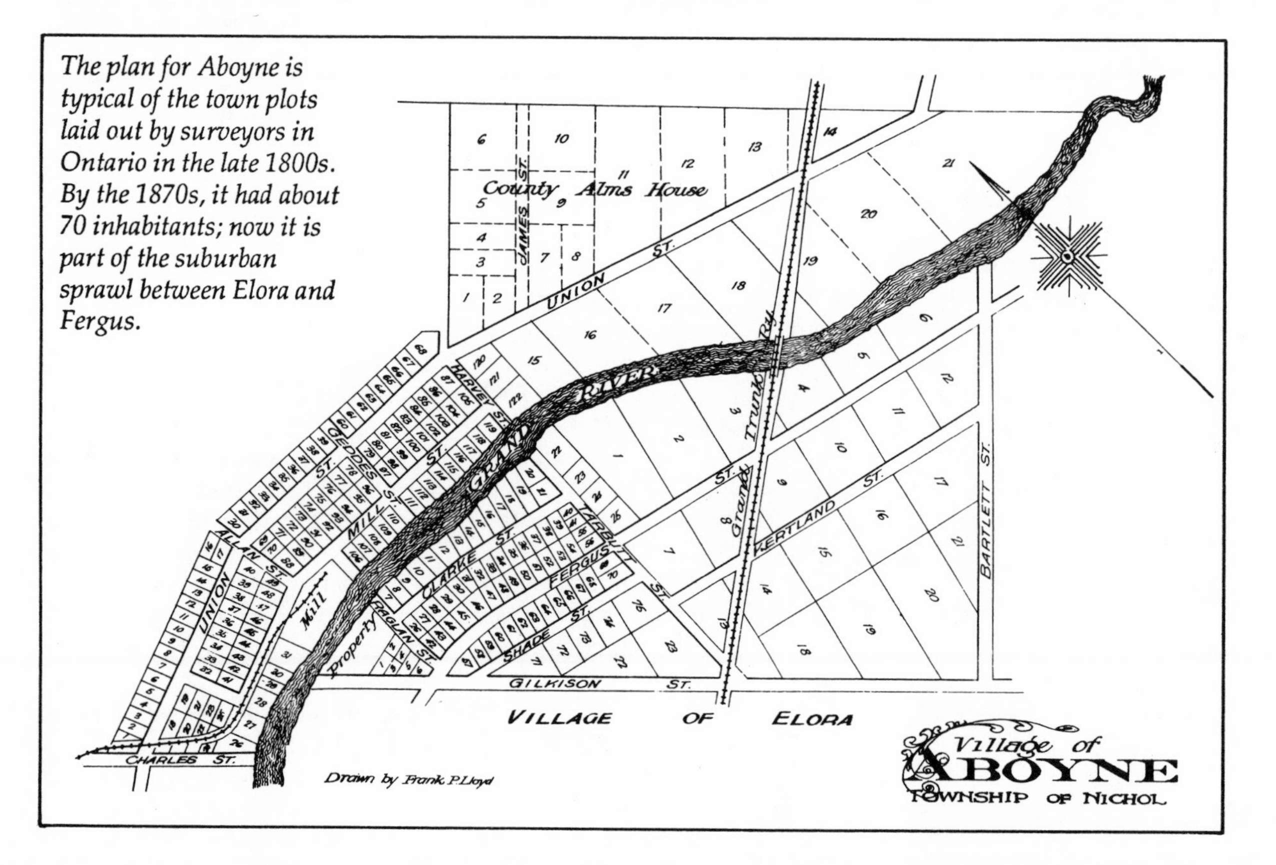

The plan for Aboyne is typical of the town plots laid out by surveyors in Ontario in the late 1800s. By the 1870s, it had about 70 inhabitants; now it is part of the suburban sprawl between Elora and Fergus.

mediate neighbours, mosquitoes, blackflies, swamp, and a hostile climate, the pioneers lived on the edge of starvation. For many, the situation was made worse by their urban origins and sometimes complete inexperience with farming. The nearest settlement where they could obtain supplies might be several days away, and the nearest neighbour some miles through the woods. Mere survival was the primary concern of everyone, and the first winter posed the greatest challenge.

A settler's primary task was to make a small clearing, and then to use the logs to construct a rudimentary one-room shelter. If there was time in that first year, the family would plant a garden among the trees which they had girdled and killed. Next summer would be time enough to cut them and remove the stumps. Progress was slow when few tools were available and there were no neighbours to help with major chores. For many, the first winter was a time of bare subsistence on the few supplies that they had brought from the nearest settlement.

If conditions were appropriate and the settler survived his first winter of cold and loneliness, the second year meant even more clearing, enlarging the cabin, and planting wheat or other crops. Sometimes a more prosperous settler would acquire an ox which could be used both for transportation and as a beast of burden. Even when more people had come to the area, supplies still had to be obtained from the nearest port or from a peddlar. It was usually several years until the local population could sustain a mill or general store. Until then, any surplus wheat had to be carried out, or sent in the winter by sled to the nearest port for grinding or sale.

The majority of the first settlements were established at water power sites where sawmills processed logs into lumber to be used for more sophisticated structures. If the area prospered agriculturally, someone would soon open a grist mill near the same waterfall. Initially, the miller would grind a settler's grain in exchange for a proportion of the crop. The farmer could take his flour to bake bread, and earned credits at the mill for the wheat that was surplus to his requirements. As time went on, a general store would be established to supply salt, sugar and other items not available locally. Eventually the economy of the settlement quickened as a black-

A settler's prime task was to make a small clearing, and then to use the logs to construct a rudimentary one-room shelter.

smith arrived to shoe horses, fabricate tools and make repairs. The inevitable distillery or brewery developed to utilize surplus products from the grist mill and to slake the thirst of the tavern patrons.

Settlements which became successful usually had a fertile hinterland, access to water power and one or more businessman with "vision, enterprise and ambition". Luck played some part, but detailed histories of many rural service centres often hinged upon the actions of one or two key people. Even in locations which were less than ideal, an excellent entrepreneur often made the difference between success and failure. The names of Adam Ferguson and the Beatty Brothers are synonymous with Fergus, just as that of the MacMillans is for Erin. Some villages such as Campbellville still bear the founder's name, while in others it is long forgotten; but how could a settlement succeed without the energy and drive of a merchant, miller, tanner, cooper, wheelwright or tavern keeper?

As population increased, the religious needs were met by churches which became among the most permanent buildings, along with the one-room schoolhouse where education was provided. Then a hotel would be built to accommodate farmers or travellers making an overnight journey. Butcher shops and tanneries were established to provide more specialized agricultural processing. Soon grocery stores, jewelers, dairies, drovers, and even doctors or pharmacists were found in the growing communities. In some, the mills multiplied to meet local needs as did the hotels, churches and taverns. An increasing number of townspeople were accommodated in houses that soon became larger and more ornate as prosperity accompanied the growth of the rural hinterland.

The merchant who obtained the postal franchise became even more prosperous than his rivals, as almost everyone visited his premises once a week to collect mail. By the late 1800s, successful settlements boasted a main street lined with two or three-storey business blocks, a number of substantial churches and even a factory or two down by the river. Of course, settlements that were not quite as strategically located or that lacked entrepreneurial talent often languished or fell into decline.

ROADS, RAILWAYS & RUIN

If a settlement did not acquire a railway by the turn of the century, conventional wisdom suggested that it was "doomed". Consequently, many schemes were developed to lure the "iron horse" to each and every aspiring metropolis. In some cases this did produce prosperity as a settle-

The majority of the first settlements were established at water power sites where sawmills processed logs into lumber. If the area prospered agriculturally, someone would open a gristmill near the same waterfall. This mill in Lakelet, Ontario continues to perform its original role.

ment gained access to larger markets, to coal for its industry and to transportation for its travellers. In others the railway had little, or at best, a transitory effect, as "boom and bust" set in. Contrary to expectations, many places were affected not at all, simply because the railway was of no value to the farmer bringing his crops to town. He still had to trek to the mill with his horse and cart to deliver his grain for processing. He still came to the local settlement to shop, to collect his mail,to visit and to drink at least once a week. Sometimes stagnation set in as a nearby town acquired new industry, and forged ahead of less fortunate rivals as a result of its long-distance import/export connections. But far fewer places actually died of "railroad deprivation" than conventional wisdom would have us believe. Another innovation in transport technology, the motor vehicle, did deal a death blow to many, but not until much later.

Motor Transport, Pubs and Rural Mail Delivery

Railways were the most modern mode of transport until the early part of the twentieth century when the car and truck began to appear in even the most remote locations. Unlike the railway, motor vehicles had a devastating effect on many towns and villages. Not only did they make it possible for anyone to bypass the local service centre for a larger place a few kilometers beyond; but they also facilitated rural mail delivery and catalogue shopping. Why patronize the local general store when the wonders of Eatons and Simpsons were only a postage stamp away? Now that mail was delivered to the end of the lane, the need to visit the local hamlet was considerably diminished and the great decline began. It is this decline that many still remember and cite as the reason for their belief in "dying villages".

To compound matters, prohibition, along with Victorian attitudes, church groups and the WCTU, conspired to close the pubs that had remained a stellar attraction in rural settlements. No more joining the boys for a whiskey or beer after the long day of planting or harvesting. No longer was it legal to quaff the spirits in order to raise one's spirits in the company of friends. Hotels, pubs, taverns and with them hamlets and villages dropped like flies. In some locations, derelict and rotting buildings remain to remind us of this carnage. Elsewhere, the old hotel has been given a new life through restoration and has become a key factor in settlement rejuvenation. Many hotels simply reverted to residences or were torn down. The abandoned hotel remains a symbol of the dying village. And between 1911 and the 1960s, the symbol represented reality as the changes in technology, attitudes and the economy reduced businesses and populations in many of Canada's smallest communities.

Villages like Sunshine, Crieff, Oustic, German Mills or Peepabun are now nothing more than a stand of lilac bushes, or overgrown ruins at the edge of a plowed field, or names on a map. Others retain the ruins of a church or school, a house or two, a ramshackle mill or a vacant hotel. They are the victims of the motor vehicle, rural postal delivery and the power of pressure groups against alcohol. Happily, others have survived, have grown or prospered; and even some of the victims are being rediscovered and resettled.

THE REVOLUTION IN FARMING

Towns, villages and hamlets aren't the only things that have changed during the last hundred years. Farming too has been revolutionized with the advent of mechanization, operations on a larger scale and agribusiness. Such changes have had their impact on the settlements; sometimes positive, but often negative.

We all agree that farms are generally bigger now and that agribusiness has replaced the family farm. This ultimately means fewer people to patronize the local store, church, school and social club. It means less local community spirit and less opportunity for the young as fewer people and more machines are required to operate a diminishing number of larger farms. Tenants and absentee corporate landlords have often replaced the closely knit farm family of the past.

The effect of these changes may be seen in the land and in the villages. Empty storefronts dot the main streets. The windows of

Snake fences built from cedar logs were durable and easy to construct.

upper stories no longer used as residences stare blankly out at the old mill which has fallen into disrepair, or at the railway station which is closed and boarded up. Abandoned farmhouses stand gaunt against the sky, close by the skeletons that have been stripped for barn board by the scavengers from the city. Woodlots have disappeared, streams have been straightened, concreted, and sanitized (only to be polluted by runoff from chemical fertilizers).

Snake fences have gone, and four or five former farms have been combined to produce corn or soybeans in the most efficient fashion. The large, high, gable or gambrel-roofed central Ontario barn has been replaced by long low metal buildings in which hapless cattle, pigs or poultry are fed the fruits of the land. Enormous blue or silver silos pierce the sky like giant fertility symbols to hold the feed derived mechanically from the earth. Between every eight or ten lots we find the ruined foundation of a church or school, or the clump of trees that shaded former congregations.

Here and there new bungalows eat away at the edges of the farms, or snuggle in the few remaining woods along the rear survey lines. No more the even, hundred acre patchwork of mixed farming, houses, barns, silver streams and picturesque hedge rows along the wooden fences. Modern technology has taken over, and it shows.

Ironically, this scenario is most frequently found in areas settled relatively recently. Our ancestors often made errors in their assessment of farmland and originally took up stony or hilly sites that appeared fertile because they were densely forested. When we search for the old rural landscape almost as it was, we need only drive to parts of eastern Ontario, southern Wellington County or the uplands of central Ontario. Here the old log barns share space with their two-bay successors or the more recent central Ontario barns. Here remain the remnants of our earliest villages, but even in these remote or infertile areas, change is coming as the wave of migrants from the cities begins to roll across the land.

CHAPTER TWO

The Land Between The Villages

The land between the villages has changed tremendously during the last hundred years. In many ways, the nucleated settlements have been less susceptible to metamorphosis than their rural hinterlands, simply because of the inertia of fixed capital. When roads, hotels, houses, mills and churches are built, they become permanent features of the landscape, far less subject to alteration or replacement than a farmstead or field pattern.

In the evolution of the countryside, fence lines, barns, houses and cleared land have undergone a continuous evolution, as farming practices have varied over time. First the log lean-to, surrounded by dense bush; later the log house in the centre of several stump filled acres; then the frame house and two-bay barn; finally a brick Victorian house and central Ontario barn commanding over 60 acres of cleared land and 40 or more of bush. In contrast, the original mill or its early replacement may remain in the village, while the main street has changed little since its origins. Houses and hotels built over a hundred years ago may have a different function now, but they are easily recognized by their form. But before we examine the changing functions of villages and hamlets in detail, we must describe the events that have occurred in the countryside around them.

EVOLUTION OF THE LANDSCAPE

The economy of the hinterland is invariably reflected in its service centres, and in agricultural areas, this economy has been imprinted on the land. Evolving farming practices responded to economic conditions in the rest of the country, just as villages responded to the needs of their hinterlands. The natural environment, so briefly described in Chapter One, set the limits and provided the potential for agriculture in eastern Canada. In each area it gave rise to unique patterns of land use and settlements. To these changing mosaics of land use we will now turn our attention.

For the first few years, there was little visual difference between the initial attempts at agriculture anywhere in eastern Canada. Almost everywhere the pioneer was faced with impenetrable bush, a difficult climate and poor transportation. Upon arriving in the new land he would normally stop at the local administrative centre to claim his property and pick up a few supplies. Then came the long trek by water as far as possible, and then overland to his plot of land. In Newfoundland, where permanent occupance was discouraged by the Crown, seasonal settlement occurred along the coast at harbours suitable for fishing. Some agriculture was practised by those who elected to remain through the long harsh winter rather than return to England, but it was meagre and never amounted to much.

In Nova Scotia the earliest settlers, the Acadians, had diked and farmed the wetlands but were expelled by the English by 1755. Only later, with the help of returning Acadians did more recent settlers manage to cultivate these lands for hay and oats. As in Newfoundland, however, most settlements in Nova Scotia were along the coasts and were associated with fishing. Clark's Harbour, Belliveau Cove, Shelburne and Mahone Bay are but a few of the hundreds that remain. With the exception of isolated pockets in favoured areas, and in the Annapolis valley near Berwick and Middleton where apples and other fruit became important, agriculture was not of major significance in Nova Scotia.

The same applied even more to New Brunswick, where forestry was paramount, and farming took a third position to it and the fisheries. There, places like Shediac or St. John come to mind much more readily than Kedgwick or Millville. Given the minor role of sedentary agriculture in these areas, few rural service centres were established but a rich legacy of fishing villages and logging towns remains. As we shall see below, many of them are now undergoing considerable change as they take on new roles as retirement centres, tourist destinations and commuter dormitories.

Prince Edward Island offered far more agricultural potential than its Maritime neighbours, with its relatively fertile, gently sloping lands providing a contrast to their thin soils and exposed bedrock. Unfortunately, land surveys in P.E.I. were not completed to the original farm level when most settlers arrived, making the establishment of towns and villages somewhat haphazard. In the other three provinces, most surveys were undertaken after settlement and no evaluation of land for agriculture had taken place. Settlers were often widely scattered, roads had to be long and sinuous, and few close-knit communities developed. Except in Prince Edward Island, neither commercial agriculture nor rural service centres were important in the Maritimes.

In Quebec, the seigneurial system and long lot surveys left an indelible impression on the land that is still in evidence. In the St. Lawrence lowland where agriculture was viable, farms were laid out along the river, with the houses closest to the water which was the main artery of transportation. They may now be seen in an almost continuous line, following the river or, if in the second "rang"

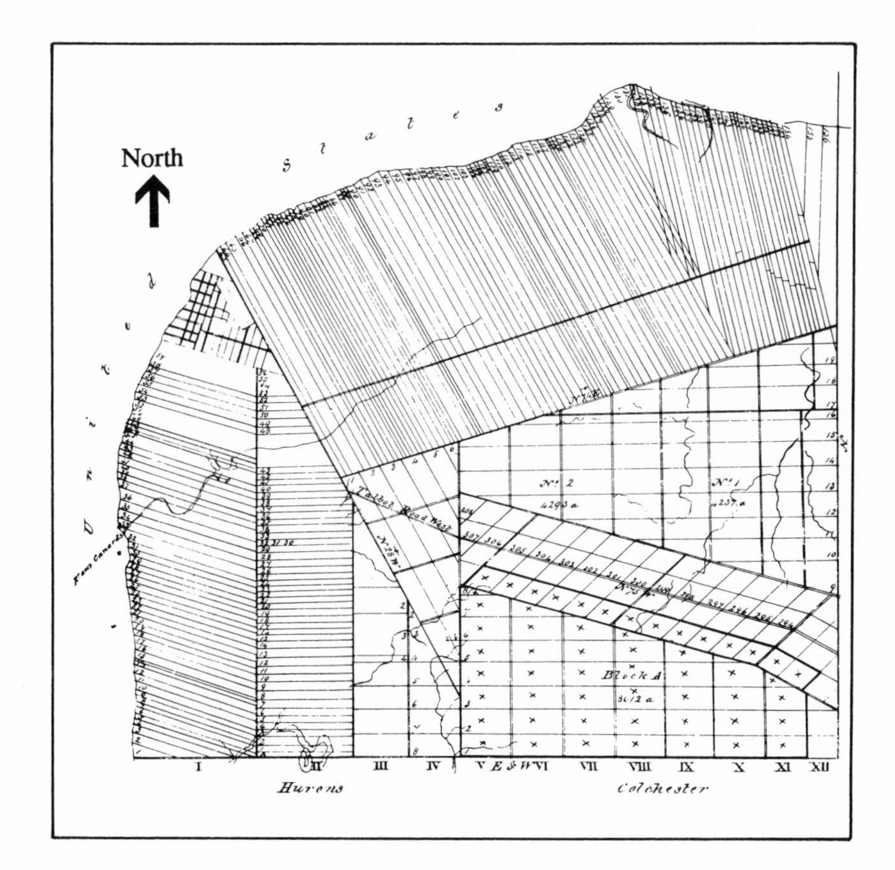

The vestiges of early French surveys still remain around Windsor, Amherstburg and La Salle. This example clearly illustrates long lots and rangs.

of settlement, following the road. Because everyone wanted access to the river, the lots were about ten time as long as wide, giving everyone water frontage as well as different soil types away from the river. The result was a linear pattern, with houses a few hundred yards apart, and little early settlement in towns and villages as we know them in Ontario.

Only in the extreme south–west of Ontario and in parts of the Ottawa Valley, which were settled originally by the French, can we find linear settlement patterns similar to the Quebec "rangs". The vestiges of such early French surveys still remain around Windsor, Amherstburg, and La Salle at one end of the province, and near Hawkesbury at the other. Otherwise, Ontario's survey system is very different from that found in Quebec. The resultant settlement pattern is also quite dissimilar, with dam sites or crossroads becoming the foci of most early villages in Ontario.

In Quebec, as time passed, service centres and resource towns did develop, either around the house and mill of a seigneur, or more commonly, near the parish church. This pattern was slow to evolve, partially because many of the first Quebec settlers spent much of their time in the fur trade, using their land only as a convenient base. This, along with inferior climate or soil in many areas, slowed the development of compact rural service centres. Even now, the impression while driving along the St. Lawrence is one of an almost continuous roadside village made up of houses, barns, and a large church every twenty kilometres or so. Of course, Quebec does have numerous mining towns and others based primarily on forestry, especially in the north. In all three settlement types, the church, usually large and having one to four spires, dominates.

Today, rural Quebec appears rustic to the Ontarionn because of its own indigenous architecture. In the oldest areas, large stone farmhouses with thick walls and steep roofs of wood or thatching may occasionally still be found. More recent structures are often two stories high, with dormers on the second floor, and a porch across the front. Others are one storey and boast the gracefully curving roof line that has become the distinguishing feature of many Quebecois houses. The combination of field patterns, house types and magnificent churches leaves no doubt that the traveller is in a part of Canada with a distinctive culture and heritage.

The landscape and character of

Ontario are also distinctive. We will explore its evolving countryside in some detail as we attempt to appreciate the subtleties of its changing character. Almost everything discussed here remains somewhere on the land today, providing a unique opportunity to explore our agricultural heritage and discover firsthand how it is related to our village legacy. An appreciation of the relationships among farming practices, farm buildings and the look of the land may turn a casual journey out of the city into an exciting adventure.

Three major physical features comprise the Ontario landscape. In the area roughly north of Barrie, the massive, glaciated granite surface of the Precambrian shield dominates and provides the topography we all associate with "cottage country". It is rough, pock–marked with thousands of lakes carved by the glaciers, and lined by the striations left when over-ridden by boulder–impregnated ice. Needless to say, little successful farming was established here, despite the efforts of the government and the colonization roads. Mining, forestry and tourism have traditionally dominated in this vast and sparsely settled region of Ontario.

South of the shield, the only major physical feature is the edge of the Niagara Escarpment, which winds its way from Queenston to Tobermory and on to Manitoulin Island. In places such as Orangeville or Flesherton, it is almost obliterated by the deep glacial deposits that cover most of southern Ontario. Elsewhere, as at Lion's Head or Milton it towers over the countryside, its magnificence dominating the local topography. To the east, below the scarp face, much of Ontario's urban population lives upon gently rolling plains that were once at the bottom of glacial Lake Iroquois, the predecessor to Lake Ontario.

During the Wisconsin glacial period that ended some 15,000 years ago, much of southern Ontario was either covered by water, ponded at the edge of vast masses of receding ice, or was under the ice itself. The bedrocks of granite, limestone, sandstone and shale were abraded, ground, pulverized and sorted, finally to be-

The glaciers that affected Ontario advanced in all directions from the Great Lakes Basins, gouging and scraping the depressions to their present depth. This is the situation at the stage of Glacial Lake Whittlesey at the end of the Wisconsin Glaciation, approximately 12,800 years ago.

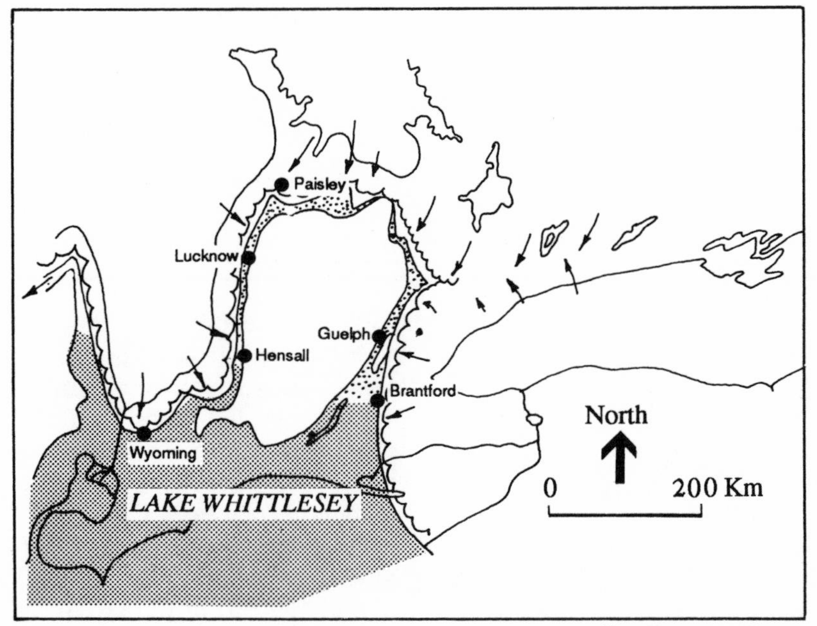

After: Chapman and Putnam.

come the ingredients of the glacial deposits now covering most of southern Ontario. The surface landscape was carved, deposited and moulded by towering, blue-white mountains of ice, sometimes a mile high. With changes in temperature and precipitation, they advanced and receded, sometimes scraping bare slashes along protruding rocks as on the Bruce Peninsula; at others they dumped enormous piles of mixed sand, silt, clay and rock called till, which is found over most of the province south of the precambrian shield.

Around the edges of the ice, tumbled rocky hills known as moraines were formed when milky water loaded with silt mingled with sand and boulders at the edge of the cold, relentless mass. Water, rock and till were left after the glacial masses receded, outlining their former position with a ring of tumbled, lake–studded hills. Where streams of water ran under the glacier, they filled with sand, boulders and silt, emerging finally as long sinuous ridges called eskers. Some remain today, but many have been destroyed by urban development, or mined for their sand and gravel.

The glaciers that affected Ontario advanced in all directions from the Great Lakes Basins, gouging and scraping the depressions to their present depth. Where water stood for long periods at the margins of the ice, silts, sand and clay were deposited to form gentle plains along the Erie shore, from London to Windsor and around Burlington. The Scarborough Bluffs and Davenport Hill are both remnants of the shore of glacial Lake Iroquois which once covered the site of Toronto. The legacy of the Wisconsin glaciation has left relatively fertile land in much of southern Ontario which remains dotted with cigar shaped hills called drumlins. They were formed when the moving ice over-rode and streamlined the till beneath its base. The best examples are near Peterborough and Guelph. The major moraines generally parallel the shores of lakes Huron and Ontario, although numerous examples exist across the province. Elsewhere, sand plains, relatively level areas of glacial till and numerous lakes and swamps provide variety in topography, soil types, vegetation, and potential for farming.

Unlike the Maritimes, most of Ontario was surveyed before the settlers were granted their land. In typically bureaucratic fashion, most of the province was divided into a neat geometric pattern that had little do with the topography. The first surveys began along the St. Lawrence and followed the lakes. Base lines were laid out roughly parallel to the lake or river, and townships were surveyed inland from the base line. Depending on the survey method used, lots for individual settlers were one or two hundred acres, forcing a dispersed settlement pattern. Farm lots were laid out along concession roads which generally trended east-west, and side roads were blazed between every fifth or sixth lot in a north-south direction. Despite the fact that a number of different survey methods were used, and that base lines deviated from an east-west orientation as surveys proceeded inland, the net result was a geometric landscape of roads intersecting at right angles, dispersed farmsteads of more or less uniform size, and a need for service centres to provide a focal point for trade and commerce. In anticipation of this need, town plots were laid out in most original townships, but more often than not, failed to become the local settlement site. Soon the practice of surveying townsites in every township was abandoned, and old maps often provide the only evidence of their intended existence.

The distinctive grid of Ontario concession line roads and sideroads was a direct result of the survey system, just as the evenly spaced pattern of towns and villages in the late 1800s was also its legacy. By then it seemed that every other crossroads had a hotel, tavern, general store or blacksmith shop. In many areas, human error compounded by the impact of swamp, rain, heat, cold, black fly and mosquito left its mark in sharp road angles where two surveyors coming from different directions didn't quite meet. Elsewhere, roads charge recklessly up the steep sides of hills or escarpments, or plunge into a lake because the line of survey crossed at that location. Where counties or townships meet, strange angles and peculiar road patterns break the consistent geometric grid. Despite these aberrations, Ontario's original survey left a lasting impression on the landscape, producing a checkerboard of farms of roughly equal size, with a house and barn near the front, and a strip of bush along the backs of lots that were never cleared.

A section of the original survey in Wellington County, Ontario.

The First Farmsteads

Settlement of southern Ontario began in earnest after 1800 when Americans came from the south to take advantage of Crown Land being offered for sixpence an acre plus survey costs and an oath of allegiance. The first arrivals came in from the south or east and generally followed the St. Lawrence and the Great Lakes. As time went on, both the surveys and the settlers penetrated the land to the north and west. A key to interpreting the settlement history and architecture of Ontario is to remember that the earliest settlements and buildings were found near the lakes, and that the progression was generally from the east to the north and west. House types built in Kingston in the 1850s would not be seen in the Bruce Peninsula until the 1880s. The same is true of barn types and agricultural practices.

The first settlers came to an administrative centre such as Newark (Niagara on the Lake), York, or Guelph and determined the location of their land. Then began the arduous journey along lake and river and then overland to their plot. In the early years there were few roads, and those that existed were nothing more than rough trails between the trees. Settlers preferred the relatively open, oak parklands along Lake Erie and avoided swamps or moraine. Since clearing was the major task confronting the settler, the lightly forested oak-hickory woods were preferred to the wetter sites supporting beech, maple and basswood.

At first the evaluation of land was somewhat haphazard, because settlers had little experience with North American vegetation. Often they would choose a heavily forested area, only later to discover that the trees had covered thin acidic soil that would not sustain agriculture. But as time went on, settlers' guides provided more useful information on site selection, and the settlers made more appropriate choices. Those from the United States had experienced similar conditions before and generally fared considerably better than those from the British Isles.

Aside from the fertility of the soil and the ease of clearing, the major factor in site selection was access to a settlement with a mill, or at least proximity to a road. Not only was loneliness a major hazard of the early forest, but settlers who wished to advance beyond the subsistence level had to have a market for their produce. For many years the main commercial crop was wheat which had to be transported to mill and market.

In his first year, a settler would clear a small area by girdling the trees, and plant a few vegetables and possibly some wheat in the clearing. His animals, which might be a pig or two and an ox, were allowed to forage for themselves in the woods. Amid the gloom of enormous trees and far from any neighbours, the pioneer would spend most of his waking hours girdling trees and clearing underbrush. His first accommodation was a one or two room cabin built of logs cut from his clearing. Later, when he had cleared more land and possibly some of the road allowance across his property, a second home, generally of squared timbers and in simple Georgian style was built. This edifice might have one–and–a–half stories, a fireplace and an earth cellar beneath. In eastern or northern Ontario, on the Bruce Peninsula and in parts of southern Ontario that were settled early and abandoned, remnants of this era remain in both houses and barns.

The barn was the chief processing point for the agricultural economy, and soon came to dominate the rural landscape. The first permanent barn was called a two-bay barn, and facilitated wheat monoculture which was the normal agricultural practice. This barn stood about 20 by 10 metres and had double doors on both long sides. On one side of the doors a bin for wheat was found, and on the other, a storage area and possibly a small stable. The wheat was threshed by opening the doors, flailing it and allowing the wind to blow the chaff away. In this system of agriculture, one field was planted in vegetables for the family, one was sewn down to wheat and another was allowed to lie fallow. The scene was untidy, with logs lying as fences at the side of cleared fields, stumps everywhere, cattle, sheep and hogs wandering in the forest, and the ever present edge of the woods awaiting clearance looming over the scene.

The successful farmer utilized all the products of his land. Logs could be sold, ashes became potash, and bark could be used for tanning. If he had cleared enough land, surplus wheat became available in the second year, and it was required by new settlers who needed food for their first year. This very rapid emergence of commercial agriculture was contingent upon one's ability to transport grain to a location where it could be milled and traded. Across Ontario, at almost

The first permanent barn was called a two bay barn, and facilitated wheat monoculture which was the normal agricultural practice. The wheat was threshed by opening the doors, flailing it and allowing the wind to blow the chaff away.

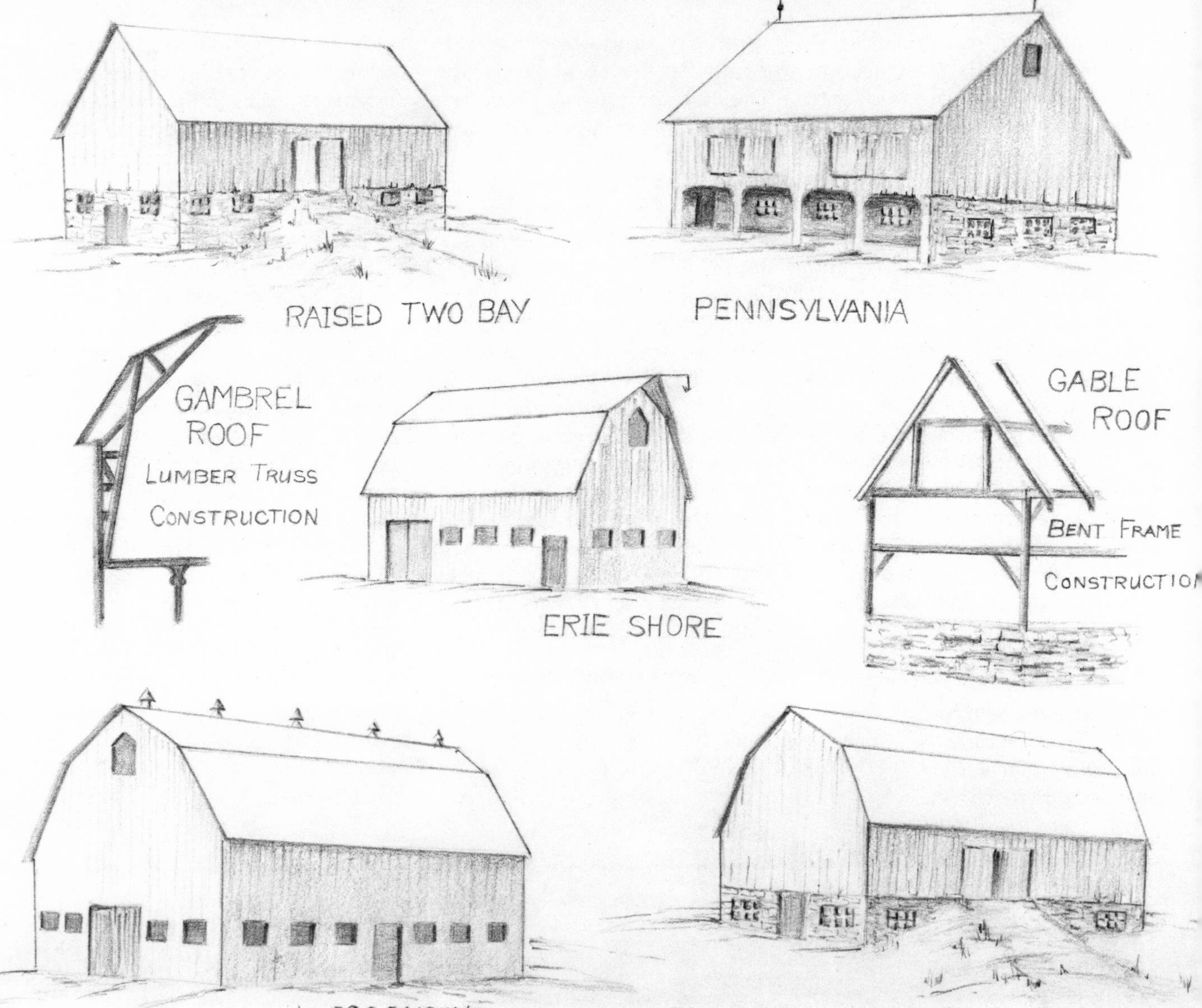

every viable water power site, mills were established to saw lumber and to grind the grain. These embryo rural service centres were established to meet the needs created by a growing commercial agricultural economy.

When more settlers arrived and the economy quickened, farmers moved into the next phase of agricultural production. Better roads and growing populations stimulated the demand for meat and dairy products, and farm buildings were modified or replaced to accommodate these needs. Sometimes the old two–bay barn was raised onto a foundation to create a stable beneath and provide space for the storage of hay above. By the 1850s, in prosperous areas, the two–bay barn was often replaced by the much larger central Ontario barn with a gable roof. This building had a large loft above for the storage of hay, a drive floor and grain bins on the main level for the storage of equipment and crops, and stables beneath. A version called the bank barn was built into the side of a hill to allow direct access to either the stable or drive floor. Later versions were built with lumber trusses rather than timber bents, and are distinguished by their gambrel roof. They provided considerably more storage in the loft and became common in the 1880s.

In Waterloo County and in parts of Bruce and Grey, the German settlers from Pennsylvania built a substantial barn with an overhang or forebay over the stable, called the Pennsylvania Barn. It had Dutch doors at the end of each row of stalls which were arranged at right angles to the long side of the barn. Unlike the two-bay barn, the Pennsylvania barn was large and flexible, and generally was not replaced. In prosperous Mennonite areas of Waterloo County, the Pennsylvania barn is now surrounded by silos and cattle sheds, and is sometimes unrecognizable, despite its persistence.

In areas where dairy farming became commonplace, the Wisconsin barn, which was promoted for scientific agriculture by the Ontario Agricultural College, replaced the two-bay barn by the turn of the century. It is a large lumber frame barn with many windows and a gambrel roof lined with ventilators. It has milking parlours on the main floor and large storage areas above. Where agribusiness has become important, the Wisconsin barn is often surrounded by large blue or silver silos.

When travelling in rural Ontario, one finds the most modern barns in prosperous areas that have undergone rapid change. Two-bay barns and early predecessors are often discovered in economically marginal areas, or in those that were settled early and subsequently bypassed because the settlers had misjudged their fertility. Everywhere, the barn faithfully mirrors the past and present agricultural economy of the area. Dairying is important where Wisconsin barns predominate, beef cattle where the Pennsylvania barn is surrounded by silos and long low metal sheds, and specialty crops such as apples are produced where the small, distinctive Erie Shore barn with its overhanging roof is found. Of course, agribusiness has changed the scene in some areas as two-storey poultry barns stretch along the ground or where hogs are found in similar structures surrounded by circular metal feed storage containers. Nevertheless, in most areas, the early legacy may be found and used to glimpse the past.

Farm houses evolved along with the barns. After the first rude shelter, a second Georgian style edifice was built of logs, and then a more ornate Victorian home of brick or batten board often became the final replacement. These now stand as Ontario vernacular architecture with their ornate fretwork and steep roof lines. In Bruce County they are built of fieldstone; elsewhere of red or yellow brick. Where limestone was abundant, many are of that material. Numerous regional variations exist, with differences in local styles or materials. Some believe that the farmhouse was a major symbol of success and prosperity in nineteenth century Ontario. More recent farmhouses are often little different from the suburban bungalow in the city or town.

The Rise of Agribusiness

The family farm has been the mainstay of the rural economy of Ontario for a hundred years, but is being threatened or replaced by agriculture that relies on corporate methods and large-scale production. Instead of planting a vegetable garden, growing some wheat to sell and some hay and corn to feed to animals and producing some cream for profit, the new farmer plants one crop exclusively in an environment that some feel is more akin to industry than to agriculture. This specialization is made possible by mechanization and land holdings of five hundred or more acres. Now huge machines chemically fertilize the land and apply weed killer, while others plow vast swaths and plant the seed over hundreds of acres. Harvesting is accomplished with self-propelled combines, corn harvesters or soya bean pickers.

The enormous investment in equipment means that extensive acreages must be cultivated to make the business profitable, and that fences must disappear to accommodate the machinery. It also means that one person can accomplish the work that occupied a whole farm family ten years ago.

As a result of the new farming technology, a way of life and a set of familiar buildings have been replaced. Now hundreds of acres may be devoted solely to the production of corn which is stored and fed to cattle which never leave their feedlot. Elsewhere, acres of soya beans, rapeseed or sunflowers have replaced the traditional mixture of wheat, oats and hay. Along with these changes has come the demise of the family farm. Corporations have bought several

Evergreen Farm, which belonged to the author's great grandfather has now been absorbed by residential development at the edge of Waterloo, Ontario. It was a typical prosperous mixed farm of the nineteenth century.

EVERGREEN FARM, RESIDE

one–hundred–acre operations, or successful farmers have taken over their neighbours' land to achieve economy of scale. The result has been a decline in rural farm populations and the disappearance or obliteration of traditional farm buildings.

In the richest agricultural areas in southern Ontario, farmhouses stand empty and abandoned while barns are stripped of boards for suburban recreation rooms. In their place we find more and more modern bungalows or split-level houses, and an increasing number of long, low metal buildings where barns once stood. Gleaming, round, metal, feed–storage containers surround the new factory farm, and enormous seed and feed–cleaning plants dot the countryside. And now the fences are gone, creating a landscape in Ontario that is sometimes more reminiscent of the Prairies than of its own agricultural heritage. The change has been profound, and the change is clearly visible on the land. Other changes, also symptomatic of the new reality, may now be observed as well.

The Rural Non-Farmers

During the last ten years, the number of farmers has dropped dramatically as new methods and urban pressures have taken their toll. In Ontario the Census of Canada classified 81.2 percent of the population as urban and 18.8 percent as rural in 1976. These figures are somewhat misleading, because 82 percent of those classified as rural were in fact rural non-farm dwellers: people living

R.M.QUICKFALL Esq., TOWNSHIP & CO. OF WATERLOO.

in unincorporated settlements of over 50, along with those in the open country who did not qualify as farmers. Put another way, in 1976, only 3.4 percent of Ontario's residents were classified as farmers.

By 1981, the last year for which detailed census data are available, the situation had changed even more. In all of Ontario, 82 percent were urban, 18 percent rural and only 3.2 percent farmers. The trend toward "demetropolitanization" (return migration to smaller settlements and rural areas) had begun in earnest, and is now widely recognized in the literature of North America and Europe. In Canada, the fastest growing settlements between 1971 and 1981 were those in the 50,000 to several hundred thousand range, and some of the smallest towns and villages. Places classified as unincorporated settlements of over 25 and rural non-farm populations also increased dramatically in many areas. Major metropolitan centres such as Toronto, Vancouver and Montreal did not grow as expected, and their old central areas actually declined in population. For example, while the Toronto Census Metropolitan Area increased from 2,803,101 to 2,988,947 between 1976 and 1981, the city of Toronto declined by 5.4 percent from 633,318 to 599,217.

Although aggregate statistics tell part of the story, they tell it bloodlessly, and without much impact upon the reader's imagination. Of much greater interest is the detailed pattern of the move back to small towns and the countryside. Who has moved? Where have they gone? Where have they come from and why did they reverse what seemed to be the inexorable trend towards the cities? What physical, social and economic impact have they had upon the countryside and how are they viewed by their new rural neighbours?

A large number of these modern-day immigrants have moved into rural towns and villages across Ontario, but many have also located in the open countryside. Now that the population of non-farmers in rural areas is almost five times that of farmers, the look of the land has been altered to reflect that fact. Within twenty miles of our big cities, especially where there is rolling or scenic land, the wealthy have built their estates. Here we find majestic mansions on ten or twenty acres, complete with riding stables, swimming pools, tennis courts and a three car garage. The owners are often affluent executives from the city who crave the solitude of the country, and can afford both the time and the money to commute daily to their workplace.

On land not quite so favourably endowed, sometimes at the edge of an existing village or hamlet, we find the subdivisions of two storey houses, bungalows and split level homes on lots up to several acres. Again, the inhabitants are often commuters who seek the quality of life and relaxed living that the country is supposed to bring. Neat, manicured lawns with sweeping driveways and landscaped streets sometimes provide a jarring contrast to the hog farm or beef feedlot only a few hundred yards away. At times the conflict is more than visual, as former city dwellers object to the noise and smells of their rural neighbours.

Contrary to conventional wisdom, commuters to the city do not constitute the majority of rural non-farm dwellers. The phenomenon of country living has spread well beyond the one–hour commuting time that some will spend to drive to the city. Non-farm people are now found in the countryside in relatively isolated areas far from the cities. Here they live, work and play, seldom having contact with metropolitan areas. The countryside reflects this new life style: here an former schoolhouse converted to a residence complete with fireplace and satellite dish; there a cottage that has been insulated and equipped with year-round facilities; elsewhere a hobby farm beside an artificial lake stocked with trout; down the road a rustic log cabin built to R40 insulation standards and boasting solar heating. All these are the physical manifestations of a major shift away from urban life-styles in Ontario.

Sometimes the rural non-farmers are less glamorous than those living in the homes described above. We still find the part-time farmer who holds a job at the local feed mill and keeps a few pigs or chickens to supplement his income. Another may drive a truck for the county and lease a hundred acres to run some sheep. Increasingly we find retirement villages tucked into the woods at the edge of productive farmland. These are often composed of prefabricated or mobile homes and boast a resident nurse and recreation hall. The senior inhabitants have sold their houses in the town or city to retire beside a lake or woods, where taxes are low and they are not disturbed by children or teen-age hooligans. Sometimes the elderly have con-

Gleaming round metal feed storage containers surround the new factory farm. This example is in Huron County.

verted an abandoned farm house, just as the yuppies have taken over some of the best examples of stone and brick farmhouses made redundant by factory farming.

In many of our best agricultural areas, a new bungalow may be found along the concession road a few hundred yards from the farmstead. Here the son has built on ten acres severed from his father's land, or the elderly parents have retired and leased farm and house to a younger person. Along the side roads, especially if they lead towards an urban area, we find everything from cottage-like chalets to substantial houses nestled into the woodlots that have been left along the "back forty". Many have retained the woodland atmosphere (complete with mosquitoes and black flies) and attempted to integrate their houses into the rustic settings. Unfortunately, these and the other non–farm residents of rural areas often demand improved roads, schools and local services; all of which increase local taxes and sometimes lead to conflicts with farm communities.

The overall impact of these non-farm inhabitants upon our rural areas varies widely. North of Toronto it is enormous, as one residential estate follows another and the rural roads are now mostly paved. Driving through these areas is reminiscent of a trip through Connecticut or Westchester County. Farther afield, along the escarpment or moraines, summer residences or converted chalets often outnumber farm houses, many of which were abandoned when the poverty of the soil became apparent. In the best agricultural areas where zoning and severance regulations are strict, the major impact is in the woodlots or on farms where a second house was built before the concern for preserving agricultural land arose. Now the non-farm residential development is encouraged to locate in or adjacent to hamlets or villages where urban type services can be provided. Farther afield, along the Bruce Peninsula, beside the lake or near to ski slopes, the process continues as cottages are converted to year round use and new homes are built to be used for winter and summer recreation or retirement.

THE NEW RURAL LANDSCAPE

A major transformation has overtaken the countryside of Ontario. We may still find the traditional farmstead with its central Ontario barn, wooden silo, abandoned windmill, brick Victorian farm house, lumber driving shed and hundred acres of mixed grain, pasture and bush. In many areas, the rail snake fences lined with raspberry bushes and wild apple trees continue to surround farms that have existed unchanged for a hundred years. But these are becoming less common as the new replaces the old, the business of farming replaces the family, the self-propelled harvester replaces the tractor and combine. This is especially true within a hundred kilometers of the major cities, where both commuters and the new rural dwellers vie with agribusiness for our rural land. Farther afield, in rugged or scenic areas, and near the lakes, farmers compete with those desiring a rural amenity area as their place of residence. Remnants of the old ways remain, especially on patches of level and fertile soil that are not appealing to the new non-farmers. Happily enough, the competition between agriculture is less severe in scenic areas simply because the very ruggedness that once discouraged agriculture now attracts those desiring a rustic lifestyle.

If present trends continue, we will observe fewer and fewer, but considerably larger farms in the future. Our rural countryside will become even more like that of New England where wealthy ex-urbanites wield more economic power and political influence than the former "locals". More of our old mills and blacksmith shops in the country will become antique shops or artists' studios, and additional surplus farm houses will accommodate those who need only a computer terminal and a modem to carry out their business. Meanwhile, the population will age, as the young leave for the city and their parents grow older and are joined by others from city or town who crave the quiet of the country.

For some this scenario presents economic opportunity. Owners of marginal farm land may find their property in demand for cottages, for ski chalets or for retirement residences. For others it presents a challenge, as they see a traditional way of life disappearing from rural Ontario and agriculture being spoiled by newcomers' demands for silence, better roads and odourless air.

Politicians and planners are confronted with conflicting demands and the need to reconcile different agendas for the countryside. Some have suggested that the pressure will decrease when the price of petroleum rises even more, but this has not yet been the case in North America. Even in Europe where fuel is much more expensive, the trend to move to the country has not diminished.

This then is the historical background and context for our journey into the villages and hamlets of eastern Canada. The size and function of these settlements may vary from one region to another, but their initial functions were similar and their evolution is often parallel. The symbiotic relationship between forest and lumber town, mineral and mining town, agriculture and market town has endured, and to a large extent, the nucleated settlements continue to reflect their hinterlands in form and function. Like the countryside however, they too have changed through time, sometimes in response to stimuli from the country, sometimes as a result of the return of population to the village. "Small is beautiful", "heritage architecture", "the clean air", and inexpensive housing have attracted people to towns and villages, just as they have been attracted to the countryside. The infinite variety of towns, villages and hamlets will be the subject of the following pages. On the road between these settlements, we will also observe the topography, farming practices, geology, flora and fauna, for they too are distinctive and have a story to tell.

The overall impact of these non-farm inhabitants... is enormous... one residential estate follows another and the rural roads are now mostly paved.

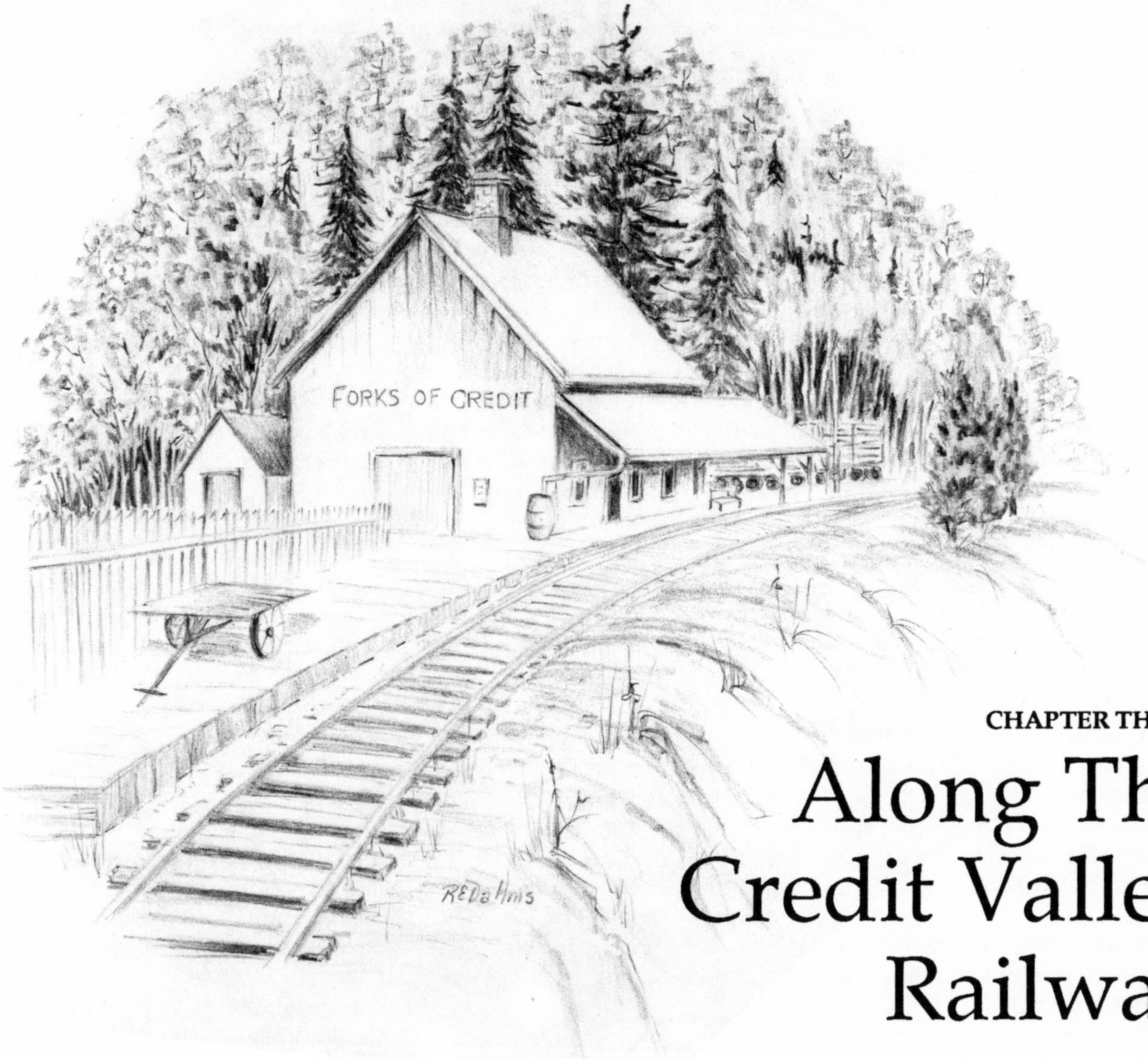

CHAPTER THREE

Along The Credit Valley Railway

The sites of ports, forts, mill towns and trading posts - these were the first successful settlements. Each was chosen because of a location which offered excellent defensive potential, access to the homeland, and later, water power to run grist mills and saw mills. But when the land was wrested from the forest, technological innovation became as important an innovation as site or situation.

The most prominent technological invention was the railway, seen in the early years as the road to prosperity. Community leaders fought and schemed to acquire a rail link; some exercising political influence, others buying the service. The evidence, as seen in railway stations, industries, rail yards and settlements that boomed during the late 1800s, remains along river and rail, awaiting those who follow these paths today. It is easy for us to trace the trail of the railway builders and experience some of the adventure that brought them to the interior of this vast forested land. Or we can recreate in our minds the struggle and romance of these pioneers simply by visiting villages within a few kilometers of Toronto.

We can penetrate the interior to explore the relics of a forgotten era of steam and stream, iron and export while we travel comfortably through the countryside. Our travels will take us back to view the hopes and dreams of the past; then into the communities as they exist on the land today.

Rail towns and mill towns were often synonymous. They lined rushing rivers along ribbons of iron like links on a chain. Wherever the railway slashed through hills or escarpments, it was forced to use the most gentle slopes. Almost inevitably it followed a trodden path or a log road along a valley which had already been a route to the interior for the settlers. Much earlier they had established dams, saw mills, grist mills and stores. Now they craved communication with the outside world. Their wheat, beef, pork, and wood required export markets. The steam train was to be their economic link to a wider world of goods and services.

The mid-1800s were a period of frantic railway building. The Grand Trunk and the Great Western were the early winners in the race for dominance, but for a few years rivals proliferated all over Ontario. The first to operate in Upper Canada was the Erie and Ontario Railway. It was chartered in 1835 and began to run from Queenston to Chippewa in 1839. It was eventually extended from Niagara-on-the-Lake to Fort Erie, and ultimately became part of the New York Central link across southern Ontario. In subsequent years, the Northern Railway from Toronto to Meaford and North Bay, the London and Port Stanley Railway, the Toronto Grey and Bruce, the Wellington, Grey and Bruce, the Midland Railway of Canada, the Whitby, Port Perry and Lindsay Railway and many others were built, competed fiercely for business and either went bankrupt or amalgamated with other lines. In the end, most surviving tracks became part of the national networks of the Canadian National or the Canadian Pacific.

One local example illustrates the wild and sometimes ruthless competition among competing railway entrepreneurs. In 1882, the Grand Trunk and the Great Western amalgamated, leaving Guelph off the main line which then ran via Hamilton from Toronto to London, bypassing Guelph by some 30 kilometers. Knowing the importance of having been on the Grand Trunk main line, Guelph businessmen quickly promoted the Guelph Junction Railway to intersect the new route near Campbellville. It was opened in 1888 and remains the property of the city, under lease to the Canadian Pacific. To increase revenues and capture business from its the western hinterland, Guelph convinced Canadian Pacific to extend the line to Goderich in 1906. There is no doubt that the Guelph Junction Railway increased Guelph's prosperity in the early years and has since made a profit for its municipal owners.

Numerous fortunate towns such as Guelph, Toronto, Kingston and Kitchener derived benefit from their early acquisition of the iron horse. Some like Fergus, London and Acton remain important today, but others, including Orton, Cataract and Alton, flashed into initial prominence, only to decline and almost disappear. They faltered when water levels decreased, when competition increased or when the motor vehicle replaced rail transport. Regardless of their present fate, former railway and river communities offer the settlement explorer important insights into past triumphs and failures.

Our explorations will follow the Credit Valley railway which ultimately ran from Toronto's Union Station to St. Thomas in one direction and to Orangeville in the other. Its right of way towards Orangeville will take us between bare rock summits, past roaring cataracts and through a myriad of contrasting communities. It was built to export goods from these places and their hinterlands to Toronto, from whence they had access to the world. Of course, it also functioned to carry supplies and settlers into the interior. Its story is one of people, entrepreneurial enterprise, promotion and promises.

We soon discover that the comic opera activities of promoters and rail builders were interesting in themselves. But the effects of rail acquisition (or lack thereof) were not always as anticipated. Two of the most interesting railway projects were the Toronto Grey and Bruce, and the Credit Valley lines. Both were promoted enthusiastically by Mr. George Laidlaw of Toronto, who has been referred to as "the Prince of Bonus Hunters". After arriving in Toronto from Scotland in 1855, he rapidly became a wealthy and influential entrepreneur.

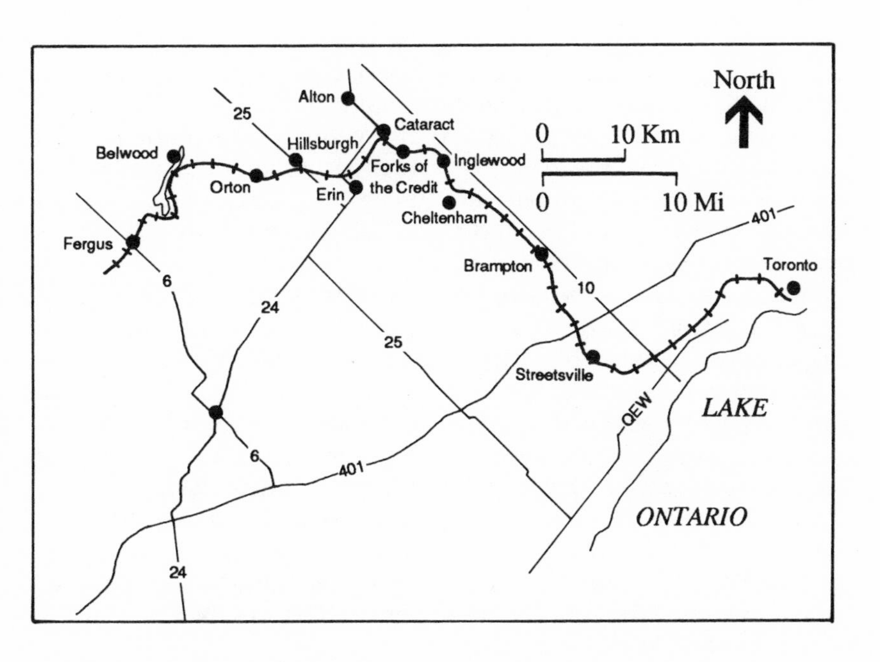

The Orangeville branch of the Credit Valley Railway.

Laidlaw had a vision of opening rural Ontario by providing export routes for its farm produce. As a byproduct he would enrich himself and his friends, all of whom sought lucrative investments in Canada. He convinced colleagues that light, narrow gauge lines (three feet, six inches), would be adequate for branch railways, and would also be inexpensive. While construction progressed, ties could be cut from the substantial stands of cedar along the route. Part of the promotion for his two schemes was Laidlaw's "Reports and Letters on Light Narrow Gauge Railways" in which he publicized the advantages of narrow tracks. In the end, another Laidlaw railway,the Toronto, Grey and Bruce, was completed as a narrow gauge line, but the Credit Valley Railway was built on standard gauge. To qualify for a government subsidy after 1874, all lines had to be built to the gauge of four feet, eight and one-half inches, so despite Laidlaw's writings, the Credit Valley line complied. Profits were still more important than principles!

Despite bitter opposition from interests in Guelph, Laidlaw used political influence to have both his railways approved by parliament. They were completed in the early 1870s, and for a time did take business away from places further south, including Guelph. Not to be outdone, Guelph promoters countered with the Wellington, Grey and Bruce Railway, later building their own Guelph Junction Railway to connect with the C.P.R. main line. Notwithstanding the early effects of Laidlaw's schemes, Guelph's competitive position was ultimately restored.

The Orangeville branch of the Credit Valley Railway was specifically intended to serve the rural areas north of Guelph. It was to begin in Toronto, linking the inland settlements to the premier port of the province. Unfortunately for Laidlaw, obtaining access to Toronto was anything but easy. The fledgling line would have to cross the tracks of the Grand Trunk and the Great Northern to reach either the harbour or Union Station. Considerable acrimony and manipulation accompanied Laidlaw's attempts to secure a right of way across the extensive lines of his rivals. Eventually he constructed freight facilities and a roundhouse near the corner of Dufferin and King Streets, and a wharf terminal south of Front Street between the foot of John and Simcoe. Access to Union Station was finally obtained in 1880, more than a year after the line had begun operating from its Parkdale facility. This event gave Laidlaw access to central Toronto and marked the end of several years of intense litigation with bitter rivals. But like the canny Scot he was, he won in the end.

The route of the Credit Valley Railway took it from Toronto's waterfront past the freight yards to Parkdale where the line had its main terminal facilities. It then ran to The Junction, just beyond Dufferin and Queen. Here the lines of the Grand Trunk, the Credit Valley, and the Toronto, Grey and Bruce railways crossed, merged and finally entered their own rights of way. From here the Credit Valley line ran to Lambton Mills, (just west of Jane and St. Clair Ave. West) and then on to Summerville which stood at the site of the interchange between Highways 5 and 27. From there it ran to Dixie station, Cooksville, and Streetsville where the St. Thomas link branched west.

The Orangeville branch, which we will follow, then headed through Brampton to Cheltenham, along the Credit River through the Caledon Hills which mark the edge of the Niagara Escarpment. On its way north it passed through some of the most spectacular scenery in southern Ontario at the Forks of the Credit, Brimstone and Cataract. Eventually it reached Elora by way of Fergus, Belwood, Orton, Hillsburgh and Erin.

Laidlaw's promotional skills were clearly evident in the financing of this line, which received bonuses totalling $1,035,000 from communities desiring its service. These included Toronto, Milton, Brampton, Streetsville, several counties and Orangeville. Elora and Fergus contributed by exchanging municipal debentures for the bonds of the railway.

Today the lasting (and sometimes transitory) effects of the early rail links may still be found in the places they were to serve. New buildings were built for commerce or industry, new economic functions were created and the appearance of towns was altered forever by the rail lines, coal depots and stations. Many of the buildings and facilities are preserved still, either in books or in fact.

Since the initial purpose of the railway was to provide easy access to Toronto, we will begin our historical trip there. Our journey from Toronto to each of these towns will follow the Credit Valley Railway, passing through the changing countryside on the way.

The sinuous, indeed, sometimes tortuous paths followed by early rail lines from Toronto to points in southwestern Ontario clearly reflect the frenzied efforts of municipal councils and local boosters to attract the iron horse. It seemed that every place offering an inducement was to receive service, and all believed that they would prosper from their new ties to the outside world. In reality, this was not always so: a retrospective look at some that succeeded and others that failed is an engrossing exercise.

Fortunately, we can still follow the abandoned tracks through the escarpment from Toronto to the northwest, passing through prosperous service centres, sleepy commuter dormitories and virtual ghost towns. Every few years, a restored steam locomotive chugs along the old Credit Valley line, carrying a small group of railway enthusiasts back to an era of steam and coal. It takes us through towns and villages, each of which competed strenuously with its rivals to serve the farmers in the surrounding countryside. Some such as Cataract and Alton had two local stations, being served by the Credit Valley and the Toronto Grey and Bruce lines. Unfortunately for many, some were just too close together for all to prosper, others were too remote from good farm land, and still others were poorly served by their local boosters. Now we find only the historical legacy of the railway, sometimes expressed through abandoned buildings and at others reflected in continuing prosperity.

A NOSTALGIC JOURNEY ALONG THE CREDIT VALLEY RAILWAY

We begin our journey at Union Station in Toronto. When we board the elegantly restored wooden cars of the Credit Valley Railway we feel a thrill as the black iron horse whistles and exhales its hot breath of steam and smoke. The once proud line has been reduced from an important rail connection to a little-used branch of the Canadian Pacific Railway. We feel almost lost as we pass through the heavily urbanized west end of Metropolitan Toronto for many kilometers. After leaving the city, we head north in the little valley of the Credit, paralleling for a time the Toronto Grey and Bruce which followed the Humber to the east. Past the high rises and technobusiness parks of Mississauga, we cross Highway 401 and Brampton where once productive farmland now produces new crops of homes for commuters to Toronto.

Soon the roadbed winds across the remainder of the Peel Plain, a fertile, level expanse of silts and clays deposited at the end of the Wisconsin Glaciation. Some 10,000 years ago, the masses of blue-grey ice that had blanketed Ontario began to recede. Contrary to conventional wisdom, the mile-thick lobes covering southern Ontario were built in the depressions now occupied by the Great Lakes, scouring and deepening them. They then oscillated across the province to join in the area between Guelph and Milverton. When they retreated, their withdrawal took them back to the basins from whence they had come. Churning, dashing, chocolate-coloured water filled the gap between the ice and the Niagara Escarpment. Here the stones and sediment subsided, creating the Peel Plain, now a rich and bucolic landscape of farms and furrows, towns and train stations, industry and highways.

We leave the plain at Cheltenham, passing through Boston Mills and Sligo, now known as Inglewood. Here the hills and obstacles begin. The road of steel clings precipitously to the ledge of shale, sandstone and limestone which forms the Niagara Escarpment. Broad plains fall behind; we wind along the Credit River towards the Devil's Pulpit, a massive limestone cliff above our first stop at the Forks of the Credit. Years ago one could walk right to the edge of the pulpit from the road above and peer at the river, but now access is blocked by expensive residential estates. An enormous wooden trestle takes us up and up, far above the raging waters of the river and over the settlement at Brimstone. Although most of it is buried today, the trestle over the Forks is still spectacular. When it was built, at 1146 feet long and 85 feet high, it was the longest curved trestle in Ontario.

The challenges faced by engineers and labourers appear everywhere as we penetrate the heartland of Ontario. Traversing dangerously steep grades and narrow trestles we hang perilously over the water. From hundreds of metres above, slumping shale slides towards the valley floor, threatening man's audacious incursion into nature's realm. We imagine the scene in the past, while our admiration for the surveyors, engineers and labourers increases tenfold. Even today the challenges are immense. Here in the valley of the Credit River, man is dwarfed and humbled by nature.

The Forks of the Credit are the focal point of our trip. Gaunt, bald fingers of limestone tower over the mingled greens, browns and yellows below. In the stream, sleek silver trout vie with salmon in the spring, tempting the rows of hopeful anglers on the shore. Carpets of purple violets mingle with fern fronds thrusting their hopeful heads through the mud. Here and there the bluejays make their cries of warning, overpowered quickly by the puff and wheeze of our engine. Down and down fall the tracks, winding and slicing through geological time and strata, finally reaching the water. Past the trestle, now mostly buried; around a pin curl twist; back again to the left; then we cross the stream at the bottom. No road existed here in the past, only the railway and a trail to Belfountain.

We use our imagination to recall the thriving collection of houses, shops, mills and factories nestled here beside the dam. Workers from the railway, officials from Toronto and settlers seeking opportunity once swelled the population far beyond its present limits. By 1859 the Tremaine map listed this little Loyalist settlement as Adjuda, but in 1877 it was labelled Credit Forks on the Pope map. When the railway came, they painted the name Forks of Credit on the station and thus it has remained.

Economic growth and prosperity came early, if ephemerally. Where the Credit had knifed through the escarpment, stone for construction could easily be dislodged. Soon the Forks became the heart of a thriving quarry business. Exposed projections of bedrock studded with bush were hacked and blasted from the ravine. Massive grey slabs, carefully cut blocks, and loads of crushed aggregate were loaded on the train to Toronto. There they fueled the building boom of the capital. Shale, sandstone and limestone were all found in the sandwiched strata along the valley sides. Nature had exposed them through erosion, leaving easy pickings for the settlers.

By the 1880s there were seven quarry operations in the area. To accommodate this growth and utilize another falls, Brimstone was created a few hundred yards upstream. Some 400 miners and their families lived here and in the Forks of the Credit. The first underground stone quarry in Canada was carved from the cliff just behind the railway station at the Forks. There building blocks were cut for the Ontario Parliament buildings and the Toronto City Hall. Workers were paid twelve-and-a-half cents an hour, averaging $7.38 for a 59-hour week.

Soon the resources of the valley attracted outside investors seeking to exploit the rich sedimentary deposits. Around 1890, Carrol and Vick of Toronto bought a number of the quarries. They then built lime and brick kilns at the end of the railway trestle, hoping to produce pottery, tiles and cement for sale in Toronto. Unfortunately, they had overlooked the climatological attributes of their location, deep in a sheltered, wooded valley. Cold air drained from above, but little moved over the hopeful stacks of the kilns. Like campers in the rain, they received much smoke but little heat for their efforts. Soon the kilns were abandoned. Downdrafts from the cliffs had doomed the ambitious enterprise. Today, remnants of the kilns remain, and we pass them where the Bruce Trail climbs the hill south of the railway trestle.

In a similar attempt around 1913, Procter and McKnight formed The Credit Forks Tile and Brick Company in order to utilize the large clay deposits. They were defeated by the same topography and microclimate, failing in their effort to produce dishes. Nevertheless, mills, logging and the quarries provided employment for many. At the peak of prosperity, four stores served the local residents with luxuries from Toronto and the old country. Busy workers laboured beside the river, dust spewed from shattering rocks and smoke from steam engines hovered over the scene. In Brimstone, the ring of the blacksmith's hammer vied for primacy with the buzzing saws of the mill which manufactured shingles and lumber. Nearby, a grand boarding house arose to house the workers who flooded to the valley.

So what did it all produce? Where are the results of the sweat, the sacrifice, the quarry deaths, the early enterprise? Why do we find so little when we peer from the trestle over the river? Where are the homes and the kilns? Why was prosperity so fleeting?

The answers are relatively easy. Brimstone and the Forks were on the railway, but they were isolated by steep cliffs, tangled forests and distance from Toronto. Agriculture was almost nonexistent within the valley. Other than industries established on a foundation of rock and forest, little local economic base was available. Ultimately the firms relying on local resources lost out to competition from others closer to Toronto. In the end, the prosperous, once vigorous industries of the valley met the fate of obsolescence and demise.

Today, little of man's work remains. Much of the valley has reverted to the magnificence of nature. The road to Brimstone is gone, washed out in a flood, but its route may be traversed on foot. Along the valley, the interplay of sun and water recall an earlier era. Deep green cedars lean from river banks to sip and drink from the stream. Frogs sing and sparrows call to their mates. Water spiders hop from circle to circle, creating symmetrical patterns on the silk smooth surfaces of backwaters, while clear rills wash around clumps of watercress. In the autumn, shimmering golds of beech and dark greens of hemlock contrast with the deep reds of the soft maples and sumacs on the slopes.

Once again, overlooking some of the most spectacular scenery in Southern Ontario we find country estates, some with acres of neatly manicured lawns and some hidden in the forest. A typical scene along the road from Belfountain to Toronto.

Our eyes follow a myriad of contrasting colours rising along the talus slopes to the sheer rock barrier. Wind rattles through deciduous branches and past the skeletal limbs of a small birch. Far above, palatial homes of commuters and city folk stand guard over green lawns or deep woods. They block access to the cliffs, preventing everyone from viewing the rugged ravine below.
Years ago we were free to walk and climb along these precipitous places. Now they all are private! Despite the fact that the settlements near the Forks had an ephemeral existence, people have been drawn again to the area to live. Just above the river, along the jagged edge of the Devil's Pulpit, and beside the roads towards Toronto, the wealthy have established their homes.

We drive along the south rim of the valley through Belfountain, a tranquil spot, early favoured as a summer resort by the wealthy from Kitchener and Toronto. On the winding road past the deep ravine we pass snake rail fences and rolling morainic pastures. Then we come upon today's equivalent of the earlier escape from the cities. Once again, overlooking some of the most spectacular scenery in Southern Ontario we find country estates, some with acres of neatly manicured lawns and some hidden in the forest. Access to the south rim of the valley has all but disappeared. Prosperous commuters from the city have fenced and posted their property to keep out the curious and the hikers.

The narrow roads leading south and east are now paved. In the early morning and late afternoon they are like busy city streets. When the sun sets or rises, it inevitably glints off the polished chrome of the BMWs, Mercedes and Audis carrying the local commuters between city and home. Nearby, Belfountain has received enough economic benefit to sustain a trendy general store and several antique shops. Trimble's Garage has long since become Belfountain Motors in an attempt to move with changing times and technology.

Belfountain continues to display much of its small-town charm. It still overlooks the site of so much early enterprise below. Its restored shops, trees, lawns, log replicas of French Canadian homes and pools of water endure. They attract commuter and tourist alike. The Conservation Authority Park recalls the days when travellers from Kitchener-Waterloo carried picnic baskets of goodies on their day trips to Belfountain. Gracious homes nearby share the slopes with cottages, some dating back to the era when Torontonians retained summer residences in this leafy retreat. Some of the ambience remains, but nearby, change is clearly evident.

In some respects, the city has come to the countryside around the Forks of the Credit. The car has replaced rail and river as the basis of the local economy. The long tentacles of Toronto and Guelph, Georgetown and Brampton, reach out to alter the landscape. New residents desire a country retreat; they are readily accommodated by local politicians and developers.

We drive down the gravel road to a less rugged part of the valley. Here ski chalets have joined the mushrooms in the woods. Along the slopes at the Caledon Ski Club, massive pylons hold sturdy cables carrying modern chair lifts to the top. Hobby farms, complete with horses, stables, pools and hot tubs occupy the "wilderness" between the hills and the streams. "Private Property" signs cause diversions in the Bruce Trail which threads its way between the rocky outcrops and the estates. Today the sale of food, real estate and gasoline to commuters generates much of the local wealth. Water power, steam, quarries and potteries have been relegated to the history books and to the imaginations of those of us who care to explore our past.

Somewhat sadly we contemplate the changes wrought by "progress" in the valley and on the land above. But now it is time to continue our trip into history. Following the Bruce Trail upstream along the valley, we traverse a section of what was the old Dominion Road, the name given to the third line between Cataract and the Forks. Now part of it is a walking trail, but the original road has long since been washed out by floods. Up, up, along the widening valley, flanked by red shale and sandstone, we walk along the turbulent water. Barely two kilometers beyond the Forks, we encounter Cataract, another name on a yellowed map.

Here the river falls precipitously over a rocky outcrop. Water swirls, foams and churns; what a superb site for dams and mills! In the early years, dense stands of birch, aspen, white pine and soft maple provided raw material and the railway offered access to distant markets. At this promising location, so well endowed by bountiful nature, the name of Richard Church from Cooksville is synonymous with early success. He recognized the excellent industrial potential of the river, and in the early 1850s, purchased the area for $100.

Years earlier, a Loyalist by the name of William Grant had discovered a salt spring near the falls and tried to exploit its economic potential. He persuaded Matthew Crooks, his former employer, to finance an expedition to package and sell the salt. Unfortunately, this valuable commodity was too deeply bedded to be extracted with primitive tools. Nevertheless, the party did erect a sawmill at the falls and built a village of shacks called Gleniffer. The salt enterprise and the community were ultimately abandoned for 25 years until Mr. Church returned to purchase it in 1858.

A former land promoter in Peel County, Richard Church realized the importance of providing inducements to settlers and potential investors. He planned to create a self-sufficient community, and immediately laid out 168 residential lots. He zoned the river flats for industry and began the kind of economic development required to stimulate growth and attract settlers. He soon opened a general store, saw mill and grist mill.

By the 1860s, others realized the potential of the water power and the local forests. They built a barrel factory, a broom factory and a brewery to supply a growing local population and utilize local resources. The brewery was almost inevitable as an outlet for surplus grain from the mill, and as a necessity for the thirsty settlers. Life was difficult, making inebriation on a Saturday night a cheap and reliable distraction.

Unfortunately for these optimistic businessmen, there were just too many competitors and too few people to sustain all their ambitious schemes. By 1865, the factories and brewery had closed for want of business. It was somewhat ironic that only Church's enterprises survived. For a time in the early years, Cataract became known as Church's Falls. Fittingly, Mr. Church was the postmaster and the leading citizen. So pervasive was his influence that the residential streets were named after his children. Now they are gone and forgotten!

Time passed and others took up

Here raging water is compressed, gathers potential energy, and roars through the narrow confines, shaking and slamming the sides. The remains of the dam at Cataract.

the tasks begun by Richard Church. The settlement was renamed Cataract and grander structures arose after fire claimed their predecessors. By 1881 a stone mill of three stories replaced the original wooden structures. This new mill was built of limestone quarried from under the falls. When it burned too, in 1885, the ruins were purchased by John Deagle and restored.

Like the ambitious Mr. Church, Deagle had great ideas for Cataract. In 1899 he managed to produce electrical power from a generator installed at the new mill. Like many men of vision, he was ahead of his time. His Royal Electric, S.K.C. model, 133 cycle, single-phase generating unit was primitive and caused many problems. Despite these difficulties, Deagle was determined to demonstrate the value of electricity. He finally was able to supply Cataract with three experimental electric lights. What a sight it must have been the first time the incandescent filaments cast their orange-yellow glow over the tiny community!

All could not be charity, and in an attempt to turn a profit, Deagle supplied power to one hotel for a cent per day per bulb. Before additional customers began to use the "new-fangled" invention, his total revenue was three cents a day. By the end of the first year he had attracted more business and made $500, fitting tribute to his pluck and determination.

By 1905, Deagle phased out the mill and the Cataract Electric Company Limited was formed. Steam power enabled other more convenient mills to grind local grain, but water remained the mainstay for the production of electricity. The Cataract plant ultimately supplied Alton, Erin, and its local customers, a remarkable achievement for a place now only a dot on a map! Eventually, a new and more reliable generator was designed and built by the Deagles, and Orangeville joined the distribution system.

Given the early success of power generation, grandiose plans were made for an underground tunnel to bring water from the lake above Cataract to an outlet near Brimstone. This would have increased the capacity of the plant considerably, but nature intervened with disastrous results. After 500 feet of a planned 700-foot tunnel had been built, mountains of ice piled against the local dams. On April 6 and 7, 1912, warm weather caused rapid break-up, and rain added to already enormous volumes of water. Swollen by melting snow, muddy torrents swirled and dashed against the feeble man-made barriers which could withstand the pressure no longer. Dams cracked and crumbled all the way from Alton to Cataract with the loss of several lives. When Deagle's dam and penstocks were destroyed, their rebuilding took precedence over the completion of the tunnel, which remains to this day buried in the hillside.

Subsequent owners of the power plant expanded it to serve Hillsburgh, Caledon, Caledon East and the Cheltenham Brickworks, but unreliable flows in the Credit eventually doomed the enterprise. The nearby land had been ruthlessly cleared for lumber or burned by careless settlers. Deforestation led to low water in the summer and to floods in the spring, necessitating diesels to augment the water power. Soon it was a struggle to provide power at reasonable rates. In 1944, Ontario Hydro bought Caledon Electric for a reputed $100,000, and closed it for good in 1947.

After the purchase by Ontario Hydro, plans were made to preserve the lake and buildings for a tourist area, but the C.P.R. objected. They feared track washouts caused by flooding. The dam was dynamited and with it disappeared much of the charm and most of the economic potential of Cataract. Recent non-local owners had decided the fate of an historic community developed originally without their assistance. Such is the way of the modern corporate world.

Today, Cataract reflects little of its successful industrial past, but for remnants of the hydro power installation and the dams. The river is still confined and crushed into a concrete channel where it passes the hamlet. Here raging water is compressed, gathers potential energy, and roars through the narrow confines, shaking and slamming the sides. Twice this happens as the river struggles against man-made barriers constructed so long ago. The ruins of the hydro installation are a graphic reminder of the innumerable private facilities providing electric power to Ontario in the early nineteenth century. Now Ontario Hydro is resurrecting some of the old sites, using space-age technology to cope with low and intermittent flows.

To view Cataract from a better vantage point we follow the Bruce Trail along the water and up the steep embankment on the eastern side of the river. The railway line still runs along the other bank, crossed by an old wooden trestle from Cataract. "Progress" in the form of sturdy fences along the cliffs hinders our access to the old mill and power plant sites. Nevertheless, we stand on the trestle and remember the booming industry and robust village that once thrived at this location. Smokestacks, wooden houses, water wheels and horse-drawn carriages dotted the valley and climbed up to the slopes above. Now, foaming, frothing, roaring water pours through the skeletal remains of the mill and plant which seem to protest their loss of potential for power and progress. In the spring the torrents continue to rage, reduced to a paltry trickle by the hot, still days of summer.

While we gaze upon this nostalgic scene, another kind of activity develops. Despite the barrier of the fences, hikers cavort in the river below the falls, drinking beer and sliding like giant white seals down the slippery shale into the rushing water. In Cataract, above the valley, a small hotel provides country style meals and accommodation for summer hikers and winter skiers. A unique home, built like a geodesic dome, stands at the edge of the settlement, and a row of "rustic" log houses lines a nearby street. Even here, commuters have joined the locals and those escaping permanently from the city. Unfortunately, the lure of the past and the Bruce Trail have attracted too many hikers and visitors. They are now perceived as a nuisance and almost every street in Cataract is posted with NO PARKING, $28.00 FINE signs. Fortunately, there are parking lots a short walk away.

We search for the remains of the other mills, hotels and stores but they have disappeared. It is now difficult to realize that a busy, important community once stood on this site. Who remembers that one of the major early enterprises was J.J. McLaughlin's bottling works which eventually supplied clear spring water to his Canada Dry Ginger Ale plant in Toronto? It was an excellent example of the combined attraction of rail access to Toronto and a local resource that was easy to exploit. In the 1950's, the building was razed and the rail siding torn out. This was both a sign of "progress" and a symptom of the demise of communities based on rail or water. Similar scenarios have been repeated time and time again in eastern Canada.

A row of rustic log houses lines a nearby street. This home in Cataract is typical of the restored pioneer dwellings found in amenity communities.

West and South to Elora

At Cataract, the Credit Valley Railway splits into two branches. Now that we have explored the main line, we are curious about the settlements on the branches. One veers sharply south to Erin, then weaves its way to Elora by way of Hillsburgh, Orton, Belwood and Fergus. It has left the valley of the Credit in favour of a route chosen by local political and business leaders. In each fledgling village, inducements such as free land for a station and right of way or the purchase of stock were used to attract the railway. For some, the strategy seems to have worked, but in others it was a dismal failure. Orton was typical of settlements stimulated by the railway as it flashed briefly into prominence between 1880 and 1911, only to become a virtual ghost town thereafter.

Great contrasts are apparent on our trip to each of these communities. To reach them we cross rolling till plains and the long sleek drumlins sculpted so long ago by the Pleistocene glaciers. Now the drumlins stand, row upon parallel row, marching across the landscape like a line of cigars, all carefully oriented north-west to south-east. Some twenty thousand years ago and earlier, ice a mile thick covered this ground, oscillating, churning, scraping and molding the land beneath it. It advanced from the Great Lakes basins and over-

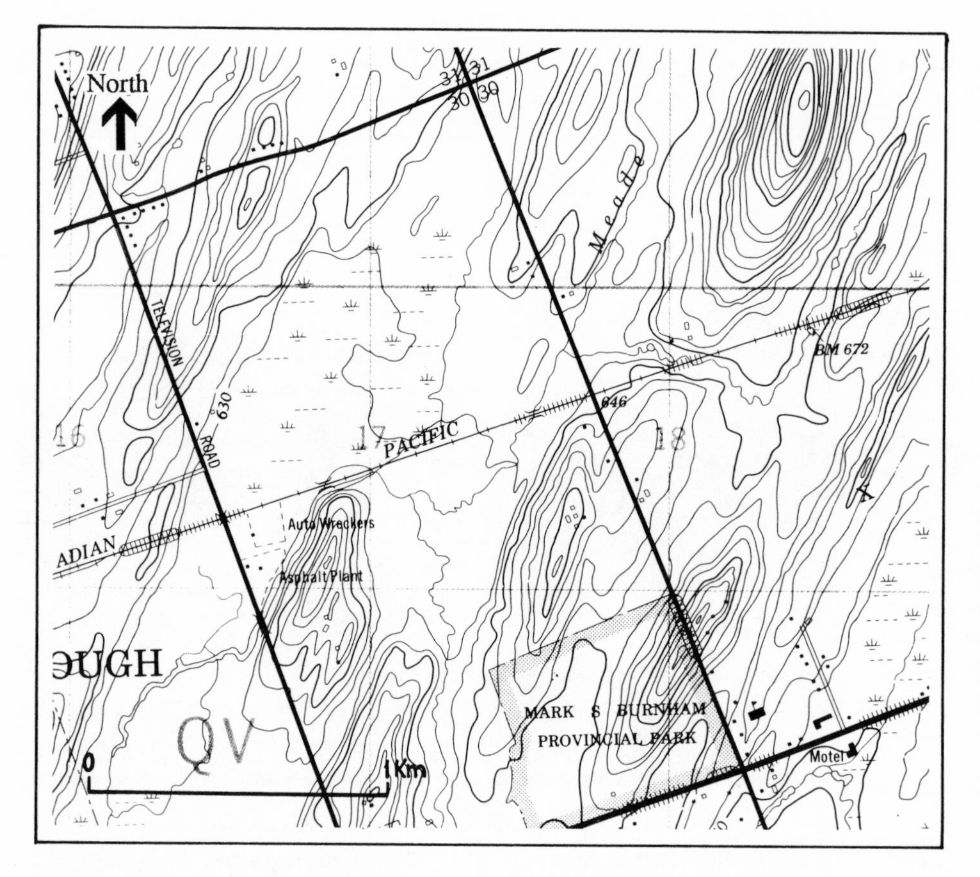

This section of a topographic map sheet near Peterborough Ontario shows the grain that drumlins impart to the landscape. Note the way in which the survey system has ignored the pattern of the lakes and hills.

rode everything in its path, depositing silt, sand, boulders and mud. Beneath the frigid, blue-green masses wreathed in cloud, deposits were smoothed and streamlined, some remaining today to remind us of the direction and power of the movement. Their stoss, or steep end, points towards Lake Ontario from which the ice advanced, and their long axes parallel the former path of the moving mass. Today, a major field of drumlins stands between Erin and Guelph, providing a peculiar grain to the landscape and a landmark at the village.

As the train enters Erin, we immediately encounter the dominant drumlin which guards the town and shelters it from the wind. The West Credit River forms a graceful loop, crossing the main street to run both north and south. It falls abruptly down steep slopes at several locations, providing excellent sources of water power. Before the white man arrived, the site was densely forested with tall, sturdy white pine, a potential settlement both picturesque and practical.

In 1862, Daniel McMillan came to the area and cleared three acres where the village now stands. He took advantage of rapids in the river to construct a saw mill. The excellent pines, said to have been up to four feet in diameter, were soon being turned into high quality lumber by McMillan's mill. Within two years, McMillan had built a house, married, and constructed a grist mill next to his saw mill. Not content with this success, he built another a dam and erected a more modern saw mill. Opposite the first saw mill he built an oat mill and nearby a dry kiln for his lumber. Even now, Mundell's Lumber Company remains on the site of the saw mill. It is the only remaining water-powered planing mill in Ontario, still manufacturing sashes and custom woodwork. Its worn red wooden exterior is unimpressive, but inside, the whir of water-driven pulleys and whine of slashing saws takes us to an earlier era. Pungent aromas of sawdust and freshly planed planks fill the air and the nostrils. When we step into Mundell's mill we take a trip to our pioneer past.

By 1840 another grist mill was erected on the second dam but was converted to a woollen mill ten years later. Just two years earlier, Wm. Cormock had constructed a distillery which made vast volumes of "good stuff". It was supplied to local farmers in exchange for their grain tailings. The products of this enterprise provided cooling relief for many a settler on a Saturday night after the weekly visit to the post office. We speculate on this early merriment while observing its modern equivalent at the three-storey Busholme Inn. Somehow today's activities seem less spontaneous and more commercial. Many decibels of noise from the giant television screen during the day and the rock band at weekends have effectively put a stop to most quiet conversations here.

Erin continued to grow and prosper for many years. A general store was established and the brothers of Daniel McMillan began manufacturing barrels, tubs, churns and coffins nearby. The best pine coffin cost $4 while No. 1 cherry went for $6; sums considered more than adequate by their makers. Somewhat later, a hotel was built and the grist mill was modernized. Given this solid foundation, it is little wonder that Erin was poised to benefit from the coming of the Credit Valley Railway.

Since its auspicious early beginnings, Erin has changed much and prospered. It was well placed to benefit from the railway when the Credit Valley Line was proposed in 1877. By then it had become the major rural service centre in the area and had grown to a population of several hundred. The village reached an early peak population of 594 in 1891, then declined, but grew to 2313 by 1981. Between 1981 and 1985 the number of business enterprises in Erin increased from 62 to 113, an 82 percent change. The traffic there on a Friday evening or Saturday morning is indicative of its firm position today. It is now the dominant settlement in eastern Wellington County.

In addition to Mundell's historic water-powered mill, we visit the partially restored woollen mill in Heritage park, and see the dams along the river on both sides of town. At the north end we discover Stanley Park. This secluded oasis just off the highway has been a recreational area and choice site for summer cottages for years. Tall dark stands of pine soar skyward to protect it from noise and traffic. Beyond, the lake is surrounded by picnic tables, now being challenged for space by new cottage and trailer developments. It retains much of its early charm, but has added an auction centre and permanent residences. It remains a pleasant setting for picnics and a great source of speckled trout for local children (who fish before the official opening of the trout season on the first of May).

The magnificent drumlin that sheltered the early settlers continues to loom over the town, but its slopes are being blanketed by the houses of commuters. A golf

Even now, Mundell's Lumber remains on the site of the saw mill. It is the only remaining water powered planing mill in Ontario, still manufacturing sashes and custom woodwork.

course drapes across its summit, and country estates dot the woods on its southern incline. From the summit we discover a panoramic view of the town and river below. We can see several dam sites, the old grist mill and the thriving business district. Along the main street we find a liquor store, supermarket, several specialty shops, a drugstore and hardware store. The town is also the location of a very successful dairy and a large fiberglass plant.

Erin supplies building lots for an increasing number of workers who commute daily to Brampton, Acton, Georgetown and Mississauga. At the eastern end of town, the influence of commuters is apparent in the rows of modern bungalows and split level houses, contrasting sharply with Gothic and Victorian structures in the older areas. We find a particularly spectacular three-storey brick mansion almost in the centre of the main street. Its opulence reminds us that the leaders of the community often chose the most convenient residential sites, near to their place of business, but a bit away from the noise of the mill. Today, many such homes have been converted to apartments.

Despite its interesting history and contemporary character, Erin has lost some of the charm of its past to modern development. Aware that progress was inevitable in such an splendid location, we leave and head west in search of a smaller, more intimate glimpse into early Ontario. Our train departs and crosses the drumlins to Hillsburgh, another of those "dying villages" (if you believe conventional wisdom). For early travellers, Hillsburgh provided a delightful stopping place and a final destination for settlers who could not acquire land near Erin. It is embraced by swooping purple hills, long ago moulded by the ice and incised by the West Credit River. We descend the steepening slope into its valley to see the main street stretching ahead, down, and then up the far side. It finally escapes over the far summit to the sky beyond.

In the verdant valley below, blue smoke curls from chimneys, and the lingering rays of the sun cast long evening shadows over the tranquil waters of the pond. The scene today is peaceful, almost obliterating our memories of the busy past. A hundred years ago, trout abounded in the Credit River and behind the dams. A private fishing club was established and water was set aside for the exclusive use of members. The large hotel provided excellent cuisine, comfortable rooms and "good stabling" out back for those who had come by stage or horse. Wood abounded to feed the mills; dozens of farmers thronged to Hillsburgh for milling or sawing. By 1881, the village boasted 26 business establishments, including a drugstore, the mills, a tailor, two blacksmiths, a saddler, a wagon maker, a tin smith, three shoemakers, a millinery shop and two bakers. Streets and shops were filled with noise and activity. Two thriving taverns provided liquid refreshment for the weary traveller, while the tin smith and tannery manufactured metal and leather goods. The population stood near 400 and prosperity seemed assured.

Although population continued to fluctuate between 400 and 500 for many years, signs of decline eventually appeared on the main street. Cars and trucks replaced the railway and horse, and Hillsburgh lost business to Erin which was on the main road north. By 1977 the 26 enterprises in Hillsburgh had diminished to a mere twelve, with the demise of those that served the farmers and their horses. In that year a couple of service stations, two general stores and a furniture store constituted the major part of Hillsburgh's business section. Vacant storefronts lined the main street, the hotel was converted to apartments, and the facade of a dying village presented itself to the world.

Is this another example of modern technology killing a perfectly viable rural service centre? Hillsburgh had grown with the coming of agriculture and thrived with the acquisition of the railway, but was the car to seal its fate? At first glance this would appear to be so, but how do we explain the doubling of population between 1971 and 1976, then an additional increase to 1065 by 1981? Despite its picturesque setting on the river between the drumlins, Hillsburgh is not really a Niagara-on-the Lake, or even an Elora or Bayfield. Why then the major new subdivision on the western edge of town and the drapes in the windows of abandoned businesses on the main street?

Answers begin to become clear on our stroll from the station along the main street. The explanation lies in the value of fixed capital, the lure of the country town for city commuters, and the ease with

The large hotel provided excellent cuisine, comfortable rooms and good stabling out back. Hillsburgh's hotel is now used for apartments.

which you can drive from Hillsburgh to Guelph, Brampton, Mississauga, Georgetown or even Toronto. Scenic paved county roads link Hillsburgh via the valley of the Credit to numerous employment opportunities to the south and to the east. The availability of large lots, many almost in the countryside and a casual approach to land use regulations make Hillsburgh attractive for many. Available space in former shops on Main Street, and a number of gracious old mansions add to the magnetism of this bucolic setting. Along the river, mills have been restored as homes, and the pond itself is surrounded by choice residential sites.

Commuters to Toronto, as we might too hastily infer, do not constitute the majority of Hillsburgh residents. A recent survey and data from the 1981 Census, show that many people from Hillsburgh drive only a few miles to work at scattered industries in the nearby township. Since 1981, many new opportunities have opened in businesses related to agriculture, while others have become available in a new restaurant, antique shops and a boutique. Commuters drive to Erin or Guelph or to jobs in the township. Mobility provided by the car allows them to live anywhere and work anywhere else.

The flexibility of telephone lines, modems and the computer enable others to sit in front of their terminals and conduct business all over the world. The result is a boom in population, and recently, even in businesses in Hillsburgh. Without its convenient location, charming setting and rural ambience, this might never have happened. More and more, this is the story of former "dying villages", even for some so far from the bustling metropolis.

We can no longer judge small settlements on the basis that they were complete rural service centres in the 1800s. Times have changed, and now they perform many new tasks, some as retirement centres, some as tourist towns and others as commuter dormitories. But neither should we resort to the conventional wisdom that most small town growth is the result of former city dwellers commuting back to the metropolis from whence they came. This is certainly true of many places near to major cities, but the vast majority of persons commuting from the settlements that we have visited find work nearby, usually no more than a half- hour's drive away. They are employed at seed cleaning depots, at agricultural cooperatives, in small-town industries or wholesale establishments, or in stores and offices. A pattern of short distance local commuting characterizes their lifestyle more accurately than the notion of hordes of exurbanites flocking daily back to the city. When we explore the countryside, we should judge the functions and population composition of Ontario's small towns by contemporary standards rather than on the basis of outmoded stereotypes.

In many towns and villages, there has been considerable growth and change. Unfortunately, one of the results of this new growth is a series of conflicts between those who oppose and those who desire additional development. Issues of pollution, traffic, costs of new services, recreational facilities and the preservation of an historic environment are becoming more common. With access and modern technology, this is a familiar story for the Hillsburghs of Ontario. Now they experience conflicts between old and new, between the past and the present, between controlled growth and massive new subdivisions. Where do they stop? Are we to convert the likes of Hillsburgh into the endless tracts of over-priced bungalows found in Brampton and Mississauga? Where do the tentacles of the metropolis end? How will we compromise successfully between history and progress, between human scale and modern urban development? These vexing questions will not go away. They must be addressed and resolved. Otherwise, former dying villages like Hillsburgh will lose much of their former integrity and character.

We ponder this important question as we board the train again and head to Orton. The trip takes us past a sprawling new subdivision spreading up the hill west of town, then on through short tumbled glacial hills called moraines. We speed past rolling fields of corn and pasture. There stands an ornate, red brick, twin-peaked restored Victorian farmhouse. We travel on, finally arriving at Orton. This settlement is also situated along the western branch of the Credit Valley Railway, but its story contrasts with those of Erin and Hillsburgh in many respects!

In Orton we find a true product of the railway age. Its tiny nucleus functioned as a minor rural service centre until the iron horse arrived. This led to its brief period of growth and prosperity. Before the railway reached it in 1879, Orton boasted few advantages. It was situated in a corner of the county known more for swamp and hill than for crops. Business for its entrepreneurs came from a few local farmers in this area of meagre production. Its location near, but not quite at, the intersection of a concession road was not particularly conducive to development of a service role. Its creek was far too small to provide power for a mill. And so it languished with a population of a hundred people until the band of wood and steel thrust new life into its sleepy streets.

Orton wasn't even listed in the *Directory of Wellington County* for 1871 and 1872. Not until 1901 did Dun and Bradstreet *Directories* record two "agents", one combined with a blacksmith and one handling agricultural implements. It also listed a sawmill, two general stores, a shoemaker, a harness maker, a hotel, a combined grocery and hardware store and another blacksmith. In 1901, the directory recorded the population as 175, Orton's peak for all time. The saw mill ran on coal, an innovation made possible by the railway. The absence of a grist mill reflected both the lack of water power and the paucity of prosperous farms nearby. Nevertheless, the railway achieved its intended purpose, stimulating a "mini-boom" for the hamlet.

Alas, this sudden spurt of growth and prosperity was soon to end in Orton. By 1921 only nine businesses remained and the popula-

Along the once busy thoroughfare we encounter four frame buildings, one a combined house/post office, the others a little worse for wear, serving now as residences. Orton's main street in the 1970s.

tion was around 100. Today we find a sorry collection of abandoned business buildings along its "main street". The former hotel has collapsed into ruin, long abandoned and forgotten, now gone completely. Along the once busy thoroughfare, we encounter four frame buildings, one a combined house/post office, the others a little worse for wear, serving now as residences. Across the street, a vacant lot has replaced the bleached and weathered cedar boards that for so long remained in a heap to remind us of the once proud pub and hotel, bursting with laughter and activity every Saturday night. Now only the silence of the land where it stood greets the expectant traveler.

Orton today is an excellent example of the "ghost towns" referred to in the popular literature. There seems to be little reason to visit, and the physical legacy of its main street is unimpressive. This is not to say that it is entirely devoid of charm. Near to the railway crossing several large old houses remain, a reminder of better days. One modern cedar home has been built near the tracks. The Anglican Church, constructed in 1901, remains on a side street. A few of the local "country estates" with their restored homes and tree-lined lots provide a pleasant contrast to the remnants of the business area. In 1977, a service station, butcher and construction company remained, but today only scant vestiges of former prosperity are found in the old business section.

Unlike Erin or Hillsburgh, location, site attractions and water power were not available to save this ephemeral product of a railway entrepreneur. Its population now stands near 70 if you count the fringes, and the main street desolation accurately reflects its much reduced status. As a service centre, Orton is even less important now than it was 20 years ago. It is just too easy to drive to Hillsburgh or Erin for anything you need.

Ironically, the hamlet gained recent notoriety and national newspaper coverage when its citizens rallied to resist the growth and change which they saw as a blatant and unwanted intrusion into their quiet residential community. In late 1986 it was learned that the Portage Foundation was planning to purchase land to build a group home facility for 70 troubled teenagers. Despite its sleepy reputation, Orton residents fought against the project which they considered a major intrusion upon their quiet rural lifestyle. And it wasn't just the people in the hamlet who got involved. According to the *Globe and Mail* "opposition to the

The former hotel has collapsed into ruin, long abandoned and forgotten; now gone completely. The Orton hotel just before it was demolished.

proposal has united fourth generation farmers and the highly paid professionals who commute to work in Toronto or Hamilton from their luxuriously remodeled farmhouses." Eventually, Erin Township Council passed a by-law to prevent the development, and Portage took the case to the Ontario Municipal Board. Before the hearing, however, the Portage directors decided to look elsewhere for land on which to build their facility.

Even once "dying" villages now have power and determination when aroused by a threat to their chosen way of life. The NIMBY (not in my back yard) syndrome is alive and well. It is not only in the city, where group homes are perceived by some as a constant threat, that we encounter this resistance. There is opposition in the remote and tranquil countryside where space should not be at a premium, and where we might expect some sympathy for the less fortunate.

The issue raises interesting questions. If rural villages are appropriate locations for commuters and ex-urbanites, would they also be desirable sites for group homes? Attempts to locate such facilities legally in cities have often met with severe opposition, even with the burning and bombing of a shelter for women in Guelph, despite the fact that it was perfectly legal. Communities like Orton would seem ideal with their open space and tranquillity, but now it appears that the "gate closing" mentality has come to even the tiniest Canadian communities. "Let us live here in peace, but don't allow any business or activity that may interfere with our lifestyle." Of course, matters of scale and compatibility must be considered, but the Orton incident gives one pause.

We leave Orton contemplating one of the important social and locational dilemmas of our time and continue west along the Credit Valley Railway. Soon we reach the watershed of the Grand, turning south to follow manmade Belwood Lake. It lies on the Grand River behind the Shand Dam which was constructed to provide for flood control in the spring and a steady flow of water downstream in the summer. Like so many other dams it conferred mixed blessings: creating a recreational area for many, but flooding farms and obliterating land for others. Today the controversy is forgotten, but the legacy remains at the lake, some

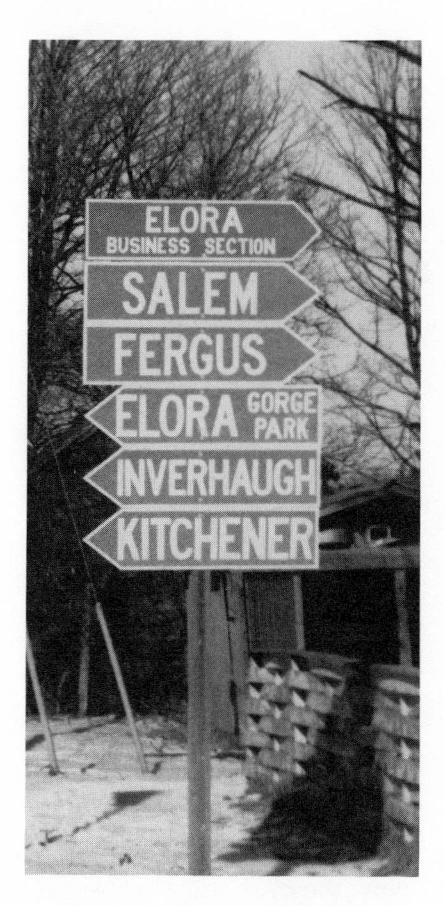

five kilometers north of Fergus.

Beside the water, stands of evergreens have been planted to replace those so ruthlessly razed in the past, and private campgrounds have sprung up to capitalize upon woods and water. Down a dip in the road, across a narrow neck of the lake, we come to the hamlet of Belwood, once a thriving community on the stage route north along the Grand River. Now it boasts a schoolhouse converted into a craft-shop-restaurant, and a number of pleasant old homes. Cottagers and fishermen are attracted to the lake while tourists patronize the restaurant and attend the summer weaving classes held at the craft shop. Little construction of new residences has occurred until recently, but some cottage development is found along the river. We enjoy the atmosphere of peace and calm which may soon be shattered by a proposed housing development just across from another recent subdivision. Soon the population could increase from 150 to 250 or more.

At 159, Belwood's 1981 population dropped from a peak of 166 in 1976, but its attractions are inducing increased building and development. Recent agricultural enterprises nearby have added to its directory entry, and the entrepreneurship of the restaurant owners might just inspire others to follow suit. The hamlet is close enough to employment to attract commuters and has the rural amenities desired by exurbanites. We feel that someone who lives here must stand on guard against the conflicts and controversies that have recently afflicted Orton and Hillsburgh. Belwood is ripe for growth and development. If it is to occur, it should be carefully planned and controlled.

On to Elora & Fergus

The train continues west and south, paralleling the Grand to Fergus. This town is now somewhat beyond the scope of our volume, simply because it has grown to 6000, above our limit of 5000. Nevertheless, it is on our route because it attracted the Credit Valley Railway. Civic fathers exchanged municipal debentures for railway bonds to provide an incentive for construction. We will make a brief stop simply because Fergus is too delightful to miss, despite its larger size. Next to Guelph, it is now the most industrialized and rapidly growing community in Wellington County. Its rich historical legacy of limestone buildings and water-powered industry have attracted our interest.

Fergus market is a stellar weekend attraction. It occupies the former Beatty Brothers factory at the intersection of the Grand River and Highway 6. There, hard by the falls and rapids that brought early prosperity to the town, we experience the industry and thrift which harnessed the power of the rapidly plunging Grand. Local vendors display their leafy vegetables, round earthy potatoes, maple sugar candy, and a vast array of household items and food. On Saturday mornings the market overflows with buyers and sellers, like a combination flea market and rural fair. Patrons travel from Toronto, Kitchener and Guelph, as much to absorb the local colour as to bargain for antiques or crafts.

Every fall, Fergus celebrates its Scottish heritage by holding the Highland Games. They began as a one day event with 300 participants in 1946, but now attract competitors from all over North America and Scotland to participate in a host of Scottish competitions. These include highland dancing, piping contests and the caber toss. Last year, some 38,000 people attended the Games.

Across the river from the market, on St.Andrew Street, we find some of the finest examples of three-storey limestone business

On Saturday morning, the market overflows with buyers and sellers like a combination flea market and rural fair. The building which houses the market was originally the Beatty Brothers' plant which manufactured farm implements and stable fittings in the late 1800s.

buildings in Ontario. They stand as lasting monuments to the Scottish stone masons who built them. The magnificent churches on the hill are part of the same proud tradition. Off the main street, Victorian mansions house many fortunate citizens. On the main street we discover the Breadalbane Inn, the restored former residence of the founding Ferguson family. Now it is an intimate, small hotel with a superb dining room exuding old-world charm. Its highly polished bannister and wrought-iron rails recall an era of elegance and gentility that has all but disappeared from the modern world.

The riverside through Fergus is lined by a park, edging the swirl of frothing water with a riot of variegated colours. At the northern extremity of the river through town, massive well-preserved mills stand above the river, overlooking their line of dams. We visit them and are reminded of the prominent importance of wheat and water, stream and dam to the economy of early Ontario. These solid old buildings, many now empty, invite some modern use, be it incubator for industry or studio for arts and crafts.

We head downstream towards Elora, trying to understand why the good burghers of Fergus have not capitalized upon their legacy. True, they have developed a formidable economic base, and are experiencing rapid population growth, but why so little attention to the potential of their site and built environment? Were the canny Scots so taken with economic progress that they overlooked the charm of the richly ornamented limestone buildings along the main street? Have they forgotten the attraction of magnificently preserved Victorian homes and several delightful churches? Don't they realize the potential of the town as a location for a festival of music, art or drama? Or has their history been so kind that they have been able to eschew such commercial exploitation of their rich and varied heritage? Just down the road, the less fortunate inhabitants of Elora have seized upon such opportunities with a vengeance!

The road to Elora follows the Grand past the Conservation Authority Park with its campsites and quarry. Then it passes the former Wellington County Home (now a museum and administrative centre for the county), to the outskirts of Elora. The break is practically imperceptible, as the two almost meet in the middle of the short distance between them. Early on, Elora was outstripped by Fergus, despite its acquisition of the northern terminus of the Credit Valley Railway. Although it was established in 1832, two years before Fergus, Elora never could keep up with its rival. By 1891 railways had brought local prosperity, with Elora reaching an all time high of 72 businesses. At the same time Fergus had acquired 84 establishments, a number that it exceeded only in 1970.

By 1981, the population of Fergus was 6065, while Elora languished at 2665. On the other hand, by 1985, the number of businesses in Elora had proliferated to 119 compared to 163 in Fergus. This resurgence in Elora requires some explanation, especially against a history of stagnation and a population that remained modest compared to that of Fergus.

For those who have recently visited Elora, its rebirth is not a mystery. Blessed by a magnificent site on a waterfall and a rocky gorge, it has always been something of a tourist attraction. For years visitors have stood at the lookout above the confluence of the Grand River and the Irvine Creek. Here we marvel at the water and the caves below. Far down in the chasm, two streams combine, freshets from each mingling and foaming as they converge. In their mad dash beneath the cedar-clad cliffs, they rush over rough rocks and between algae-covered boulders. The earliest pioneers stood at this very site, awestruck with wonder at one of nature's spectacular showplaces. We share their admiration before continuing our exploration.

We climb down the stairs to the river. This walk has been a popular local pastime for years. In the cool of the gorge, water drips from the overhang to trickle slowly to the river. During the winter, long, sleek fingers of ice reach to the valley floor, clutching at the snow below like giant frosty hands. Water swirls under the ice, making delicate patterns, eddies and whorls as it struggles to the few open patches below. Stalactites and stalagmites of crystallized precipitation cover the grey limestone chasm, imparting mystery and icy charm to this world of white and green. For time immemorial, the gorge has attracted locals and tourists alike.

Across the river from the market on St.Andrews St. we find some of the finest examples of three storey limestone business buildings in Ontario.

At the northern extremity of the river through Fergus, massive well preserved mills stand above the river, overlooking their line of dams....These solid old buildings, many now empty, invite some modern use, be it incubator for industry or studio for arts and crafts.

Finally we leave this secluded retreat to visit the rest of Elora. The town's real renaissance came only when several entrepreneurs realized the potential of Mill Street and began to restore its derelict industrial buildings. The lure of natural phenomena alone was inadequate to attract crowds of well-heeled visitors. So entrepreneurs took over, to enhance (or exploit, if you listen to the critics), the already attractive local environment.

We remember clearly the restoration of the mill, at a reputed cost of several million dollars. This crumbling eight-storey structure, strategically poised above the plunging falls, was lovingly rebuilt from top to bottom. Inside the bar, along an exposed rocky outcrop, the penstock remains to remind us of its origins as one of the largest grist mills in Ontario. The exterior walls, almost five feet thick, protect us from the water below, while tongues of orange flame flicker from the fireplace. From the balcony we observe the limestone "Tooth of Time" which seems suspended in the centre of the churning cataract. The restoration which we now enjoy was not accomplished in a day. Financial hardship and opposition plagued what ultimately became the cornerstone of the "Mill Street Revival".

After a number of years of struggle, and more than one owner, the mill began to prosper. Then several old factories across the street and business blocks along the river were also restored and converted. The mill became a hotel, pub and restaurant, while shops, a cinema and other delightful eating places began to fill the renovated Mill Street structures. At first it was tough. Numerous businesses changed hands and others went bankrupt. In the beginning, the suspicious, skeptical, negative, and sometimes hostile attitude of locals towards the newcomers didn't help.

Slowly at first, and then with increasing momentum, the initial risks paid off. Tourists were attracted to purchase antiques, to view the scenery and to dine on the balconies and patios by the river. Soon artists and artisans joined the local shopkeepers, making and selling their wares in and around the original Mill Street nucleus. Then buses from Toronto and Kitchener began to crowd the village with shoppers and tourists from June to October. From its Mill Street genesis, the original nucleus has crept up the hill to town, almost reaching the main business area. In the words of one scholar, Elora has become an "amenity community" attracting visitors from far away.

My wife and I return in the winter to sample the scenery and skiing at the Conservation Authority Park. In summer it provides campsites and swimming; in the winter there are groomed trails. With its improvements, Elora has become a year-round attraction. We ski atop steep cliffs along the frozen river, then thread our way through the woods. Cold clutches at our lungs and ice begins to form a freezing barrier in my beard. Chilly winds finally penetrate our clothes and turn our thoughts to food and warmth. Fortunately, it is but a few minutes to the home-baked pastry at the Café Flore or the Wellington County Stew at the Mill. We are torn between a hot toddy to warm our hands and a cold beer to slake our thirst. The beer wins out and we order our lunch.

After lunch, filled and satisfied, we take time to observe the ice on the falls and stroll along to the shops. Many are now open year-round to serve the winter visitors. Our interest in residential architecture convinces us to drive

along side streets lined by historic homes. Today we are lucky enough to stumble upon a guided interior tour. This presents a wealth of historic Ontario history. In much of Elora, careful attention has been paid to the restoration of significant architecture. We are pleased to find that the liquor store has joined this trend and occupies a carefully renovated schoolhouse. The excellent selection of wines available there is a direct reflection of the increasing sophistication of the residents of Elora.

Despite its obvious charm, Elora has not yet reached the status of Niagara-on-the-Lake as a tourist attraction. On the other hand, it appeals to increasing numbers and could become too "touristy". On some summer afternoons, the crush of tourists is oppressive. Buses and cars jam Mill Street making access almost impossible. There is additional parking across the river at the end of the restored foot bridge, but at times even this is inadequate. Notwithstanding these minor inconveniences, arts and music groups have promoted the successful Three Centuries Festival which presents local and international artists in Elora's churches and restaurants.

A particularly attractive event has been the quarry concert. On a warm summer evening we take to bleachers lining the cliffs above a man-made lake. Far below a brass ensemble prepares to play from a barge. Under looming cliffs, torches cast faint flickering light upon the placid water. The scene is like a fairy tale, slowly rising mists, brilliance seeping slowly from the sky, a creation of summer magic. Strains of Mozart waft across the water. Solid colours, devoid of shape or shadow, spill over the landscape, then moon and stars sweep the empty expanse above. A choral group materializes from the darkness, adding resonant strains to the night sounds of brass and cricket, swallow and frog. Finally, cool fingers of creeping mist completely envelop the scene, capturing the moment forever in an ecstasy of music and nature. Such are the joys of the quarry concerts; successful syntheses of music by man and settings by nature.

Next morning, snug as snails in our beds above the falls we luxuriate in memories of the evening concert. Soon we realize that all in Elora is not music and romance, scenic beauty and pleasurable visits. It is also a place of work and residence for many, rural service centre, commuter dormitory, generator of wealth and enterprise. Elora has attracted families which formerly lived in Kitchener, Waterloo, Guelph and even Toronto. Its small-town atmosphere, riverside sites, and Conservation Authority Park have enticed many from other municipalities. In the past, lower house prices were also an attraction, but the gap has narrowed since more and more commuters have discovered Elora. It remains a quiet and pleasant village with much to offer to resident and visitor alike.

The very real danger for Elora is that it will be spoiled by its own success. More businesses, tourists and residents have the potential to change it from an unspoiled country town into a "tourist trap." The balance between becoming a Niagara-on-the Lake, where development has radically altered the social and economic fabric of the community, and retaining original charm is delicate. Only though consultation, co-operation and foresight will its citizens preserve the best of Elora while avoiding the worst excesses seen elsewhere.

Reluctantly we wend our way to the next stop on this historic journey. A few hundred yards to the north and west lies another historic, but considerably less successful, community. This is Salem, now almost a suburb of Elora. It prospered mightily for a few years in the 1830s, until Sam Wissler, its chief promoter and businessman, died and his estate was frozen. An additional blow occurred when the railway bypassed Salem for Elora.

We make the necessary detour into Salem by following Geddes Street to the Irvine Creek crossing where more history awaits. Here we are rewarded by discovering the remnants of the once thriving mills along the creek. Their limestone ruins cling precipitously to cliffs near the bridge. At this point the river gushes madly through a narrow obstruction into the bowels of the limestone depths below. It plunges into the gorge, unleashing the power that provided incentives for major business ventures in the 1800s. But all is not in ruin; just downstream, several former factories have been renovated into apartments now inhabited by commuters. An enterprising potter molds his clay in the shop he has established nearby.

Immediately before the river enters Elora, we find a delightful residential estate developed around a former stable and mill. Near the gates, a home and artist's studio fashioned from an industrial building extend down towards the water. Slightly farther on, a carefully landscaped subdivision of newer homes blends into the river valley.

Soon artists and artisans joined the local shopkeepers, making and selling their wares in and around the original Mill Street nucleus. The Elora Mill and the back of Mill Street from the Grand River bridge.

Here we are rewarded by discovering the remnants of the once thriving mills along the creek. Their limestone ruins cling precipitously to cliffs near the bridge at Salem on the Irvine Creek.

Across from this exclusive enclave, others have built their country retreats, near to the river and handy to the amenities of Elora. A few artisans have also established themselves in Salem which has never become as commercially successful as Elora. But it has provided some delightful residential settings. All one needs to qualify is time to commute and the cash to acquire increasingly scarce building sites near the river.

Additional growth will require full (and very expensive) services for water and sewage in Salem. Parts of the community have already experienced the agony of these sudden and major costs. Meanwhile, with fond memories of our sojourn at the confluence of the Irvine and the Grand, we continue our trip along the Credit Valley Railway. Our final destination is but an hour's travel to the east.

The Orangeville Branch

Alton is an overlooked jewel in the crown of the Credit Valley Line. Just past Cataract, the Orangeville Branch follows gentle slopes north-west along the river valley. We continue our journey by rail but could cut across country by car, following county roads to the east and north from Elora.

Regardless of our route, the discovery of Alton is a pleasure and a treat since it occupies one of the most captivating sites in Ontario. It was established beside the Shaw Creek, directly under "The Pinnacle", a rugged hill called a kame by geologists. Approached by rail, Alton retains much of the rustic charm of days gone by.

Artifacts found on the Pinnacle indicate that Indians had inhabited the area for some 3000 years before the white man came. They hunted caribou in this fertile locale and used the valley to travel inland from Lake Ontario. They had recognized the potential of an area destined eventually to become a thriving industrial community. Beneath the tumbled mass of sand and stone, hard beside a clear rill washing clumps of new watercress, this site gave birth to the village of Alton. Its topographic and architectural attractions make it well worth a day trip, despite the fact that it is bit off the beaten path. Steep slopes, swift water, languid pools, cedar-lined shores, and a legacy of historic architecture lure us to a settlement only now being "discovered".

When the first settlers arrived in 1834, power provided by Shaw's creek was the basis for Alton's initial development. But early growth was slow, and it was not till the 1840s that the Wright Brothers erected a grist mill nearby. The full potential of the Alton location was realized only when Benjamin Ward built a woollen mill in 1845. In a few years other mills were constructed. By the First World War, Dods Knitting Mill of Alton supplied socks and other woolens to thousands of Canadian and British troops. This business became known as the "Upper Mill" and was eventually taken over by the Toronto Millstock Company which ran it until 1965.

Eventually the upper mill was sold and the equipment auctioned to be used again in Woodstock. The upper mill has been rebuilt and restored as the Millcroft Inn, a luxurious hotel. The three stories of the original 1881 stone structure now house cozy lounges, snug bedrooms and a glassed in balcony for diners. Today we relax above the millpond and falls and feast upon exquisite cuisine in a rustic atmosphere. Quail, pâté, riesling, stuffed veal and fresh fruit topped by sherbet - we are more than satisfied. Endless cups of coffee from fine white porcelain complete our gourmet adventure. We depart with full stomachs and considerably thinner wallets. The thick stone walls, heavy dark beams and pine furniture recall a more gracious era from the past. Beyond the restored mill, additional accommodation is provided in wooden chalets across the river. Millcroft has become a year-round resort and retreat.

Nearby, the palatial Dods home continues to stand, reminding us of the wealth and prosperity once generated by the upper mill. Its ornate gables, soaring peaks, and handsome patterned brick recall the wealth and sophistication of those who guided Alton's early growth. The home is now being insulated to modern standards and completely renovated. The "Pinnacle" behind the Inn, which was also sold with the property, has been developed for skiing in winter and hiking in summer. Trails circle the peak, swooping steeply down the slopes to the stream, affording panoramic views of the town and hills beyond.

Just downstream from the Millcroft Inn, another historic structure remains. This is the lower mill, built by William Algie in 1881 but burned and renovated many times since. It eventually became the Beaver Woollen Mill and was run by the Dods family until 1935. It was then purchased by the Western Rubber Company, and continued to function as a rubber factory until a few years ago. It has recently been purchased by a company which plans to use it for artists and artisans. Just across and down the street, the large stone factory that once housed Barber Brothers Carriage Works has been restored to its 1894 condition and is used for a general store and antique shop. During the First World War, over 150 employees produced munitions here. The workforce consisted primarily of women who toiled for two shifts a day to assist in the war effort.

We stroll along the now gentle stream and contemplate its violent history. In November 1889, it precipitated an event that caused grievous harm and was long remembered. Rain had been falling for days and the stream was filled to capacity. Local dams strained and bulged in valiant attempts to restrain the boiling, surging waters. Finally it happened. The McClelland Brothers' mill dam heaved, cracked, and finally gave way, releasing a wall of water 16 feet deep from a pond of seven acres. The debris-laden torrent plunged over the pond at Dods Mill, smashing the dam and unleashing an additional five acres of water to plunge down the valley. Fortunately, the Beaver Knitting Mill dam held for half an hour, but the wall of churning water dashed relentlessly against the barrier, eventually gutting the mill and destroying much of its machinery.

The then enormous wall of water advanced again, dashed against the Dominion Foundry and threw it into the turbulent muddy mass. Then the flood continued its wild rampage to the dams below. Unable to withstand the shattering power unleashed by tons of churning, heaving, oily, debris-laden liquid, the last dam at the Alton Flour Mill heaved, crumbled, and finally gave way with a resounding roar.

The dams and the mills of Alton were almost totally destroyed, necessitating a major effort of reconstruction. Nature had done its work and obliterated in hours that which had taken years for man to construct. Unfortunately, we have not yet learned the lesson of the flood plain. Regardless of

The former Lower Mill (Beaver Woollen Mill) in Alton. Parts of the building are now being used by artisans.

the care with which we build and protect our structures, we will forever be subject to floods. Despite the precautions we take or the strength of our dams and dikes, nature is capable of producing even larger and more destructive storms to challenge our ingenuity. If we continue to remove the forests, plow the land and channelize the streams into concrete ditches, we increase the potential for yet greater disasters in the future. Today the creek is calm, but this is not a guarantee for the future.

In the Alton tragedy, three small frame houses were dashed to pieces by the raging torrent. Fortunately, only one person was killed in the flood, while three others experienced a harrowing escape. (After their home was inundated, they were carried to the ceiling by the water before being swept to safety.) Only two of the dams were rebuilt after a flood greater than that accompanying Hurricane Hazel removed much of the industrial legacy of Alton. Fortunately, other structures remain to help us recollect its industrial and cultural achievements.

Down the street we discover the former Science Hall which was the scene of numerous lectures, plays and concerts. It may be found, now a private dwelling, just across the river from the former Beaver Woollen Mill. The Mechanic's Institute, or local library, which was constructed in 1882 is at the intersection of Amelia and Queen Streets and continues with its original function. For a time such buildings were the intellectual hearts of Ontario communities, bringing books and learning to the workers and their families. The general store, just across the street, also continues as it has for years. At the corner we find the former Palmer House Hotel at Queen and Main Streets, now occupied by several apartments and a number of artisans and artists. Today a glass blower and boat builder ply their trades, along with several purveyors of antiques and crafts. A stroll through its spacious rooms recalls the legacy of its past and its potential for the future.

Alton had early aspirations to greatness, some of which left their mark for us to observe today. In 1904, concrete sidewalks were installed on Main and Queen Streets all the way to the Credit Valley Depot. This modern innovation welcomed the traveller in style and gave the settlement a sophistication far beyond its time. The Toronto Grey and Bruce Railway also served Alton, but its station was on the edge of town, beyond the limit of the concrete footpath. Nevertheless, the service of two important railways assisted its rapid rise to local prominence.

Central Alton has changed little, despite disastrous floods and ruined industry. Or is this genteel stagnation because it has been bypassed until very recently? Even the upscale Millcroft Inn manages to blend well with its small-town character, despite a renovated interior and relatively stiff prices. Now Alton seems poised on the verge of a renaissance. With its rich heritage of nineteenth century architectural treasures it is waiting to be discovered by the masses from the cities. Seeds of gentrification and commercial development have already taken root along Queen Street. Potential is evident on Main Street as well. Several new subdivisions have been built on the outskirts, no doubt a harbinger of growth and development to come.

In a way, Alton is the quintessential Ontario mill town, protected until now by its location and relative obscurity. We hope that those who do exploit its remaining commercial potential will do so with the care already exercised by their predecessors. Alton is a treasure that should not be despoiled by insensitive commercial development, or by unscrupulous residential developers. Unfortunately, the recent experience with residential subdivisions has not been good.

The recent events in Alton prompt us to contemplate the future of the towns along the Credit Valley Railway. It is time to pause again to recall intrepid pioneers and railway builders who "opened up the soil". They had the courage and vision to go "where no man had gone before" risking the wrath of sometimes hostile Indians, the dangers of cold and starvation and the ever-constant summer plague of mosquitoes and blackflies. Today the fruits of their labours remain -- some now trendy, gentrified villages like Elora, others thriving service centres such as Erin, still others, like Brimstone, nothing more than names on a map. Yet all have potential and all have a future. The direction taken by each will be the result of decisions made by many; businessmen, planners, government bureaucrats, town councils and ordinary citizens. Before plunging wildly ahead into continuous growth, renovation and development, let us take stock of both our future and our legacy. Each is embodied in the communities along the Credit Valley Line, and each is worthy of careful contemplation.

Diversity, complexity and change are the characteristics lending ambience and charm to Ontario's rural communities. Before we cast them all into the same homogeneous mould, let us assess their distinctive local character to determine whether some are worthy of preservation while others may benefit from change. Careful thought and measured progress are to be preferred to precipitous schemes. It takes only a day to destroy the legacy of two hundred years.

CHAPTER FOUR

To The Agricultural Heartland And The Land Of The Mennonites

Thoughts of floods, dams, historic buildings and village heritage remain as we continue our exploration of Ontario. We have left the rail line and river valley to plunge into the heart of Ontario's productive farmland. Here we will discover settlements with distinctive forms and diverse functions -- those concerned primarily with the provision of service to the local farmer.

In the beginning, the rural service centre was the heart of the agricultural land in which it stood -- a place of meetings and exchange, of friendships and commerce. Some had much in common with their railway counterparts, eventually attracting the iron horse and sometimes possessing a mill. Others stood at crossroads in the midst of fertile fields of wheat. They existed for no purpose other than to be depots of exchange, mail pick-up places, the locale of a pub, or centres of socialization and Saturday night flirtation. Many came and went in a few short years; ephemeral products of ambitious promoters and an uncertain economy. Others stood, and grew, and endure today. All have a story to tell and many have left a physical legacy. Others remain only as entries in business directories or as names on a map.

Throughout Ontario, location on a stream was by far the most frequent "raison d'être" for the earliest settlements where wood was sawed and first crops of wheat were ground to flour. But when the pioneer period ended, surpluses developed, the economy diversified and population increased. Some farmers grew wheat, others oats and potatoes; others raised cattle and pigs; many mixed them all. Wheat monoculture gave way to a diversified economy requiring frequent trade and exchange. In locations where no stream existed, but where crops flourished nearby, service centres proliferated like mushrooms after a September rain. It seemed that every other crossroads had acquired a tiny settlement. By the 1880s, a day's return journey by horse took any farmer to his local hamlet. Many didn't include a mill, but each boasted a general store, post office, hotel, blacksmith, tavern, and church. When the post office and general store were combined, they became a social centre to rival the most popular tavern. Farmers and villagers gathered there regularly to talk, to play cards and to smoke. The village post office became a veritable institution that endured for decades. Between 1860 and the turn of the century, these tiny, bustling centres provided the link between the farmer and the outside world.

By the 1930s, changing technology took its toll when rural mail delivery, prohibition and motor transport combined to destroy most of these hamlets. They dropped like flies in DDT. The car and truck had replaced the horse as a primary mode of transportation. Victorian women's groups linked drink with all evil, thereby killing the pubs, and catalogue shopping by mail pushed the general store to the wall. This was a sad era in the history of Ontario settlement. Modern technology had shattered the dreams of land developers and ruined the lives of local merchants. On the other hand, the car, the post office and the radio changed the life of the farmer forever. They brought him into the mainstream of local and national life, improving his access and communications as no innovations had done before.

Because they were so typical and numerous, it is difficult to find a link that binds a group of service centres together. This is now especially true, since many have changed to commuter dormitories or have become economically specialized, while others have disappeared completely. Service to agriculture was their initial function; one that enables us to appreciate their common legacy. On our continuing journey, we will travel through some of the best agricultural land in Canada, beginning just north of Waterloo, and ending at the tip of the Bruce Peninsula. This trip will take us to several towns that have been "gentrified", to others with a distinctive Mennonite flavour, to some that have become resort or retirement centres, and to others that have almost entirely disappeared. We will seek their origins and attempt to explain their diversity. Along their streets we will observe the complexity and change that have made them interesting and unique.

The short drive from Alton and its mills to St. Jacobs and its German heritage takes us through cool tree-clad hills, then past square fields of wheat or hay waving in the summer sun. When we reach St. Jacobs, the differences between the two communities become immediately obvious. The contrast between the rugged, rolling, boulder-studded environs of Alton and the gentle till plains near St. Jacobs is reflected in local agricultural pursuits.

Millennia before St. Jacobs was founded, glaciers smoothed and sculpted, oscillating over the limestone bedrock, depositing fertile layers of silt, sand and clay. On this inviting foundation stand Pennsylvania barns with recent wooden additions, tall blue silos, and long metal sheds. Now they command acres and acres of corn, hay or field crops. What a contrast to the rustic two-bay barns and rough hillside pastures surrounding Alton. In place of cattle or sheep grazing on the slopes, we find feedlots crammed with hapless steers or broiler chickens, mooing or clucking their lives away in hot tin sheds. Nearby, a major poultry processor wrings the necks and plucks the feathers of the unlucky fowl before they are frozen and sent to market. In contrast to this carnage, peaceful countryside rolls to the horizon. It is dotted with barns, cattle, tidy homes and wheat, corn and hay rippling in the wind. Enterprise and prosperity are everywhere obvious.

Like Alton, St. Jacobs did attract a rail line, and had its mills, but today these features have faded and new enterprises have replaced the old. St. Jacobs is the happy beneficiary of its handy location, much nearer than Alton to major concentrations of population, both urban and rural. Its functions have recently metamorphosed to accommodate the economic realities of the 1980s. Squeaky clean streets leading to the heart of this Waterloo Region village slide past rows of brown and white bungalows surrounded by carpets of groomed green grass.

No carnival atmosphere of plastic fast-food outlets greets us at the entrance of St. Jacobs. Instead, an ornate sign proclaims our welcome to this community of 1189 industrious souls. The drive past agricultural implement dealers and then along streets sheltered by canopies of maple leaves takes us to the busy business area in the river valley. Here we immediately become aware of an historic role as a rural service centre. One of the first buildings we notice is Martin's blacksmith shop, just as it must have been a hundred years ago. Sparks fly from the anvil while a local Mennonite awaits the repair of a shoe for his horse. Outside the shop, two black carriages stand like messengers from the past. They are driven by bearded old-order Mennonites from farms who make such a business viable today.

Just down the street, the former grain elevator of a mill has been transformed into a shop selling

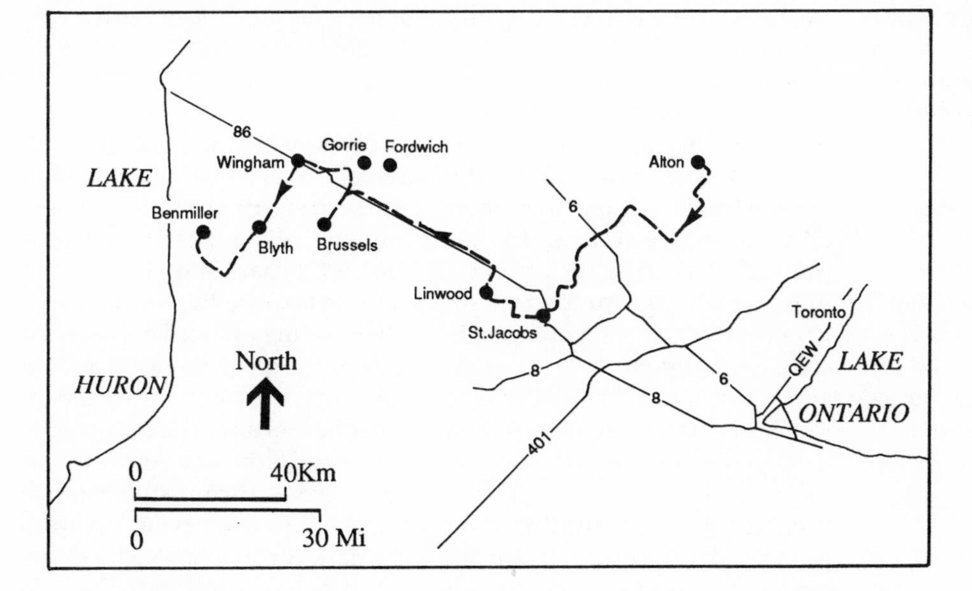

Our route through the Agricultural Heartland and the land of the Mennonites.

One of the first buildings we notice is Martin's Blacksmith Shop, just as it must have been a hundred years ago. This business in St. Jacobs continues to shoe horses for local Mennonite farmers.

trendy furniture. We enter the former silo to view the wares and experience local agricultural history. A pungent odour of grain and chaff permeate the atmosphere to recall for us its original function. Down the street we discover boutiques, a gallery, gift shops and several restaurants. Of course the ubiquitous hardware and general stores remain to supply the local farmers with their needs. The combination of old and new, service function for the farmers and shopping attractions for the visitor, exist harmoniously side by side in St. Jacobs.

Once again, the efforts of an entrepreneur have contributed significantly to the success of a community whose functions have changed. Prominent on the main street is the Stone Crock, a folksy, unlicensed Mennonite restaurant renowned for its generous portions of home-cooked food. Here on a Saturday or Sunday, patrons from great distances line up to sample the pork and sauerkraut followed by apple strudel, or the roast beef and mashed potatoes accompanied by freshly picked vegetables and preceded by generous bowls of home-made soup. Shoo-fly pie (mostly sugar and maple syrup), strawberry or raspberry tarts, puddings and local ice cream tempt the dessert eater. Authentic nineteenth-century furnishings and waitresses in pioneer dress complete the illusion of stopping in an Ontario country inn, circa 1897. Needless to say, it didn't take long before other local entrepreneurs began to cash in on trade drawn initially by this restaurant which attracted far more business than we would expect for a small town enterprise.

A block or two west of the main street, we notice that another entrepreneur has taken advantage of the rustic setting to convert a charming old mansion into the Jakobstettel Guest House. Here we may relax for a night or a week. Its green lawns, trees and flowers combine to create the atmosphere of an exclusive residential neighbourhood in a prosperous turn-of-the-century village. Crocuses push up from the dark earth, while snow drops lift their heads to the spring sun above. Later in the summer, geraniums drip blood-red blossoms and a profusion of lilacs

We notice that another entrepreneur has taken advantage of the rustic setting to convert a charming old mansion into the Jakobstettel Guest House.

scent the air with their pungent essence. Soft maples and a few remaining elms cast their soothing shade over the tranquil street. The proprietors have created an enchanting atmosphere at their village inn. With Kitchener-Waterloo and Guelph so close they are on to a good thing, and it may well lead to more of the same.

St. Jacobs has not yet been spoiled, but its location and potential for additional gentrification make this a possibility. A recent survey conducted by Philip Coppack to measure the appeal of the village has documented the attractions of St. Jacobs. He found that most people who visited came because of its rural atmosphere, friendly people, good restaurants and attractive homes. A survey of residents revealed that country-type living and friendly neighbours were rated as St. Jacobs' most pleasing attributes.

Such attractions will remain important as long as the scale and pace of population growth do not overwhelm the village. Excessive economic development, especially if it attracts MacDonalds, the Colonel, or a Pizza Hut may also pose a threat. When tourists and their attendant economic functions become more important than traditional activities, a settlement becomes a less attractive residential location. And when congestion and traffic replace rural atmosphere, it loses appeal for day-trippers as well. Along with their success, some diversifying communities sow the seeds of their ultimate demise.

TO THE HEART OF MENNONITE COUNTRY

The transition from St. Jacobs with its Mennonite roots and modern businesses to Linwood is accomplished within a few short kilometers. We drive north and west, across the tranquil river, through rolling fields of corn, and into a region where farms are without power connections. Here we find solid red brick or stone farmhouses devoid of the usual ornamentation. They stand proud, commanding lush pastures which contrast with the warm brown tones of freshly plowed fields. The unmistakable, pungent, all pervasive odour of new manure assaults our nostrils as we enter Mennonite country in the spring.

In this prosperous corner of the Waterloo Region, old-order Mennonites eschew the conveniences of the modern world to preserve their traditions and way of life. When the slumping sun has spread its final flash of fiery red upon the sky, they read by the flickering yellow flame of a kerosene lamp. In the spring their dark brown maple syrup froths and bubbles in vast metal vats, licked by fires of oak or maple. Entry to their homes transports us to the past. Here the dry sink, pine sideboard and harvest table are standard items of furniture rather than antiques. Blue smoke curls slowly skyward from the iron cook stoves, wafting like feathering clouds into the breeze. Cattle call their mournful cry, demanding relief from milk-gorged udders. Chickens and geese scrabble for grubs in the barnyard beyond.

Sturdy draught horses draw iron plows across the fields, cutting furrows through the crumbling black loam, straight as an Indian arrow. Warm manure, bubbling and seething while it oozes through the augers, spills onto the field from the spreader, returning organic nourishment to the soil from whence it came. All is recycled, and that which is taken from the earth is ultimately returned. No chemical fertilizers here; nor pesticides nor herbicides. Weeds are plucked from between the crops and gardens carefully tended by hand. Such is the husbandry that has made this a region of agricultural production unparalleled in Ontario.

Work is the major agenda for the Mennonites, but spiritual enrichment also looms large in their lives. On Sunday they drive, pulled by snorting, high-stepping stallions, to the plain white church. Here horse and buggy line the wooden stable as the devout file into their stark and simple place of worship. Inside, women wear cloth bonnets over white net coverings and sit apart from the men. Hand-made clothes of black material are fastened with hooks and eyes, buttons being too decorative and thus too "worldly" for the faithful of the old order. Children are educated to the age of leaving in religious schools, while OHIP is left to modern Canadians.

When we visit an old-order Mennonite homestead to purchase

On Sunday the Mennonites drive, pulled by snorting, high stepping stallions to the plain white church.

some maple syrup, we step a hundred years back into time. The children, wearing glasses at an early age because of generations of intermarriage, play quietly with their wooden toys. Their mother, dressed in her formless frock, white apron and white net head covering is kneading the dough from which to bake bread over the glowing coals in the wood stove. A wooden churn is used to produce creamy, pale yellow butter. A new batch of cottage cheese drains from a cloth bag over a wooden bowl in the summer kitchen. Meanwhile, the father repairs his implements in the barn after returning with his horse and wagon from a trip to the mill.

These are the hardy souls who patronize the Linwood General Store. Here we discover black homburg hats, high black lace-up shoes, vast bolts of dark blue material, and wood stoves for sale. Leather harnesses and hand churns are still available, along with sausage presses at $365. The shelves are filled with black stockings, German language hymn books and wide brimmed black felt hats for $69. Of course, some modern hardware is also available, but the shop girls are Mennonite and the store is clearly not for tourists. Across from the church, a convenient shed is provided for parking the horse and buggy.

The village has a community centre and lighted ball diamond like many Ontario settlements, but it is well off the tourist track. This fact has enabled it to remain a archetypal, unspoiled rural service centre. The former hotel has been converted to apartments and is now for sale, and the local population has declined. This characteristic is shared with many communities developed primarily to serve the surrounding farmers. Even here in a remote and traditional area of the Waterloo Region, some farm enlargement and consolidation have occurred. This has led almost inevitably to rural population decline and to the demise of local service functions.

A number of years ago, Robert Murdie conducted a study to compare the shopping habits of Mennonites with those of modern Canadians. Its results exemplified the differences between the two cultures. Although both banked in Elmira or Waterloo, Mennonites shopped for clothes in Linwood, Heidelberg, Hawkseville or Wallenstein, while modern Canadians went to Kitchener or Waterloo. These differences reflect both culture and technology. Both societies banked where they did because no other banks were closer. Modern Canadians pursued fashion and variety by travelling up to 80 kilometers to buy clothes, whereas Mennonites went to the nearest town with a general store, normally less than 20 kilometers away.

Of course, the Mennonites purchase only yard goods from which to make their clothes. These are available in every self-respecting general store. The major constraint is the distance of a return trip in a day by horse and buggy; the same limitation that produced the dense pattern of rural service centres in the late 1800s. In Mennonite country, little has changed since those days. Only when forced to participate in modern institutions, such as banks, have the Mennonites changed their ways. In the area of Linwood, the nineteenth century is alive and well.

BACK TO THE TWENTIETH CENTURY

We don't have to drive too far in order to observe the devastation wrought upon once prosperous service centres by really large-scale farm consolidation and agribusiness. Only 55 kilometers west of Linwood in Huron County we encounter Brussels, once the bustling, prosperous centre of a region dominated by hundred-acre farms. Now we find a settlement of 961, situated in the midst of some of the richest farmland in Canada. But for the farm buildings we might be in the Prairies. Unfenced fields of long green corn and yellow canola blossoms stretch to the far horizon. Here and there we discover the bleached cedar boards of a central Ontario barn, elsewhere the gaunt skeleton of a crumbling Victorian farmhouse. Among the trees, covered in vines, festooned with overgrown lilac bushes and almost hidden from the sun, stands a former hamlet. Now it is abandoned and crumbling, forgotten by all but the locals and a few settlement explorers.

Down the road, a squat modern bungalow with aluminum siding stands surrounded by modern gambrel-roofed central Ontario barns and a forest of silos. Several self-propelled harvesters are poised in the yard, ready to swallow up the corn and spew it into waiting trucks. Beside these mechanical monsters we find the pick-up truck and an enormous air-conditioned tractor, complete with stereo sound and sheepskin-covered seats. Farm consolidation by successful locals and some corporate agriculture have combined to produce this new rural landscape. If we ignore the abandoned farms and hamlets, signs of prosperity are everywhere on our approach to the village of Brussels.

What a sight this must have been in the 1880s! Horses and their riders clattered down the streets while the shops overflowed with people and goods. The tavern produced a steady stream of whiskey and profanity when its patrons rolled into the street on a warm Saturday night. Doctors, pharmacists, lawyers and shipping agents vied to serve customers and clients who thronged to the village. The mill converted mountains of wheat or oats to flour, while down the street the cooper's hammer could be heard as he fashioned his barrels from wood and metal hoops.

After its auspicious beginning as Ainleyville in 1856, Brussels acquired a blacksmith shop, saw mill, grist mill, woolen mill and many other industries. By 1863, when its population reached 780, it was a thriving industrial village and an important local service centre. Carriages were built, woolens were woven and spun, turnips were waxed and doors were fabricated. Brussels boomed!

In the next year, the arrival of the Wellington, Grey and Bruce Railway linked Brussels to export markets for its agricultural and manufactured products. By 1891, its population stood at 1204 while the directories listed 84 economic establishments. Modern new business blocks, three stories high, some ornately decorated, extended the length of its main street. Given its location on a dam site for water power, served by the most contemporary form of transportation and in a fertile agricultural hinterland, its future seemed assured. What then has happened to cause its recent decline?

We immediately experience the fading fortunes of Brussels. The magnitude of change since its heyday strikes us as soon as we enter the village. Along Turnberry Street, the scene is almost one of desolation. Rough boards cover the windows of once proud and thriving businesses. The formerly grand hotel has closed, standing like a ghost in the midst of a graveyard. Down the street, two battered industrial buildings, wearing their faded signs like bandages, sink and sag while they fall into disrepair. The street is not entirely deserted, but what was once a splendid vista now lacks the colour, sound and bustling activity of its glorious past.

We find a third of the main street business spaces vacant in Brussels. The population has fallen to 962, a 20 per cent drop from its 1891 total. According to the Directories, Brussels lost 53 business establishments from 1891 to 1981, a decrease of 63 per cent. Even if we look at a shorter period, things seem bleak. In 1961, Brussels had ten food stores, five clothing out-

We find a third of the main street business spaces vacant in Brussels.

lets and three furniture businesses, most of which have closed. One of the survivors is a magnificent five and ten cent store, complete with its large wooden window frame and bright red paint. Inside, pine boards, worn smooth by generations of bargain-seeking customers, cover its floor. The smell and feel of yesterday linger in this slightly faded throwback to the past.

But today there is a disparate note in Brussels. The population has increased by 118, or 14 percent from 1961 to 1981. How do we explain this apparent contradiction? When we look again at the settlement and the statistics, another story begins to emerge. Brussels has certainly suffered from rural depopulation and the advent of agribusiness. And like many similar places, it has been dealt a devastating blow by the motor car which has taken away former customers who now shop for more variety and better prices in the city. But it retains its scenic location on the river, its quiet tree-lined streets and its small town character. Unlike the business buildings, the houses are not boarded up. In fact a few new dwellings have been built on the outskirts, and a number of turn-of-the-century beauties have been gutted and renovated.

But who would live here, relatively far from either the city or the lake? The age profile of the residents provides a clue. In 1981, some 22 percent were over 65, compared to 14 percent for Huron County. This is not a large difference, but it does illustrate the attraction of Brussels for retirees. Special tabulations from Statistics

Canada show that most people who moved to Brussels from 1976 to 1981 were from nearby townships, no doubt retiring farmers.

We must not paint too bright a picture for Brussels, which has certainly lost both business and population in the last hundred years. Even a major study and a campaign to paint up the main street sponsored by the Huron Planning Department did little to reverse the trends. Elsewhere, non-farm people have sustained rural service centres, but in Huron County the attraction of the lakeshore lures many to settle by the water. In an attempt to protect agricultural land, tough planning regulations have kept them away from the fringes of places like Brussels.

There really aren't many attractive and available residential sites in the midst of prime farmland. Furthermore, Brussels isn't close enough to major centres of employment to become a commuter dormitory. Consequently, local population growth has been slow, and there are few rural non-farm dwellers nearby. In the final analysis, Brussels may grow slowly to accommodate retiring farmers and a few fugitives from the city. But in many respects it is a typical victim of the changing technology of transportation and agriculture. Ironically, improvements in both have adversely affected towns in most rich agricultural regions.

WE TRAVEL TO A "DYING VILLAGE"

After our visit to Brussels, it is time to move on. This time we choose the small community of Wroxeter characterized as a "Ghost Town" by Ron Brown in his book, *Backroads of Ontario.* He noted that of the dozen and a half stores on the main street, more than two-thirds were boarded up. This certainly seemed to be excellent evidence for the existence of a dying village, corroborated by the abandoned 1972 Chevrolet on blocks in front of the former general store. To us, the street appears devoid of both businesses and people on a quiet Saturday afternoon. And yet there seems to be a puzzle here. We find a spanking new playground and lighted ball diamond on the outskirts, along with a number of modern new bungalows. On the main street we see a recent brick structure that houses a bank and real estate agency. The Maitland Con-

The street appeared devoid of both people and businesses on the quiet Saturday afternoon when we visited Wroxeter.

servation Authority occupies a building on the same street as well as a former school building across town. Clearly something is happening in Wroxeter.

What is the answer to the dilemma seemingly posed by this once thriving community? It lies inland from the lake, near to Highway 87, just a half-hour's drive through moraine and rolling pasture. We stroll across the bridge that passes the former mill site and millpond, where we detect the reason for its previous prosperity. In the early years, farmers would travel by horse and cart from as far as Neustadt and Mildmay to have their peas ground into meal at this mill. Some even walked, heavy sacks of wheat, oats or peas slung across their backs. Blacksmiths, bankers, gunsmiths, tanners and a woollen mill were among 36 businesses in 1881 when the population stood at 560. Prosperous merchants mingled with Saturday night visitors to the pub, gossiping and making business deals over a whiskey or beer.

After the railway bypassed Wroxeter a bit to the north and the highways looped around it, the community began to suffer. Its plight was not helped by the presence of Fordwich and Gorrie, competing centres a few miles to the west. When mills, family farms and horse transportation were predominant, such proximity mattered little. Farmers continued to patronize the nearest local service centre. But by 1987, rural depopulation, farm enlargement, access to larger places by car and subsequent one-stop shopping trips had taken their toll on Wroxeter. Its plight has not been improved by the local access from the highway, which could charitably be described as baroque. For the uninitiated, the local road pattern is truly a mystery!

The population had declined to 276 by 1976, and by 1981, only 11 businesses operated in the hamlet. What a far cry from the old days when the mills hummed with activity and local merchants built block-long three-storey business establishments on the main street. The physical evidence and statistics seem surely to point to a dismal future. One lonely grocery store remains viable, while an attempt at a craft shop has failed, leaving only the cedar siding to remind us of its short life. On the walls of several buildings, faded signs, now almost illegible, proclaim their former functions. The remnant of a blacksmith shop remains, now mostly devoted to repairs of cars and tractors. But why then has the population risen to 350 in 1981, a 27 percent increase since 1976? Somehow, the statistics don't corroborate the evidence seen on the street. Or do they?

We head back to the outskirts of town, along tree-lined streets towards the highway. Here an older home has been turned into a duplex and there stand several new Manitoba splits. On a hill close to the playground, additional homes have been constructed during the last few years. The former village hall has been converted to apartments to accommodate those who have moved here from somewhere. Did they come to escape the city or to retire? The answers are not apparent without additional investigation.

The only way to discover definitively what has happened is to ask the local people, and that's just what we did. Last summer, two students from the University of Guelph administered a questionnaire designed to discover what really made Wroxeter tick, and to probe the attitudes of its residents to a whole host of issues. Our findings belied the image of a dying village, notwithstanding the sorry state of the main street. Upon a closer investigation, even this street didn't appear so bleak. The buildings had not been demolished, but were mostly functioning as residences.

Once again the value of the capital fixed in structures became evident. Rather than being demolished, abandoned shops were converted very easily into apartments. This alternative has served many who could not afford to build or had found no other rental accommodation. In a town like Wroxeter, the main street goes nowhere, and with the decline in business activity, is a quiet location for a home. Why not utilize all those solid two and three-storey buildings? And that is exactly what they did.

Almost everyone interviewed expressed satisfaction with life in Wroxeter, citing its country atmosphere and quiet nature as attractions. Many were retired farmers from nearby, but others had found employment in Wingham and at numerous business enterprises in the surrounding countryside. Major grocery shopping, visits to medical services and comparison shopping were generally done in Wingham, less than half an hour away by car. Banking and convenience shopping were almost always done locally, despite high prices in the convenience store. On balance, respondents were content with their access to necessary goods and services. Their trips to work, shop or visit the doctor generally took less time than they would have taken on busy city streets or highways. When asked about the future, many believed that growth and development were desirable. Many respondents would like to see both a larger population and more stores in the future.

These answers may seem at variance with those from Alton or St. Jacobs, but the situations are vastly different. Even though Wroxeter is a picturesque village on a millpond, it has neither the historic architecture of an Alton nor the economic potential of a St. Jacobs. Aside from visiting friends or just exploring Ontario villages, there is little reason to travel to Wroxeter, and its location does nothing to encourage chance encounters. You whiz by on Highway 87 before you notice it's there. Unlike many other communities, growth poses no threat for Wroxeter but additional people might sustain more local shops and social organizations. At the moment, its lovely churches reflect the past but are far from filled on Sundays.

A NEW FORM OF COMMUNITY IN ONTARIO

Wroxeter may well be part of what scholars now refer to as the "dispersed city" in Ontario. More and more, this new pattern has taken hold. Now, numerous formerly dying villages function primarily as residential neighbourhoods, tied by the car to work and shopping a few miles away. These places are not dormitory suburbs, and function quite independently of the major metropolitan areas that some of their residents have abandoned.

Employment, goods, services and entertainment can all be obtained nearby, often at relatively isolated outsized functions that attract customers from both near and far. Geographers have given the name outsized function to businesses in small towns that attract far more trade than one would expect in a settlement which some consider to be dying. Usually an enterprising businessman has taken advantage of a former mill, blacksmith shop or hotel and has used his entrepreneurial talents to create a business that draws people from far afield. Pubs, res-

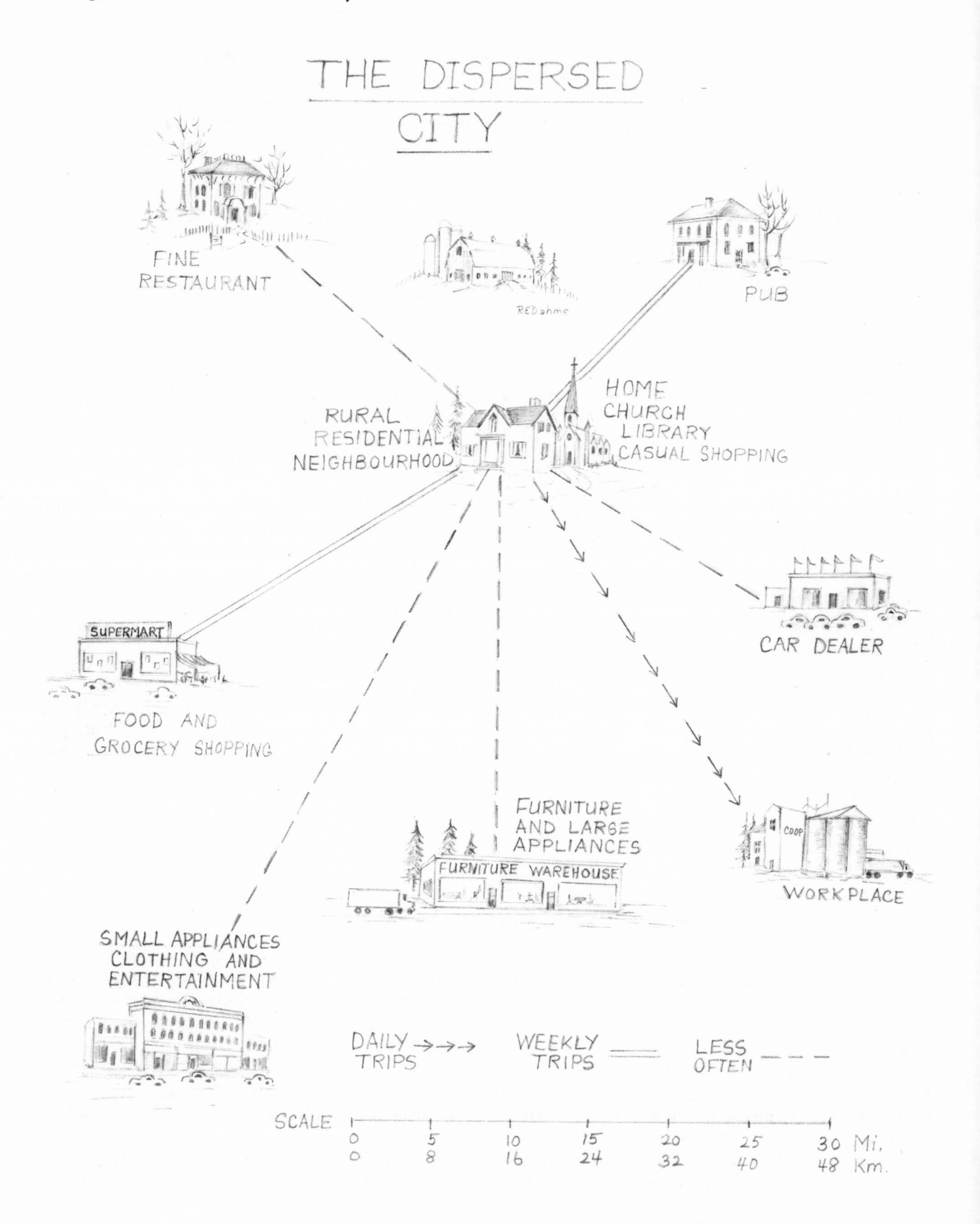
THE DISPERSED CITY
FINE RESTAURANT
R.E.Dahms
PUB
RURAL RESIDENTIAL NEIGHBOURHOOD
HOME
CHURCH
LIBRARY
CASUAL SHOPPING
SUPERMART
CAR DEALER
FOOD AND GROCERY SHOPPING
FURNITURE AND LARGE APPLIANCES
FURNITURE WAREHOUSE
COOP
WORKPLACE
SMALL APPLIANCES
CLOTHING AND
ENTERTAINMENT
DAILY TRIPS
WEEKLY TRIPS
LESS OFTEN
SCALE
0 5 10 15 20 25 30 Mi.
0 8 16 24 32 40 48 Km.

taurants, general stores, flea markets and implement dealers often qualify as outsized functions in rural Ontario. Sometimes they are the only local economic function, but they often employ many people and generate considerable business. The Benmiller Hotel complex, the Maryhill Hotel and the Aberfoyle Mill Restaurant are but a few examples.

Pleasant, relatively inexpensive residential accommodation and outsized functions are often the secret of population growth without extensive local economic development. It is no longer essential to live where you work, or to live near a major industrial centre and commute. Employment and local shopping are not necessarily prerequisite to population growth in towns or villages with attractions such as large old homes, a millstream, a nearby forest or a hill, and access to other places by a reasonable road. It is easy to reach all the necessities of modern life from even the remotest agricultural village in western Ontario.

Wroxeter for example, now functions essentially as a residential neighbourhood, set in a matrix of productive farmland. It poses no threat to our rural resource base since it has plenty of room for additional housing within its boundaries. Its mobile inhabitants range beyond it on tranquil county roads to work at a seed cleaning plant or feed depot in its rich agricultural hinterland. Others find employment in the stores and factories of Wingham or Fordwich, while a tiny minority travel as far as Tiverton to work at the Bruce Nuclear Complex. On Sundays they can drive easily to the Benmiller Hotel for an elegant dinner out, or to the restored pub in Neustadt. Satellite dishes and the TV station in Wingham keep everyone abreast of the latest news and fashions.

The mobility provided by the car, which originally created so many ghost towns has enabled many of these places to function efficiently in a new role. Now many form a component of increasingly common dispersed cities in the countryside. Together these groups of settlements, some entirely residential, others having a few businesses, provide all the facilities of the city, at lower costs. They exist all over Southern Ontario in relaxing rural settings. Most are without the majority of the "urban hassles" we have all come to despise. So are the Wroxeters of Ontario really dying villages? Or do they represent the wave of the future --- an invitation to more of those who require only a car or a computer to conduct their daily business affairs?

THE REBIRTH OF A COMMUNITY

We leave Wroxeter somewhat sadly, still pondering the ultimate fate of our rural service centres. Happily, we conclude that the largest probably possess enough fixed capital in homes and business blocks to assure their continued existence. They will continue to be places of residence for the retired and locally employed and will offer a small range of goods and services.

The drive south and west takes us towards another settlement in the heart of agricultural Ontario. On our trip to Blyth we pass gentle slopes, plowed fields, fodder crops, beef cattle and dairy cows. But in this new agricultural landscape, the cattle are cribbed and confined, penned in their low, humid shelters, unable to roam and graze as in the past. Where the landscape was once dotted with herefords or holsteins, it is now rudely punctuated by the towering steel repositories of their feed. Day after day they eat, defecate, eat again, eventually to be milked or slaughtered. These physical changes to the landscape are somehow symptomatic of the parallel alterations in the farm economy that have given them birth.

Blyth has much in common with Brussels, but several additional factors affect its present and future prospects. Blyth too is on a stream, was a once thriving rural service centre, and has declined since 1891. The same explanations we deduced for Brussels are relevant to Blyth: but then why and how are they different? First let's look at population. In 1981, Blyth's population of 926 was only one less than its total in 1891. This small decline is unusual for former service centres, many of which have dropped by over half their earlier totals. Between 1961 and 1981 Blyth increased by 202 people for a 28 percent gain. This too is surprising in a period when losses continued for many rural communities. But even this does not tell the whole story.

When we drive through Blyth it seems more prosperous than Brussels, even though it is

Farther down the street, we discover the Old Mill, an industrial building that has been converted into a major outlet for leather goods and clothing. It is one of the enterprises that has contributed to the recent prosperity of Blyth.

smaller, and it appears far more vibrant than Wroxeter. Main Street is alive with people shopping at a boutique, a potter's shop, and a craft shop. Several restaurants seem to be doing well. Along the main street, fresh paint clings to old buildings, bringing them new life in the fading summer sun. None are abandoned or boarded up. A stroll along the street takes us past the busy pub to the former town hall, an ornate brick edifice surrounded by mature trees. Here we begin to discover the secret of Blyth.

The old town hall has become a summer theatre, where excellent theatrical productions may be seen. Some of the plays are written by local authors and many deal with well-known problems of the farmer or village dweller. From a modest beginning, the Blyth Summer Theatre has achieved international acclaim, attracting audiences from Detroit, Buffalo, Toronto, Kitchener and Guelph. Farther down the street we discover the Old Mill, an industrial building that has been converted into a major outlet for leather goods and clothing. Somewhat ironically, it stands just in front of a large and prosperous flour and feed mill that continues to serve farmers from miles around. Inside, the Old Mill is crowded with buyers looking at racks of furs, long and short leather coats, gloves, sheepskins, seat covers, blankets and baby booties. This is a big business which has an additional outlet in Annapolis Royal, far away in Nova Scotia. Someone must have done something right, for parking is difficult and customers appear even on weekday evenings.

More exploration uncovers a large, new, "old mill" near the former railway station just out of town. In modern spacious quarters it too displays sheepskins, leather coats, gloves and many other items, often at prices below that of a city store. Blyth's rural service centre roots have been exhumed and nourished in the theatre and in the "old mills". Today they have grown, flourished and produced a new and vital prosperity. Success has bred success in Blyth.

Once again, the old story of individual initiative and entrepreneurial activity that promoted so many settlements in the early years has been repeated. People with a dream and determination fought hard to establish the Blyth Festival in a remote location and in the face of skepticism and struggle. They persisted however, and are now well recognized across the province. Recently, a film based on a play produced in Blyth was made in the village. For a few weeks it experienced all the excitement of becoming "Hollywood North". Other entrepreneurs saw the potential of a delightful old building near the playhouse and began to retail leather goods at times which enabled play-goers to combine shopping and entertainment in one trip. When business increased, another leather outlet jumped onto the bandwagon to become a complementary function.

Now you can go to the festival in Blyth, stop for a bite and a beer, and do some comparison shopping for leather goods. Not bad for a relatively remote and obscure country town. New jobs have been created to augment its traditional service role, and the "snowball effect" seems to have set in. Time and the efforts of local businessmen will tell whether the success will continue. So far things look good.

ON TO BENMILLER

A mere twenty kilometers farther west of Blyth in Benmiller, luxury awaits us. There on the banks of the Maitland River we find a world-class hotel complex with a gourmet dining room. Nestled beside the water, the former grist mill provides sports facilities and luxury accommodation. The former woollen mill used to produce those famous Benmiller blankets, but now dispenses exquisite culinary delights. After our busy day, this classic outsized function entices us inexorably.

The reason that this luxury hotel has such a salubrious setting has to do with events that occurred over 10,000 years ago! The end of the Wisconsin Glaciation marked the last major incursion of glacial ice into what is now Ontario. During this final episode in the Pleistocene era, events conspired to produce the geomorphology which resulted in the attractive physical features surrounding our next destination. When mile-high mountains of blue-green ice began to retreat into the lake basins, small advances continued to occur during periods of heavy precipitation. New falls of snow fed and nourished the slowly oscillating mass. These forward sorties were followed by retreats when melting exceeded the build-up of the crystalline flakes. As a result, ice crept forward from the edges of the Great Lakes basins, only to retreat again as the climate inexorably warmed.

Vivid blue skies outlined towering frigid mountains covered in puffs of white cloud. When these vast ice mounds moved forward, they consumed everything in their path. But as they melted, the retreating glaciers regurgitated immense amounts of sand, silt, clay, water and stone. Torrents of turbulent murky water poured from fissures and ran beneath the ice. Great, jagged, frozen, scarp faces calved and cracked, leaving their rubble of rock and mud, water and ice upon the ground. Swirling, crashing, foamy milk-hued streams carried sand and silt, to be deposited and then run over again by the relentless ice. Time and time again this happened, until finally the ice was gone and only its product remained. For thousands of years it had ground the granite or limestone boulders into tiny particles and pebbles. These now blanket the landscape as outwash plains, till sheets or tumbled moraine. When the ice had receded sufficiently and the temperatures became more moderate, the vegetation that we now recognize was established and the animals returned.

We find the evidence of this cataclysmic glacial action on our topographic maps, and on the ground. It can be detected in a ring of moraines roughly outlining southwestern Ontario, generally paralleling the shores of Lakes Huron and Erie. These moraines are tumbled scenic hills usually covered by woods, and pock-marked with sudden depressions called kettles. Many have filled with water to form ubiquitous little lakes and ponds. Steep slopes, punctuated by granite boulders called erratics, constitute a scene that is wild and unkempt. Birds nest in the trees and jays squawk their raucous calls as if to proclaim the freedom of seclusion in the hills.

These remnants of the continental glaciation stretch along much of the shore, just a few miles inland from Lake Huron. We will encounter this topography not only at Benmiller, but also around places from Wyoming in the south to Lucknow in the north. The moraine is also the location of numerous villages that are now nothing more than names on faded old maps. Early agriculture just couldn't support either farmers or settlements which were scattered through much of this rugged terrain. What a contrast to the carefully cultivated, green-carpeted fields of the fertile farms lying on the till plains nearby.

When the Maitland River recovered from the vast volumes of meltwater flowing from the receding glaciers, it found itself in a deep and twisting valley. Near Benmiller it cut through the moraine to empty into Lake Huron. Because of this accident of nature, and because of the idiosyncracies of our township survey system, our drive from Blyth to Benmiller is a little more difficult than one might expect.

Topography and the survey system have conspired to make our journey longer. The first obstacle is the sinuous path of the Maitland as it cuts through the moraine. Despite the resolve of surveyors to lay out a neat geometric grid of concession lines and sideroads, most roads stop abruptly at the river. Originally they were shown on maps as crossing the river, but the cost and difficulty of bridging the river soon intruded.

Our second problem of direct navigation lies in the boundary between Hullett and Colborne Townships. Theoretically, base lines for original surveys in Ontario were laid out parallel to major lakes or escarpments. In practice, the configuration of shorelines changes, and surveyors after all are only human. Unfortunately for us, roads in Colborne form a pattern parallel to the Huron shore, but such is not the case in Hullett where they tend to run NW-SE, rather than NS-EW. Where the townships join, we encounter a crazy-quilt of sharp angles that completely destroys the rectangular symmetry we have come to trust. To further complicate matters, Highway 8 cuts across everything, its alignment having nothing to do with either survey. It was a colonization road built to open up the Huron Tract before the township surveys. Consequently it tends to ignore completely the pattern of the subsequent surveys.

We finally find Benmiller, a luxurious country retreat and the object of our search. We wind through the woods and farms and come to the rushing Maitland. Around another bend we see a group of buildings, some finished in natural wood and others built of stone. Between the rustic wooden structures along the shore, a small stream gurgles forth and bubbles happily into the wider river. Manicured lawns sweep from the front of the old stone grist mill, culminating in a sunken garden profuse with fragrant flowers of every hue. A table and umbrella invite us to sit beneath the towering pines and sip our well-deserved drink.

The settlement we are visiting (now really no more than a gracious hotel and a few shops) was named after its second inhabitant, one Benjamin Miller. He stopped on a tributary of the Maitland in 1837 to open a tavern in what was called the Hollow. This business was continued by his son Jonathan who gained notoriety as the largest man in the county at six feet two inches and 468 pounds. Of much greater importance to the Hollow was the large woollen mill established to utilize water power at the falls, where Sharpes Creek descended to join the Maitland. Here for years the famous Benmiller blankets were made until newer technology and competition ended the business.

Once again, entrepreneurial activity has transformed a "ghost town" which had lost its industry and its population. From 200 people in 1891, the hamlet went to almost nothing in the 1960s. This was a far cry from the original bustling community that boasted a large woolen mill, several general stores, a tanner, tailor, shoemaker, blacksmith, hotel, sawmill and builder in 1891. In 1987, most of these functions are still extinct, but a trendy boutique has been opened, and the Benmiller Hotel has become the centrepiece of the former Hollow. The woollen mill buildings have been restored using heavy beams, straw plaster and mill machinery as chandeliers and partitions. Here a dining room seating 100 offers delicacies such as quail, local smoked trout and lamb loin cooked with rosemary and port wine. The list of wine is interesting and extensive.

Down the road beside the river, additional accommodation is supplied in rustic apartment-style units which once housed the former grist mill. This complex is complete with efficiencies, an indoor jogging track and a pool. The former millrace runs under these buildings and drives a high-efficiency generator that provides power for the complex. High technology and the most common Ontario power source have been combined successfully in an ex-

We finally find Benmiller, a luxurious country retreat and the object of our search. Manicured lawns sweep from the front of the old stone grist mill, culminating in a sunken garden profuse with fragrant flowers of every hue.

periment that could be repeated at innumerable dam sites across the country.

Benmiller has become a favourite hideaway for politicians on retreats and for patrons of the Blyth and Stratford Festivals. The shiny new BMWs, Mercedes, Porsches, some with American licence plates, attest to its appeal for an affluent clientele. They run on its indoor track, play badminton or ping pong and then soak in the whirlpool or sauna. Occasionally, when on an expense account, my wife and I mingle with the fortunate. Once after a refreshing swim, we strolled through the grounds past the stately home of the former miller and down to the water rushing in the millrace. On that quiet summer evening, soothing sounds of running water mingled with the night cries of birds and the gentle chirp of crickets. Yellow light from shimmering candles danced out the windows and onto the terrace of the woolen mill. Inside, diners partook of paté and pheasant. Rural and rustic, the Benmiller soothed the soul and emptied the pocketbook. But what a delightful experience it was!

In the winter time we came for a ski package, but stayed at Cherrydale Farm, a short drive down the river. Here at the end of a lane lined by cherry trees, country-style accommodation and meals are provided for somewhat less than the prices at the inn. Crisp, groomed trails followed the river, cutting between stands of cedar and through the maple-beech woods. Icicles hanging in matted clumps reached from the shore to the water below, outlining the bank in off-white opalescence. Above, billowing puffs of cloud were pushed across the deep blue sky as the dry air crackled and stole the moisture from our lungs. Benmiller in the winter had a magic attraction and gentle charm; a product of man's enterprise and nature's glacial endowment.

Situated in the middle of nowhere, the Benmiller complex is a perfect example of the outsized functions now providing employment in the countryside where none existed before. The directories list this as one function, in the same category as a tiny craft shop or potter. In economic terms, Benmiller is infinitely more important than these other small businesses, as it attracts patrons from all over the province and the adjoining U.S.A. It employs cooks, dishwashers, busboys, bartenders, waiters, cleaners, clerical staff and groundspeople.

In an area where populations have declined and agriculture never really amounted to much, Benmiller Inn provides economic stimulation and a reason for some local children eventually to find a career near their homes. The combination of woods, water, an historic building and considerable entrepreneurial effort has rescued a former ghost town from oblivion. Although not the solution for all similar settlements, the Benmiller example is becoming increasingly common in eastern Canada. The technology of motor transport which originally destroyed these places has given us the mobility to utilize and appreciate them once again.

CHAPTER FIVE

Along The Huron Shore And To The Top O' The Bruce

After our delightful dalliance at Benmiller, we head for the lake. On the way to our next destination we pass fish-smoking enterprises, antique shops and plowed fields. At the mouth of the Bayfield River we encounter a village of the same name; one that has been well-known to boaters and fishermen for years. More recently it has become the destination of both tourists and retirees. A short stroll through the settlement explains why it has become so popular with such diverse groups of people. When we enter from the south, ancient maples forme a dark green canopy over the quiet street, providing a cool welcome to this historic village on the Huron shore.

We progress into Bayfield and discover the Albion Hotel, constructed in 1857. It continues to cater to the locals as well as to settlement explorers like us. Its dining room takes us back to the turn of the century. A massive oak sideboard lines the wall, complementing the spindle-back chairs surrounding the ancient tables. The highly polished original bar dominates a room that serves as a breakfast restaurant, meeting place and drinking spot, functions it has fulfilled for years. Here the postman stops to chat with the local trucker, and the farmer covered with dust from his fields quaffs a cool one after a hot day on the tractor.

In the evening, visitors from the marina fill the dining room to savour home-cooked splake or whitefish from the nearby lake. In the morning we share the breakfast bar with local tradesmen while feasting on sizzling bacon strips, golden orbs of egg, and brown, crusty bread. Upstairs, the rooms are old and creaky, most sharing communal facilities, but the beds are comfortable. And it is quiet unless you choose to stay when a rock band occupies the bar. Little has changed at the Albion over the last hundred years.

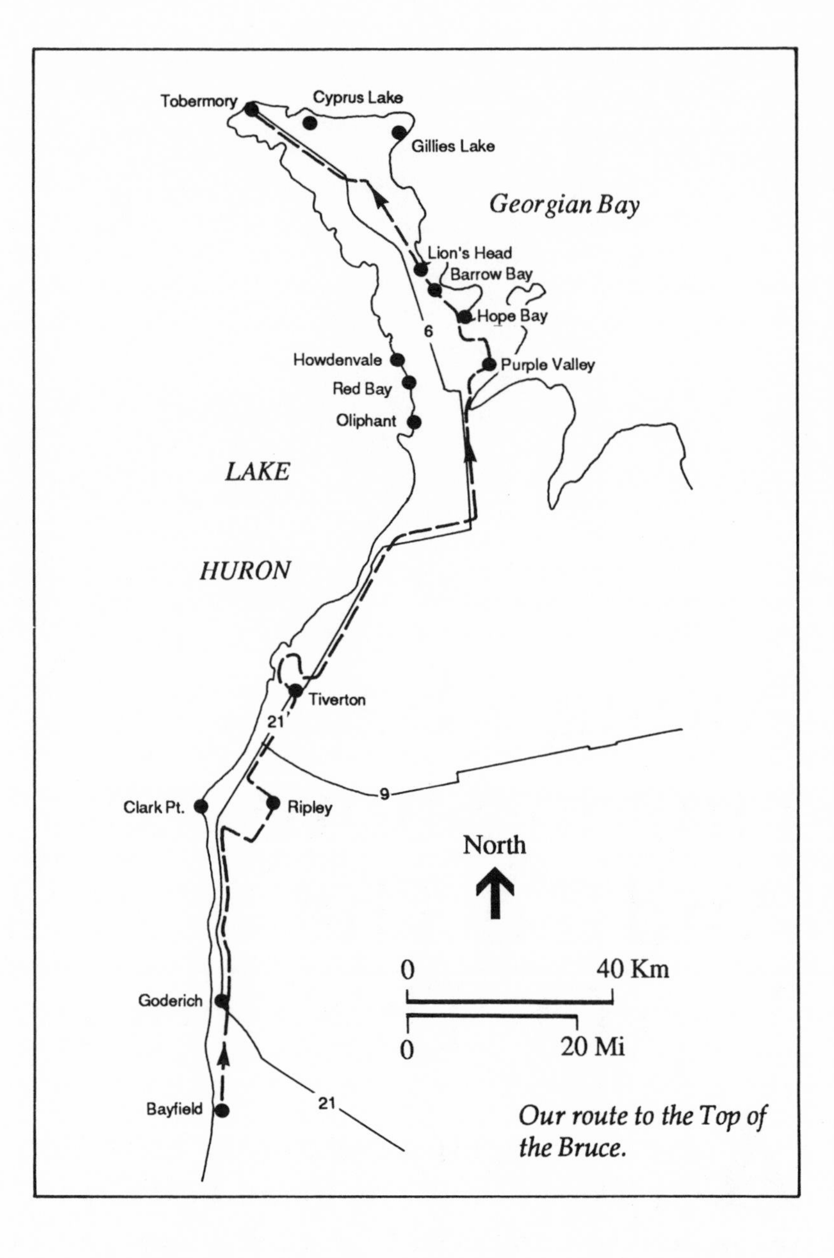

Our route to the Top of the Bruce.

A stroll down the main street takes us past carefully restored homes and shops. Many date back to a few years after the establishment of Bayfield by the aging Belgian Baron de Tuyle. He had heard about John Galt's Canada Company and thought that he could make a tidy profit when the Huron Tract was settled. To implement his scheme, he hired Captain Wolsey Bayfield who had surveyed the lake for the Royal Navy. Bayfield was to find suitable land and survey it for de Tuyle's new settlement. As instructed, Bayfield surveyed two plots of land in 1828, one at Goderich and one at the present site of Bayfield.

The Baron purchased 1500 acres on either side of the Bayfield river for 3s.9d. an acre and laid out a town there in 1832. The first structure was a cabin that served as a boarding house for the captain and his men who worked and cleared the land. Under the old Baron, little was accomplished and he soon lost interest in the scheme. The first real progress came when John Morgan built a store in 1834, and the Baron died in 1836, leaving the enterprise to his son. After that, the settlement grew and prospered, becoming an important market town, mill site and port.

By 1891, Bayfield was a thriving community with some 26 different businesses and a population of 595. Its harbour was filled with lake boats, their sheets slapping in the wind as they waited patiently for their cargoes to be loaded or to be unloaded and stacked on the docks. The bustling community boasted a bakery, a carriage maker, a fish store, four mills, a tailor, a wagon manufacturer and the usual hotel and general store. Smells of baking bread mixed with the pungent perfume of fish and fertilizer. The blacksmith's hammer clanged as sparks flew red and orange from his anvil. Tradesman and merchants hurried along its streets, lending it an air of busy vitality that was soon to fade.

Meanwhile, permanent residents built fine structures of white wooden clapboard while seasonal inhabitants constructed more modest cottages and summer homes. Almost all were tucked carefully in among the trees, as if a deliberate attempt had been made to preserve the natural setting for posterity. Much of what is now the business section was lined by delightful Victorian structures, their pointed gables adorned with wooden fretwork; their porches providing shelter from the sun and rain.

Today most of these buildings remain, converted to modern businesses but retaining their historic form. After suffering a severe decline in business after its early peak in 1891, things began to turn around for Bayfield. By 1961, there were still only 19 enterprises operating there, but by 1981, the total had risen to 25, just slightly below its earlier total. Now, with the addition of a number of completely new buildings devoted entirely to commerce, there are over 30 businesses, an all time high. Things are happening so quickly in Bayfield that we expect to find two or three new enterprises every time we visit.

When we leave the Albion to stroll towards the lake, the first business we encounter is an antique shop located in a restored home. Here we find brass door knockers, German porcelain, oil lamps from ships and an assortment of tables, chairs and dressers. Farther along the street, houses are intermixed with a pizza parlour, a number of gift shops and an excellent restaurant.

In contrast to Brussels, there are no vacancies on the main street of Bayfield. Every building is occupied and almost all have been renovated. The other major difference is the number of residences mixed with businesses in Bayfield. So far, shops and boutiques have not driven the people out of adjoining homes in Bayfield. Many of the homes that have commercial uses at the front continue to accommodate people above or behind. Houses, stores and fancy restaurants serving everything from seafood to chateaubriand mix easily on this street with pizza patios and ice cream take-out stands.

Farther along, elegant boutiques offer an array of expensive designer clothing that would make most husbands wince. One new shop is devoted entirely to chocolate and fudge. Even outside the door on the street, the delectable essences make it impossible to pass without sampling at least one or two of the products. A little farther on we find a craft shop carrying exotic hand-made woollen products and genuine soapstone carvings. Although a few "made in Taiwan" souvenirs of Canada have appeared, most in Bayfield are actually original handicrafts. The rampant commercialism of a Niagara-on-the Lake has not yet overwhelmed the gentle rural charm of Bayfield. We hope that its continuing success will not begin to destroy the very attractions that lured visitors here in the first place.

Down the road we come to the Little Inn where we experience gentle breezes on the patio, excellent wine and wickedly delectable desserts. The renovated hostelry was a coaching inn by the 1830s, catering to travellers who visited the little village, bypassed by the railroad (and with it by "progress"). Its pine floors, antique furniture and cozy fire contribute to the grace and leisure that recall another era. A long, lacy porch surrounds it on two sides, blending gracefully with the weeping willows whose wispy leaves provide shelter from the sun and wind. Recent additions and renovations have retained the old-world charm of an establishment which preserves the best of our village heritage. Cross-country ski packages and summer sojourns by sailors and thespians assure its continuing success.

Across the street from the Little

A long lacy porch surrounds The Little Inn on two sides, blending gracefully with the weeping willows whose wispy leaves provide shelter from the sun and wind.

Inn, another lovely wooden building has been converted into a hotel, providing competition and additional accommodation in the village. Just beside it, the proprietors of the Little Inn have built a rustic wooden annex to accommodate the overflow from their old hotel. Several more restaurants, a bakery, wafting its fragrance of bread and pastry into the air, and several other specialty shops complete the picture of Main Street. True, it is getting a bit crowded and difficult to park on the main street on a summer Saturday afternoon, but at least it is not yet overwhelmed by bus loads of tourists from Toronto as in Elora and Niagara-on-the-Lake.

But, to truly savour authentic attractions of old Bayfield, we stroll along the side streets, under the chestnut trees and beside the gardens. The lawns are sprinkled with violets, lilies of the valley, tulips and daffodils. It is spring! The bouquet of chestnut blossoms mingles with the sweet aroma of lilacs, lilies of the valley and hyacinths. All is shaded and serene away from the business activity and the shoppers. Here we encounter a delightful melange of splendid old permanent homes and smaller summer cottages, some of which enjoy spectacular views of the lake or river. A brick mansion hides behind its tall surrounding wall, recalling a scene from the south of England.

Below lies the marina, with its restaurant and tennis courts, yachts and fishing vessels. Here there is a mix of locals and wealthy tourists, charter operators and teenaged tennis players attempting to imitate Martina Navratilova or Boris Becker. On the outskirts of town, some new homes have been constructed, along with more commercial businesses on the highway, but as yet they have not destroyed the magic that makes Bayfield a joy to visit at any time of year.

Visitors aren't the only ones who appreciate Bayfield. Local residents have increased in number since 1891, a trend that differs from that in many small communities. Despite a drop in population to 464 in 1961, Bayfield counted 649 permanent residents in 1981, 29 percent of whom were over 65. Compared to the 14 percent in Huron County over 65, this makes Bayfield a retirement community, as well as a thriving business centre. Since 1976, over 30 percent of those moving to Bayfield have been over 60. A number have moved "to town" from local farms, but

The Marina, with its mix of fishing boats and pleasure craft reminds us of Bayfield's former functions and present prosperity.

detailed migration data indicate that many have come from places as far away as Toronto, Ottawa and London.

Given its location on the lake, excellent marina and availability of building lots, Bayfield is a logical choice for retirement. A variety of comparison shopping and medical facilities in Goderich are but half an hour away, as are its larger grocery stores. Persons who boat or vacation at Bayfield or even just visit on day trips can find pleasant living in a bucolic small town atmosphere in this charming village. It is an excellent example of the "amenity", "small is beautiful," "location" and "heritage" factors that have contributed to village renaissance in favoured areas. It is not only a pleasant place to visit; it also offers much for the permanent resident, especially in the off-season. If recent trends persist, the proportion of its population over 60 will continue to increase.

We cannot help but compare Bayfield now with Niagara-on-the-Lake a few years ago. The history of Niagara-on the-Lake is as old as the history of settlement in Upper Canada. In 1792, Colonel John Graves Simcoe, the Governor of the new colony, made Newark, as it was then called, the capital. By 1794, the town plot, complete with a location for Fort George, clergy reserves and 412 lots had been laid out. In typical military fashion, the settlement was arranged in a rectangular grid pattern with provision for lots of one acre and others of one-half acre.

Since it was the seat of government, Newark grew quickly with the influx of government administrators and their families. High society and wealth came early in its development. Military and government demands combined with a location at the head of Lake Ontario assured early commercial and industrial success. By 1808, travellers reported that the town contained some 200 houses.

Newark eventually attained its present name and endured both depression and prosperity. The war of 1812 dealt a major blow when the Americans burned many of the buildings. By the 1830s, however, shops lined Queen Street and a substantial boat works had been established. Following the opening of the second Welland canal in the mid 1840s, the village was doomed as a manufacturing and transportation centre, bypassed and on a road and river going nowhere. Nevertheless, the excellent stock of grand homes remained and the settlement persisted as a residential community and summer resort. Its population reached 3,340 by 1851, a total not exceeded until a major annexation increased its area and population after 1961.

By the end of the nineteenth century, a network of rail and tram lines once again made Niagara accessible, laying the foundation for it to become an important summer resort. Wealthy families came to enjoy the views of the river, the clean air and the genteel tranquillity remaining from the early days. Frame houses that were already large were expanded to accommodate children and guests. New enterprises arose on Queen Street; boat building returned and the place boomed. Despite this economic growth, population had not yet regained its early total. By 1911 the settlement boasted some 1,318 souls, well below the level of 1851, but higher than the 1901 count.

After World War I, Niagara-on-the-Lake once again retreated to its former residential status. Rail and tram services were being replaced by the car and the village was bypassed again. Population declined to 1,228 in 1931. By the end of World War II, general economic prosperity returned with the development of new boat building and other industries. Niagara-on-the-Lake became to some extent a commuter dormitory and retirement centre. By 1961, the population had increased again to 2,712. In the final analysis, the legacy of fine architecure and historic buildings combined with entrepreneurial initiative led to major economic growth in the 1970s and 1980s. Niagara-on-the-Lake remains the foremost example of what early nineteenth-century Upper Canada was like at its best. With increasing mobility, affluence and promotion, its architectural heritage became the basis of its contemporary success. The renovation of shops, the advent of the Shaw festival and the promotion of hotels and restaurants all played a part. The scene had finally been set for the real boom in a once quiet community.

During the last ten years, Niagara-on-the-Lake has become a tourist town "par excellence". Its broad main street is bordered by historic buildings dating back to the 1700s, while elegant Georgian mansions line its shady side streets. Nearby, restored Fort George attracts those interested in history, while the Shaw Festival draws throngs of theatre patrons.

In the past, Niagara-on-the-Lake was a sleepy semi-rural community in the midst of some of our best orchards and vineyards. Like Bayfield, it too was a desirable retirement location for those escaping from the city. These attributes endure, but are now overshadowed by restaurants, hotels, motels and trendy shops tailored to the loads of eager tourists transported there by bus and car. On a summer afternoon, Queen Street seems as busy as Yonge Street in Toronto, and there is nowhere to park. Worse still, the restaurants are jammed, and anyone without reservations made months earlier is out of luck for accommodation.

Although local and Canadian-made arts and crafts are still available, more and more souvenirs produced in the orient are appearing to compete with indigenous articles. Congestion on the streets and sidewalks is so severe that the locals no longer enjoy a stroll on a Sunday afternoon. Many also object to visitors peering into their gardens and windows as they tour past these gracious homes.

We wonder whether Bayfield will suffer the fate that is threatening Niagara-on-the-Lake which has almost been wounded by its own success. Niagara-on-the-Lake remains a quiet county town in the winter, but the summer crowds are close to overwhelming. No longer do visitors escape noise and congestion. Instead they may encounter more traffic and larger crowds than they experience at home. There is a local move afoot to slow or stop commercial development, but this may prove difficult.

As long as profits roll in, entrepreneurs tend to continue to exploit their advantage. The moment of truth may come when tourists begin to go elsewhere because they cannot find accommodation, or parking; or have to wait too long for lunch; or cannot stand the busy rush on the streets. Of course, at a population of over 12,000, Niagara-on-the-Lake is now much bigger than the other places we visited, even though much of this apparent "growth" is the result of boundary changes. Recently it has grown rapidly from a sleepy little town to what it is today, and to some extent its enlarged boundaries reflect its increased importance. All settlements with similar attributes have some of the same potential for growth, especially if they are promoted by ambitious entrepreneurs.

In a sense, the attractions of such communities may ultimately be self-limiting. To us, Niagara-on-the Lake seems close to this limit; but what of Bayfield? Will it also be spoiled by its own success, or will development be limited to preserve the very virtues that engendered success in the first place? Maybe the good citizens will pause, look carefully, and learn from the lesson of Niagara-on-the Lake. Or maybe they won't. A visit in ten years will give us the answer.

Elsewhere along the Huron shore we find another important trend in settlement development. This is the proliferation of new and rejuvenated communities catering almost exclusively to the elderly. Among the established resorts, Bruce Beach and Port Albert have witnessed the wholesale winterizing of cottages for year-round use. R 40 insulation, new, air-tight aluminum or vinyl windows and efficient wood stoves convert former cottages into snug winter retreats. In other locations such as Boiler Beach or Point Clark we discover similar transformations. There is now an almost continuous string of new subdivisions on the lake from Grand Bend to Southampton. These cater almost exclusively to those (retired or otherwise) desiring urban-type dwellings in a country setting on the lake.

Waterfront locations, sweeping vistas of the water, golf courses and tennis courts attract new buyers. They combine with easy

access to goods and services by car to make the Huron shore a desirable retirement locale. In time, catering to the needs of additional affluent arrivals will become big business in the county, as it has already for the builders and developers in the area.

Despite attempts to create integrated communities, many subdivisions along the shore are more like displaced urban suburbs than towns or villages. Despite their manicured lawns, imposing gates, wrought-iron fences and fancy names, they have not yet developed a separate identity or local cohesiveness. People from many distant localities have come here, sometimes lured back by memories of vacations spent by the lake, sometimes attracted only by the glossy advertisements of the developers.

We ponder the future of these places and their possible prospects. Someday as they age, the new arrivals will require enhanced medical service, meals on wheels, help with the cleaning and gardens, and finally institutional care. Their presence today is a boon, but it may become a slowly ticking time bomb unless we plan ahead. We must soon provide for the increased social services that the newcomers will inevitably require. Some communities such as Bayfield Village, with its recreational complex, resident nurse and delivery services, are preparing for the future. Others have not shown such foresight. Given the age profile in Canada, problems of services for the elderly will become a problem everywhere. But in settlements where most of the citizens are over 60 when they arrive, the crisis will occur sooner than elsewhere.

Following our visit to Bayfield, we head straight north along the Bluewater Highway to Goderich. Situated at the mouth of the Maitland, it is one of the prettiest towns in Canada and has a unique central area. Its history is as interesting as any in Canada.

John Galt founded the community in 1827 to open up his Huron Tract. He laid out a plan with streets radiating from a central square. Today the Octagon, as it is known locally, surrounds a green space containing the County Court House. This in turn is circled by a wide street lined by superb buildings from the turn of the century. The town abounds in homes built by the wealthy in the late 1800s and early 1900s, many of which overlook the harbour. The restored Huron County Gaol is on the northern edge of town and worth a visit. The former home of Samuel Sloan, built in the late 1700s, is now occupied by Robindale's Restaurant where gourmet food is served in antique surroundings, another example of successfully recycled heritage architecture.

On our stroll around the spacious Octagon, shops crammed with fashionable merchandise lure us in, despite our vow to conserve our cash. We enter the Bedford Hotel, rebuilt after a fire in 1895, now carefully restored. In the lobby, a curving staircase, its banisters carefully polished, spirals to the floors above. Old-world charm exudes from this historic structure, which has a link to our previous stop. From the fire until 1905 it was operated by none other than the notoriously overweight Jonathan Miller of Benmiller fame.

The Bedford Hotel is captivating. It is a reminder of the vast potential of these buildings which we were so anxious to demolish even a few years ago. And the Bedford is not alone in this community. Many of the shops, the library, the houses along the lakeshore, all are ripe for re-use and a new lease on life. For many, only minor modifications are required to effect restoration and impart vitality. Even though Goderich is the county seat and a thriving port with considerable industry, it has significantly more potential than has been realized. With a little more promotion and investment to maximize its attractions, Goderich could become one of the premier tourist attractions along the Huron Shore.

Well, enough academic musing! Let's get on with the trip to the "Top O' the Bruce". Highway 21 north takes us towards yet another "dying village" at Ripley. Here grain storage has taken over a former store, and the main street reminds us of a ghost town in Arizona. On a hot Saturday afternoon, not a soul stirs as we inspect the cob-webbed windows protecting dusty sacks of feed and grain in a former store. Paint peels, the Co-op is silent and the "antique shop" seems to be filled with rusting junk from abandoned farmsteads. Once again we despair for our lost heritage of rural service centres.

On closer inspection, however, we discover that the picture may not be totally bleak. We drive along the back streets and away from the centre of town and find that local employment appears to be available at the mill, with the drainage contractor or at the township's local depot. The large primary school obviously employs a number of professionals and support staff. At the edge of town, a spanking new retirement home caters to the elderly. And along the back streets we discover square, red-brick Georgian homes over-run by trumpet vines, tall peaked Gothic mansions with their ornately carved barge boards, and numerous smaller new homes of nondescript lineage. Clearly there is some life in Ripley, despite our initial impressions.

Once again we have discovered the secrets of a small town by prowling about its streets, rather than bypassing it entirely or

An elegant mansion overlooking the harbour in Goderich . Such residences are but one of the attractions of small-town Canada.

The restored Bedford Hotel and the County Court House on the Octagon in Goderich.

merely following the highway through its centre. Ripley has enjoyed considerable new construction, some by "infilling" lots which were bypassed for many years, some in new subdivisions at the outskirts. The population increased by 27 percent from 1961 to 1981, standing at 590 by 1981. This was in the face of a major decline in businesses following the boom years of the 1800s. But recently, three new businesses have opened. The percentage of people over 65 has risen from 19 to 24 since 1976, no doubt providing potential customers for the medical clinic, grocery store and ultimately the rest home!

Ripley may not yet have attained its former status, but after years of stagnation, it is on the way to recovery as a retirement centre providing local employment. We stroll its tranquil streets, far from the dust and noise of city or factory, and savour its intimate charm. Scenes of childhood in other small towns flood back, as we remember the friendly "Good day" extended to native and visitor alike. No doubt the same is true of Ripley where the pace is reminiscent of the forties or fifties. This is reflected in the casual mix of land uses and lack of sidewalks on most streets. We understand why local farmers have come here to retire, and we know why refugees from the city have swelled its population.

In Ripley, mobility has provided easy access to the lake, to goods and services and to employment. Its ambience is of slow-paced enchantment on a sunny summer afternoon. Streaks of light filtered by leaves fall upon lawns of cool, damp grass. We feel no need to hurry, or to rush in order to participate in the local lifestyle. People here proceed as they have for a hundred years -- slowly, steadily and happily. If you don't want to live and work in the city, why not move to Ripley? If it has been your local market town, why not retire here? You know the people and will find familiar surroundings. Given the costs of housing and taxes in the noisy city, or the prospect of lonely isolation on a farm, you might do a lot worse. We leave somewhat reluctantly, having come to appreciate this sleepy little village.

To reach the Bruce Peninsula from Ripley we jog west and then head north along the Bluewater Highway, ultimately joining Highway 6, the only major route north to Tobermory. When we drive north, we pass Kincardine, a busy town with tranquil side-streets and a pleasant beach. Here

Streaks of light filtered by leaves fall upon lawns of cool damp grass. We feel no need to rush to participate in the local lifestyle. One of many tranquil scenes on the back streets of Ripley.

we discover large homes, some almost mansions, inhabited by farmers and wealthy local businessmen. At one time it was feared that the boom created by the construction of the Douglas Point nuclear complex would die, and with it Kincardine, but this has not occurred. Tourism and retirement by the lake have seen to that.

A short drive to the north leads to Tiverton, a dormitory settlement for workers at the Nuclear Complex. In contrast to the solidity of Kincardine, it has the look of a frontier resource town which has boomed from the recent influx of inhabitants. Raw, barely landscaped subdivisions stretch down the road to the power station, seemingly held together by hydro and telephone lines. In the centre of the settlement (if it can be called that) a bank and appliance store have opened to serve new customers.

Tiverton isn't much, but it's worth the short drive west to view the vast and somehow ominous Douglas Point nuclear installation. This is especially spectacular when the sun is setting, casting shimmering orange spears across the water between the shadowy shapes of heavy water towers and reactor containers. An eerie calm envelops this massive power potential locked within concrete pods squatting beside the glassy lake. Nearby, Inverhuron Provincial Park has been converted from a camping area to day use only. Years ago it was a popular haven for city folk from Guelph or Kitchener, myself included, but we invariably shuddered at the roar of steam escaping during the venting of the turbines. This inevitably occurred at three in the morning, just after an evening of heavy partying; enough to sober up the most frivolous of revellers. It is probably just as well that Ontario Hydro erred on the side of safety by banning overnight camping at Inverhuron.

Our trip north along the Bluewater Highway takes us past Port Elgin, which has long been a resort attracting beach lovers from all over Ontario. Its gracious summer mansions mingle with newer chalet-style homes fringing the sand. Down the main street, pizzerias, chicken dispensaries, pubs and patios have proliferated to accommodate the summer crowds. At night summer residents join the locals and the newly retired to stroll the streets and beaches. A boys' brass band wafts mellow tunes across the lake as surf-boarders challenge the waves and teens flirt in the sand. Port Elgin endures, thrives, and continues to attract both residents and tourists.

We head towards the Bruce Peninsula, leaving the glacial deposits of Huron and Southern Bruce County behind. The sweeping, open fields of corn, sunflowers, soybeans and flax in Huron and the patchwork of pastures in South Bruce are soon replaced by more rugged terrain. Driving towards the peninsula we come upon the remnants of the distant past, the limestone plains and thin soils atop the Niagara Escarpment. At Wiarton we follow a long slope through the arch over the road which proudly announces the entrance to the Bruce Peninsula. Here we catch our first glimpse of Georgian Bay as we ascend the Niagara Escarpment to the north. At the top of the long steep incline we realize that we have emerged into an area where nature has created a different topographic design.

A TRIP TO THE TOP O' THE BRUCE

The jagged ridge of Lockport Dolomite which we encounter at Wiarton bisects Ontario from Queenston to Tobermory. It is in reality the edge of a tilted basin of limestone laid down in the Palaeozoic Era over 250 million years ago. This topographic break, called the Niagara Escarpment, was formed when water differentially eroded hard and soft rocks. The end result was the resistant edge that rises to the surface as southern Ontario's most visible landscape feature. From the northern outskirts of Wiarton, the edge of strata that dip gently into the Michigan Basin to the west are clearly visible.

Eons ago, layer upon layer of sediments were deposited at the bottom of warm inland seas to form "cuesta and vale" (ridge and valley) topography of limestone, sandstone and shale. Some of these strata contained salt found at Goderich or Windsor; others contained oil found at Petrolia. Almost infinitely later by man's reckoning, but in a short period of geological time, glaciers abraded this early landscape, smoothing the projections and depositing masses of till and boulders in their wake. As a result, the mighty Niagara Escarpment is almost buried in places where it crosses southern Ontario, but is clearly visible at others such as Milton, Collingwood and the Bruce Peninsula. The more recent glacial event has hidden the much older escarpment in many areas of the province.

In fact, the Bruce Peninsula is the backbone of the Niagara Escarpment. Its steep (or scarp) face forms the rugged cliffs confronting Georgian Bay; its dip slope plunges under Lake Huron, covered by sand or swamp. In places such as Owen Sound and at Colpoys Bay (the site of Wiarton), extensive gashes knife through the sediments to remind us of enormous pre-glacial valleys cut by the rivers that once drained the land. Now we see them on the map, and when we pass, we see them as major hills exposing the pre-glacial topography. A drive along the Bruce Peninsula reveals limestone plains scraped bare atop the cuesta, and rugged cliffs that withstood the mightiest efforts of the glaciers. They remain --- skeletal fingers projecting boldly into the chilling waters of Georgian Bay, standing guard against the crashing waves of this turbulent, boisterous body of water.

The "Indian Peninsula", which was the name given to it by the pioneers, was settled late for southern Ontario. It was not until 1854 that the whites acquired the Indian territory north of Wiarton, at the time when land sales were beginning in the south. Thin soils on the peninsula would not be conducive to farming, a fact that many settlers discovered too late, but the forests were magnificent. Red, white and jack pine, white and black spruce, white cedar, tamarack and hemlock covered the land. Elsewhere, stands of hard maple, beech, white elm, red oak, ash, grey birch and basswood could also be found. Sailors circumnavigating the peninsula marvelled at the unbroken expanses of giant trees and at the ferocity of the waves lashing the rocky grey cliffs. In the winter, grey clouds hung like muslin sheets over the stark white of the snow, punctuated by the dark green evergreen spears along the shore. This was a foreboding and mysterious land -- one that yielded its secrets slowly and with reluctance.

The pines were particularly valuable as spars and square timbers for export to Britain. This led to the development of a thriving lumber industry. Sadly, little care was taken and waste was rampant. Vast stands were clear-cut while fires destroyed others. Dense, murky clouds of acrid smoke clung to the tree tops like smothering layers of smog from hell. Vast acreages of prime timber were devastated by this careless, wanton waste.

The logging boom lasted till the late 1890s, after which the land remained "a patchwork of wilderness, arid barrens, small farm clearings, and a struggling second growth of forests." The millions of board feet of timber shipped in huge rafts from almost every port on the peninsula offered little benefit to the settlers. Their claims did not include the right to log, a privilege granted to major corporations which ruthlessly exploited the forests on these embryo farms. Needless to say, this led to bloodshed and strife when pioneers saw the only economic value of their land being stripped away by others. With the trees gone, many farms were reduced to small patches of soil in the midst of limestone plains. They had already been scraped bare by the glaciers, now they were stripped again by the loggers. Little wonder that times were hard and life expectancy was short for the early settlers of the Indian Peninsula.

The premature devastation of the Bruce Peninsula becomes apparent soon after we climb the long, steep incline north of Wiarton and follow the roads to the north. In many areas, forest regeneration has reclaimed the land, while elsewhere abandoned farms stand on thin soils which barely cover the bedrock. The peninsula is infinitely more interesting when we leave the highway and skirt either shore. On the west we encounter sandy beaches, resorts, cabins, lodges, new retirement subdivisions and swamp. On the east we follow the stark outcroppings of limestone escarpment, passing through settlements like Hope Bay which once boasted mills and industry. Nearby, Purple Valley, which had once vanished without a trace, now boasts a riding stable and antique shop. Several ancient log houses are to be found across the road from the antique shop. Here a general store had once served the surrounding farms, but given the poor agricultural conditions, its life was short. In contrast, Hope Bay has become a summer resort. A potter has taken over and restored the former mill for his home and workshop. Even in this isolated area, enterprise and the desire to leave the city have combined to create a successful business. Of course, a setting beside the lake in sight of spectacular cliffs is more attractive to development than Purple Valley's location amidst scrubby woods and former farmland.

The minor roads on the Bruce can be confusing, especially when they wind endlessly among dense pine woods and over rocky outcrops. The one consolation is that if you do get lost, all roads eventually end at the water or within a few kilometres across Highway 6. This makes it safe to venture off the beaten track to view the delicate local orchids, to visit the Cape Croker Indian Reserve with its excellent camp ground and spectacular cliffs, or to explore Oliphant, Red Bay, Howdenvale or Pike Bay on the opposite shore. Everywhere these former "dying villages" are being given new life by year-round tourism based on the snowmobile (unfortunately, it seems to have displaced cross-country skiing in these parts), or by people returning to retire in a former vacation community. Fortunately for these settlements, renewed interest in year-round sports and the winterizing of cottages for retirement have brought new business to the area. This occurred soon after rising fuel prices had decreased weekend trips to summer cottages and resorts.

Along much of the peninsula, the ground appears to be dry, even though amounts of precipitation are adequate. This is the result of underground drainage created by streams which have dissolved the soluble limestone and sunk into crevasses, taking the runoff underground with them. Along the Georgian Bay shore, many "caves" may be found, some cut by waves from earlier, higher lake levels during the Pleistocene. Others are merely major fissures in the limestone, while still others are genuine solution caverns. The latter are a sign of karst topography, a name given by geologists to areas where drainage is underground and limestone caverns abound.

The most famous and spectacular caverns along the Bruce are those at Barrow Bay, approximately half-way north on the eastern side of the promontory. While there, we stand atop the cliff and imagine prehistoric men building their cooking fires in the shelter of the caverns, after hunting their prey in the forests beyond. In fact, this is exactly what many did see when attending the movie Quest for Fire, much of which was filmed here and in the swamps above. A few of the props remain.

Soon we discover bridges and walkways built to give the movie crew easy access to the scene of action. Several paper-maché clubs and boulders remind us of the visitors from Hollywood, but it is the awesome beauty of the overhanging cliffs, the talus slopes and the wild, white, water below that draw us to this site. Tumbled boulders, green clinging vines, clefts cut from limestone as if by a giant saw, deep branching valleys thrusting into the land -- this is the Bruce at its most glorious.

Continuing north along the bay side, we come to Lion's Head. It is one settlement that has derived great benefit from the recent retirement of former summer vacationers. Nature has assisted in its rejuvenation by supplying a delightful harbour which overlooks a limestone peninsula in the shape of a sleeping lion. Lion's Head was once a thriving fishing port that exported lumber to customers around the world. Then isolation and farm abandonment took their toll as the population fell from 425 in 1921 to 358 in 1951. Similarly, the number of businesses recorded by the directories was six in 1881, which rose to 24 in 1901, and then fell to 15 in 1941.

In the prosperous years, activities associated with the lumber industry, such as mills and sash makers, shared the economy with general stores, blacksmiths, hotels and clothing stores. By 1941, all vestiges of the lumber industry had disappeared, along with every hotel but one. Of the other businesses, only one specialty store remained. Lion's Head had been reduced to a minor local service centre with a gas station, several general stores and a bakery. The garage and chopping mill were the most common functions with two of each in the hamlet.

By 1981, the population of Lion's Head had climbed back to 476, and would be much higher if we counted the extensive residential subdivisions along the shore to the north. By 1985, 30 businesses were listed by the directories, including the largest former hotel converted to a retirement home. Several additions made this the dominant structure on the main street. A two-storey general store on the road to the waterfront supplied almost every conceivable need, while a district hospital stood on the shore of the bay. Fishing boats lay beside the pleasure craft at the marina, and much of the waterfront had be-

Purple Valley disappeared, but now boasts a Tea Room and Riding Stable. Note the light standard which formerly illuminated the gasoline pumps. Even in remote areas such as this a few new functions have been established to serve the tourist.

come a park.

Lion's Head is a pleasant destination for a day trip or a summer vacation but has also become an important retirement community for people from all over Ontario. Special census tabulations prepared by Statistics Canada show that 43 percent of those moving to Lion's Head between 1976 and 1981 were over 60, as against just under 10 percent for the county as a whole. Many came from as far away as Toronto and London, instead of only from local farms. Interviews revealed that former cottagers had returned to take up permanent residence in their former summer retreat. The village housed 175 persons over 60, or almost 38 percent, in 1981, compared to 16 percent for Bruce County. By any standards, its role has shifted from that of a rural service centre and tourist attraction to that of a retirement community.

The village offers spectacular views of the lake and cliffs, along with convenient, local medical services. It may be more than coincidence that the undertaker is located across the street from the retirement home! Nevertheless, most goods may be purchased locally, and it is a relatively easy drive (in the summer at least) to Wiarton where a wide range of goods and services may be obtained. In the village and along the north shore, many permanent, large and luxurious residences have been built to take advantage of the views and the tranquillity. Some surpass in size and elegance any normal city home, and are certainly intended for year-round use. In addition to this new construction, numerous older cottages have been insulated and converted into permanent dwellings.

As the population in and near Lion's Head increases, so do its prospects for economic growth. Many of the elderly have substantial pensions and bring considerable economic stimulation to nearby businesses. Others are former professionals who will become leaders in local administration and politics in order to further their own ambitions for the settlement. These people bring money, ideas, business and intellectual stimulation to the village, but require neither schools nor playing fields. On balance they will become a lasting asset that will improve the chance of future growth and prosperity. And with the local availability of medical and retirement home facilities, they will find care available as they age. Such is the story of Lion's Head and many communities like it which offer scenic attractions combined with a relatively accessible location and a history of summer residents.

On the last leg of our trip to the top of the Bruce, we traverse the road out of Lion's Head. From Isthmus Bay we climb a steep ridge following the brink of a lofty limestone bench which skirts the wave-swept shores. Here the views back over the retreating bay are as impressive as any in Ontario. Dense, tangled forest frames a scene of magnificent waves pounding the variegated cobble beaches. To the south, the shoreline sweeps in a graceful arc, stretching away to the sun. Inland, pine and cedar forests extend to the horizon, apparently without end. Below, water ebbs and flows, tugging at the coast as if trying to pull the shore back to its depths. Driving ahead, we find ourselves among the Forty Hills, a plunging labyrinth of tumbled soil and rock. Corkscrew twists and sudden dips lead us through the tangled maze of this tumultuous terrain. Finally we find our way back to the highway, having experienced some of the most tortuous roads and spectacular scenery in the province.

Our ultimate destination is only an hour or so away, but much lies between. The ensemble of log barns and outbuildings on the west side of the road reminds us of those hapless pioneer farmers who saw the trees disappear from under their noses while the loggers and mill owners got rich. Farther on we pass the turn-off for Gilles Lake, once known by the Indians and early settlers as Ghost Lake because of its white marl bottom and immense depth. And how did lake trout manage to arrive, much less thrive in a lake several hundred feet above Georgian Bay? One suspects that eggs were dropped by gulls or by the rain during a small tornado.

In the 1880s, the Lymburner family cut trees near Gilles Lake and channeled its water two hundred feet down the cliff to operate their mill. An ingenious log chute was constructed to transport the logs from the cliff-top to the mill. In the best years, their establishment cut up to 25,000 board feet of lumber per day and sent it by steamer to destinations all over the lakes. Unhappily, by 1905 the denudation of the forests put an end to the operations.

The village offers spectacular views of the lake and cliffs. Fishing boats lie beside the dock at the marina and much of the waterfront has become a park. Lion's Head is now a Retirement-Amenity Community, accommodating tourists, cottagers, retirees and day visitors.

Farther north we cross streams teaming with trout, protected from anglers by mosquitoes and poison ivy; not to mention the Massasauga Rattlers. On the right a road leads to Cyprus Lake Provincial Park, from which a well-marked walking trail crosses several former lake terraces to the sparkling white cliffs and blue vastness of Georgian Bay. Icy cold and crystal clear water beckon the scuba diver or hardy swimmer, while we the hikers enjoy this, the most spectacular stretch of the Bruce Trail. Here the magnificent limestone spine of Ontario dominates everything. Frost-shattered, house-sized remnants of the precipice complement the stark three-hundred-foot cliffs. Only the bravest hikers follow this trail to the top, where views and vistas stretch endlessly across the crystalline waters of the bay.

When we trek back from the bay, we silently thank the hikers and conservation groups who fought for the Bruce Trail, making it possible to follow this great escarpment from Queenston to Tobermory. Before we reach the smaller Cyprus Lake, our path takes us across spongy brown carpets on the shady forest floor. Scrambling up the precipitous slopes, slithering like snakes down the other side, we pass two swampy lakes. They lie still and clear, fringed by blue iris, newly formed cat tails and arrowheads, dotted with water lilies of assorted colours. At the end of our hike to the bay, we relax on the sandy beaches and swim in the warm water of Cyprus Lake.

The remainder of the drive to Tobermory crosses limestone plains and swamps, emerging finally at the site of the Big and Little Tubs. These are the local names for the two canal-like inner harbours cut from the limestone as if by a knife, and providing safe havens for any craft with shallow draft. The outer harbour is a circular basin almost four miles in diameter, sheltered from the gales by an arc of lofty islands. In days gone by, many a sailing ship found refuge here from the autumn gales that raged and whistled across the top of the Bruce.

In Tobermory we find a delightful mix of lake port, tourist resort, underwater park and port for the Chi-Cheemaun ferry to Manitoulin Island. Although now primarily a pleasure destination, Tobermory was once important to the commerce of Ontario. Between 1890 and 1898, it was the premier lumber port on the peninsula, shipping vast quantities of pine logs to mills in eastern Michigan. The greatest proportion of the 301 million board feet of wood rafted from Ontario mills in 1884 passed through Tobermory. If this occurred today, economic nationalists would scream loudly about the sale of our natural resources to the Americans. In the 1800s however, no such sentiment was uttered. In those days, trade came before politics.

Off the end of the peninsula, Flowerpot Island with its strange geological formations and caves beckons the hiker. Since the days of the Indians, these oddly shaped limestone columns have been held in awe by their beholders. In 1827, John Galt, who was sailing on the Gunboat Bee from Penetanguishene to Goderich, ordered the boat to divert from its course so he could view these grotesque twisted monoliths. Now Flowerpot Island with its 300 acres of cliffs, forests and depressions is a national monument, preserved from desecration and commercial exploitation.

The National Underwater Park off Tobermory attracts enthusiastic scuba divers from across the continent. Below the surface in the eerie depths, skeletons of wooden sailing vessels lie preserved for all time in the icy waters. In a rare instance of federal-provincial co-operation, a new national park has been created to encompass much of the northern tip of the peninsula. It will preserve the natural state and make formerly inaccessible areas available to visitors. In Tobermory proper, numerous hotels and motels cater to those who have come to await the ferry or just to look around. There is no lack of eating places for the hungry, or viewpoints for the sightseer.

We decide to join in the fun of observing the passing parade. From a strategic bench beside the wharf we watch the "Big Canoe" or Chi-Cheemaun open its gigantic prow and swallow 115 cars. Some six hundred passengers embark for the delightful voyage to Manitoulin Island. In the inner harbour, fishing boats putt-putt softly on their way to the open waters of the bay. An American tourist, bulbous belly matching his bulbous nose, argues with his wife about a motel. Two tanned, lissome, athletic hikers doff their rucksacks and chug-a-lugg a coke. Across the inlet, rubber-suited snorkellers looking for all the world like frogmen from another planet emerge clumsily from their cluttered craft. The sun is bright, the day is delightful, and we are pleased to be at our destination; the "Top O' the Bruce".

We continue to loaf and contemplate the scene. Fishing expeditions, trips to Manitoulin Island, voyages on the glass-bottomed boats, and just plain relaxation are the favourite indigenous occupations. In tune with the locals, we purchase triple vanilla cones, and spend the next half hour protecting them from the swooping, screeching gulls. What a way to pass a summer afternoon!

Our trip through southern Ontario has taken us through virtual ghost towns, declining service centres, yuppie havens and retirement villages. The time has come to move to "something completely different". Having arrived at the top of the Bruce, we have sampled many of Ontario's changing communities. Now we must leave them behind to head north and east. After this meandering trip around southern Ontario, we will travel along the Trans-Canada Highway and then into eastern Ontario. Our next journey will take us into shield country very different from the tills and hills of limestone that we have experienced in southern Ontario. Contrasts and similarities await us as we prepare to sample the towns of the near north, the eastern edge of the province and the frontier fringe.

CHAPTER SIX

A Trip To The "Near North", The East And The Frontier Fringe Of Ontario

So far we have explored settlements that began as rural service centres, mill towns or rail depots. In southern Ontario, such places were often close together, a direct result of the prosperous agriculture nearby. Now it is time to venture into a different world -- that of the "near north" and the frontier fringe of Ontario. Here distances are vast; resources consist of forests and minerals; soils are thin and acidic despite the appearance of fertility induced by their lush cover of conifers. And here the links were originally by lake or river, later by rail and, finally, by road. Communities now thrive if they have a mine, if they provide supplies to tourists, or if they are truck stops along lonely stretches of road.

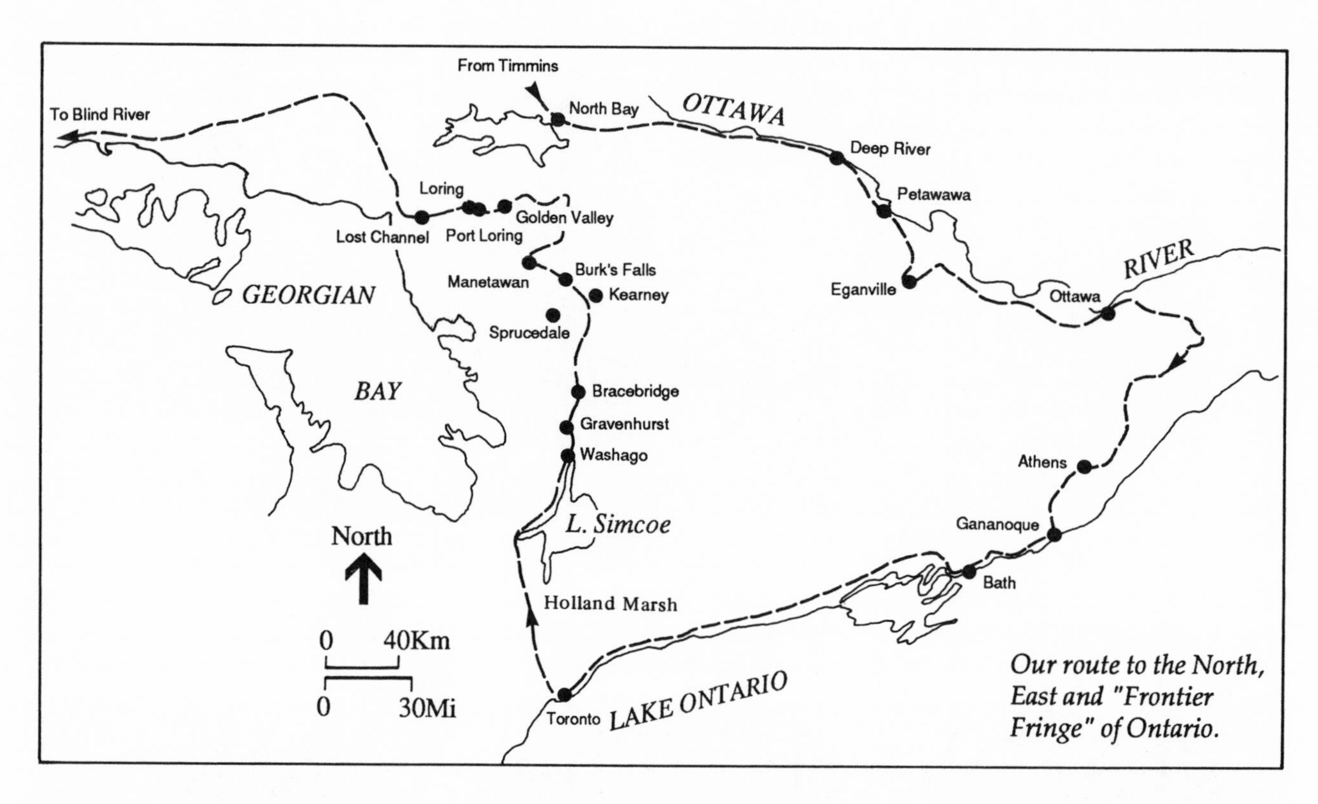

Our route to the North, East and "Frontier Fringe" of Ontario.

There is more land between the villages in the north than in the south, and the links between them are longer and more tenuous. Often the success or failure of a community is related directly to its location on a highway, lake or river. The physical assets of the hinterland are just as important here as in the south, but the economic base is seldom agriculture. Instead it is mining, forestry, catering to tourists or supplying those in the far-flung reaches of the bush. Here we will take a look at that vast land. We will consider the physical features that are so vital to northern communities. We will examine the scattered settlements, and in doing so, will journey back in time as well as in space, for the lives and the settlements of those in the north today possess many similarities to the lives and communities of the pioneers in the south a hundred years ago.

We will begin our trip by heading straight north from Toronto. Highway 400 is woefully overcrowded on any summer weekend, and practically suicidal on a holiday. But between times it is a rapid and picturesque route to a land of lakes, rocky shorelines and cottages. It passes through the lush Holland Marsh where the dark black soil has been drained and turned into the vegetable garden of Ontario.

Over 15,000 years ago, the Wisconsin Glaciers were retreating from North America, pouring water from an estimated nine million cubic miles of ice onto the land. During this process, which took about 9000 years, vast lakes and rivers were formed around the edges of the melting ice sheets. One of these was Lake Algonquin, an expansive body of water occupying the Lake Huron Basin and the depressions south of what was to become Lake Simcoe. Lake Algonquin covered the area now known as the Holland Marsh. When it finally retreated, it left behind a vast swamp of some 20,000 acres. This marsh which is now drained by the sluggish Holland River is covered by fertile black peat over six feet deep. Its central portion originally supported a vegetation of sedges, cat-tails and reeds, while its margins were cloaked in white cedar woods. During the early part of the twentieth century, this muddy wilderness was traversed by only one lonely road, Highway

11. After 1925, reclamation began, and in 1935 a group of Dutch settlers came to the eastern side of the marsh to establish the village of Ansnorvelt. Dikes and drains were installed, turning this former wilderness into a vast and productive vegetable garden.

Passing by, we see the lines of young onions, beets and celery which march in lock-step across the flat, black, fields. Later in the season, fat orange carrots, spinach flying dark green leaves like flags, and mounds of subterranean potatoes push on to the far horizon. In the spring, drains, ditches and irrigation channels share the landscape with stooping planters. Massive mechanical harvesters come in July or August. Then, fruit and vegetable stands display tumbled heaps of red, green, and yellow produce beside the road. It is a pity that over-use of the land and the occasional drought have caused many inches of irreplaceable topsoil to blow away in the wind. The long, straight black furrows continue to produce enormous cabbages, succulent beans, juicy tomatoes and slender green zucchinis, but without more care, their productive life may be limited. The vegetable stands, packing houses and fields that depend upon this rich abundance will not survive forever. Now is the time to care for the soil that took so long for nature to produce.

Heading north through Barrie we join Highway 11 to Orillia and climb on to the shield. That thrill of being in "cottage country" returns, as glacial sediments are replaced by the smoothly polished granite and gneiss that form the basement of the province. Here the vegetation changes subtly; maples and oak gave way to white pine, tamarack and birch. Beside the highway we encounter the first of the thousands of lakes formed when runoff and rainwater filled the glacial scours. The feel of the land is different. We are in a freer, less populated, more inspiring part of the planet. We hurry on, anxious to discover more.

Soon we encounter the first canoe and camping outfitters; another sign of the changing scene. Ahead to the right looms Webers, a veritable fast-food institution on the road to the north. Here business has been too good to suit the Ministry of Transportation and Communications. A traffic hazard was created by people crossing from the busy southbound lane of the highway to the hamburger heaven on the other side. When a high fence failed to stem the tide of ravenous travellers, a pedestrian overpass was constructed to take them to their food. Regardless of the weather, long lines of hungry travellers seem always to stop at this restaurant, lured undoubtedly by the insidious aromas that always waft across the highway from the grill.

We too succumb, but once past this barrier, overstuffed, and contented, we resolve to pause no more before we reach our destination in the South Parry Sound District, or as it is known to most, the Huntsville-Burk's Falls area. For years this has been a popular locality for children heading to summer camp, for campers going to Arrowhead, and for cottagers seeking relaxation for a week or a month. Much earlier in history, it was also the scene of frenzied economic activity. Then, logging and ill-conceived agriculture opened the land creating numerous settlements, few of which exist today.

Long before Highway 11 sliced through the woods and granite hills, the settlers came to Kearney, Cecebe, Sprucedale and Magnetawan. Lured by the prospect of a plot of land from the government for 50 cents an acre, they arrived by steamer and by colonization road. By the early 1870s, economic potential south of the shield had been exhausted and the pioneer was forced to head north or west to make his fortune. Most of the good land in the south was gone, and economic competition was keen. Some settlers could no longer find fertile land in Southern Ontario, others had failed, and others were professional pioneers seeking yet another windfall.

When the Parry Sound District was organized in 1870, free land was offered in 100-acre lots. Much of it was taken by settlers from Waterloo and Wellington Counties. Later, several settlement schemes lured unsuspecting Europeans to the dense pine woods which covered the glacially scoured, granitic terrain. In the early 1870s, a private temperance group planned an experiment to colonize the area near Sprucedale with teetotalers, but abstinence was rare and not particularly popular among the pioneers. Soon the land was opened to all comers.

In an area west of Burk's Falls, incentives were provided to attract settlers. One such scheme was the Donaldson Plan under which ready-made farms were prepared for the new arrivals. The government would clear five acres and build a small house on each plot which was then sold for $200. After 18 more acres were cleared, the settler received title to the land and house. The program was to be self-financing using the original deposits, but few were ever collected and failure resulted. Nevertheless, people did arrive, first by rail to Washago and then by colonization road to the area near Burk's Falls. The other route was from Washago to Gravenhurst, then by water to the head of navigation on Lake Rousseau. There immigration sheds were provided for families while the men travelled the Nipissing Road to the Magnetawan area. By the turn of the century, the population of most of these settlements had peaked and has been declining ever since.

Why so many failures, even when the Government sponsored the settlers and the land looked so lush? In hindsight, the answer is simple. The thin glacial soils that supported such magnificent stands of red and white pine dissipate and erode quickly when the cover is removed. Prospective farmers quickly cut the trees to free land for crops, while lumber companies removed the forest as fast as they could ship out the logs. After a brief spurt of population growth and prosperity based on the lumber industry, most places began a period of long decline. Unfortunately for them, the seemingly lush vegetation, undisturbed by man for centuries, concealed an unpleasant surprise. Under the thick, spongy layer of needles, twigs, brambles and brush lay thin acidic soil. Not only was it inhospitable to many crops, it washed away when the trees were cut. Just as in the supposedly fertile tropical rain forest, successful plant life here depended upon an appropriate mantle of trees and underbrush to sustain its vigour.

Even though governments had actively promoted settlement of the shield, the settler faced almost insurmountable odds. Discouraged farmers headed for the west to farm the prairies, or to the north in search of gold. Almost everyone was sadly mistaken in their assessment of the agricultural potential. But it was the hapless pioneer, not the bureaucrat who suffered in the end. Some things never change! Now tourism sustains some of these former settlements while others have all but disappeared.

Kearney is one such example. To reach it we leave Highway 11 just beyond Huntsville and follow the scenic parallel route 592 to the intersection of 518. The narrow blacktop strip twists and turns between watery ditches, weaving and intertwining with the Little East River. It follows this tangled skein of dark brown liquid almost to its source. Although we are only a few kilometers off the major route north, we are truly in the wilderness. Beyond us to the east are wild, forested, granite hills, inhospitable and uninhabited for miles. Here on the edge, frogs sing in the swamps as a great blue heron lifts ponderously from the teeming bog. It finally gets airborne; a wriggling, hapless minnow in its beak. Sedges, cat-tails, a fancy of spongy bushes and a tangle of wild raspberries -- all vie with the eggy bog beside the road for life and dominance. Infilling has created a place of sluggish conflict as vegetation creeps inexorably waterward to construct new land in the former lake.

Civilization appears again in the form of a general store, several churches, a credit union and a group of houses at Emsdale. Passing along 518 towards Kearney we encounter "The Doghouse". Here a local craftsman manufactures custom paddles from cherry wood for prices ranging from $30 to $40. Hand hewn, they are a thing of beauty, smooth and shiny, recalling again the aquatic heritage of this lake-studded forest. We head east, seeking our first destination on the shield; a place called Kearney, reputed to have been a thriving community some fifty years ago.

Twenty minutes later we top a rise, pass through clouds of pleasantly acrid smoke produced by burning grass, continue by some shacks and reach our destination. As the day fades rapidly into gloom, we catch a view of Kearney on our right. Its small dark lake is ringed by a necklace of cottages, their docks projecting like so many pointing fingers into the water. As darkness slowly rolls across the lake, light from windows angles down to be reflected from the slick surface below. Above, wisps of stringy mares' tails form symmetrical orange arcs along the horizon. The final flickers of fire from the sun fade into blues and blacks, and night comes quietly to the village.

The scene now appears idyllic, but the first settlers here had an exceedingly difficult time, starting with their trip. First they came to Gravenhurst by train, then by boat to Bracebridge, by road to Port Sydney, by boat to Huntsville, and finally, by what passed for a road to Kearney. Initially Kearney thrived when loggers assaulted the trees with reckless abandon. The settlement became a town of 812 in 1911. Since then, things have declined, despite a flurry of activity in 1919. In that year, enough radioactive material was discovered nearby to claim a government reward, but little more was ever found. A gold rush at about the same time produced more talk than gold, so when the forests declined so did the population. By 1920, two local sawmills and several others nearby employed a few dozen workers, but until very recently, the path has been steadily downhill for the village.

From a low of about 400 people, Kearney has recovered to 565 today. Much of this has been the result of improved transportation bringing in tourist business. Cabins for rent surround the lake and a fishing camp is found on the outskirts of town. A general store and fast food outlet supply sustenance for the body, while several churches feed the soul. The most interesting of these is St. Patrick's Roman Catholic Church, a delightful fieldstone structure on the outskirts. With its mix of pink granite, salt and pepper gneiss and grey dolomite, it recalls a church in an Irish village. Aside from the churches, little remains to remind us of Kearney's past, despite the superb setting and a few older houses.

Kearney has declined but is not dead. A major woodworking company at its edge now manufactures sashes and doors from local wood. The LCBO outlet will undoubtedly add to its attraction for hunters and fishermen. From here they have unlimited access to vast stretches of white water, woods and wilderness. Algonquin Park lies only a few miles east. With a little imagination and promotion Kearney could become an increasingly attractive tourist destination. The new road should help considerably. This dream will be realized as the more accessible settlements become even more crowded and polluted. So far Kearney remains relatively unspoiled.

About fifteen kilometers farther north we encounter another of those bypassed communities – literally and figuratively speaking. Here Highway 11 skirts Burk's Falls in its rush to reach North Bay. Cars accelerating along the bypass carry their passengers around a delightful town that has been spared the noise and pollution of diesel fumes and traffic. Here the Magnetawan River

Burk's Falls railway station, now used for storage. In 1885, the Northern and Pacific Junction Railway came to this community and gave it an insurmountable advantage over its rival Magnetawan.

plunges over a falls that in times past forced the Indians, fur traders and explorers to pause and portage around the obstacle. This same barrier also became a major source of power for sawmills and factories. The town boomed when the local wood was cut, milled and made into sashes, doors and lumber for export. After 1902, water power produced electricity to light the streets. In that same year, this important event encouraged optimistic citizens to register a plan for the "City" of Burk's Falls in Parry Sound.

Burk's Falls was overshadowed by its local rival, Magnetawan, until 1885 when the Northern and Pacific Junction Railway came to Burk's Falls. After this happy event, lumber, veneer, broom handles and doors from local factories could be shipped all over the word from this thriving industrial centre. The population rose to 800 at the turn of the century and a bright future seemed assured. Alas, the Great Fire of 1908 burned most of the town, with damages costing $170,000, an enormous sum at the time. This blazing inferno, which started in the Knight Brothers Kiln, quickly spread to engulf two hotels, a church, most of the stores and several residences. Burk's Falls was rebuilt but the setback of the fire, along with the depletion of the forests ultimately took their toll. The population slipped to under 700 by 1941. Today it stands at 895, despite the highway bypass which was predicted by some to leave it stranded without business from passing motorists.

If the number and quality of local motels is any indication, Burk's Falls is no tourist resort. It supports only one motel with eight tiny units. It is, however, a thriving service centre once again. On our stroll along its main street we encounter a Stedman's, a hardware store and a handsome post office built in 1935. People bustle past with a cheery "Good morning" for local and stranger alike. Several rambling clapboard homes of former lumber barons stand on the hill near the river. One major wood-working factory remains to utilize the power, and a plaque identifies the former electrical generating plant.

Below the dam we find the moorings for the steamers which faithfully plied the river from Burk's Falls to Magnetawan. From 1870 until 1934, passengers and freight were carried by boat along this historic water route to the interior.

Burks Falls is far away from major cities, bypassed by the highway and no more attractive than many other towns, in spite of the river and the dam. On the other hand, it offers access to an almost unbroken wilderness of trout, trees, water and tranquility. Posters in a realtor's window advertise lakefront cottages for prices ranging between $27,000 and $39,000; a far cry from those a hundred kilometers south, which often run to six figures. Farms with a hundred acres of land are going for similar amounts. If one has the time to commute, or to come here for the summer, the area is very alluring. Fast roads, telecommunications and increasing numbers of retired executives seeking solitude may well restore the fortunes of Burk's Falls.

We decide to follow the river route of the pioneers to Magnetawan. The name has a ring about it, conjuring up images of rugged, bearded trappers, burly loggers and an old Indian chief. Lacking a canoe, we follow Highway 520 downstream along the river. We pass the former steamship landing, and after a few more minutes of driving, arrive at Cecebe. Little except a sawmill and cottages mark this site today. It is not mentioned in the directories and now has a population of only nineteen. The lake from which it takes its name sweeps gracefully away from the highway, followed by a ring of resinating pines which hide some cottages upon the shore. The water is flat and calm. Bleached clouds move high, and above us gulls slip over the updrafts and yaw in the wind. Beyond there are the trees, rocks, water, bush, and the road to Magnetawan.

Across the road from the lake stand several farms. They mark one of the infrequent areas where agriculture has lasted more than a few years in this rugged land. Ramshackle sheds painted green, red or white list and sag beside the few small houses. Tumbled cedar barn boards punctuate fields spotted with rusty boulders dropped by the glacier. Here and there sheep graze on the rough pasture, joined occasionally by beef cattle. The houses, with their peeling paint and ornamentation of abandoned farm equipment, look none too prosperous. Yet one or two newish sport cars and well-kept yards appear along the road. The struggle continues as man attempts to tame this inhospitable terrain.

The road to Magnetawan winds through the hills like a black, twisted belt. Along it we pass two

Below the dam in Burk's Falls, one major wood working factory remains to utilize the power, and a plaque identifies the former electrical generating plant.

porcupines pressed like fossils into the pavement. Finally we reach the locks on the outskirts of the village. Here we pause to observe the site of so much early activity and to read the inscription on a cairn in the captivating Centennial park. It commemorates the 20 families of Swiss settlers brought to Magnetawan by Madame von Koerber in 1885. They followed the first government-sponsored settlers who came in 1868, hoping to farm or to make their fortune from the forests. By 1873, the Dodge Lumber Company had cut the Rousseau and Nipissing Road through Magnetawan in exchange for lumber rights from the government. This primitive route crossed the river at a point where it narrowed to 75 feet, setting the stage for the early prosperity of the village, which by 1879 boasted a number of hotels, stores and several sawmills. In contrast, an early traveller reported no hotels and only one store in 1867.

The steamer from Ahmic Lake to Burk's Falls reinforced Magnetawan's early prosperity. It slowed to pass through the lock, then docked to embark passengers and furs, and to unload supplies. The original lock was built by the Ontario Government between 1883 and 1886 from stone-filled timber cribwork measuring 112 by 28 feet. The structure raised or lowered steamers by 10 feet and over 700 passed through it each season until it was replaced by a concrete structure in 1911. The lock and river greatly facilitated trade and settlement of the area as far as Ahmic Harbour where navigation on the river ended.

The river had other uses as well. Loggers removed vast quantities of trees from the surrounding forests, squared them, and floated them down the river to Georgian Bay. Ultimately they reached Portsmouth England or the United States. Logging boomed for a time, but the glowing reports of farming potential that attracted European settlers were not realized. By the mid 1880s, much of the land had been cleared to reveal only a few inches of topsoil which were easily washed away and far too shallow for commercial agriculture. In most places, the land didn't even provide a decent subsistence for the hapless settlers.

By 1885, the Canadian Pacific Railway had completed its transcontinental line and was encouraging settlers to head west. In

Near Cecebe, tumbled cedar barn boards beside sagging structures punctuate fields spotted with rusty boulders dropped by the glacier.

1891, the railway's agent came to Magnetawan to promote the western exodus, but was met with skepticism by people who had already been fooled once. Finally, four free passes convinced a cautious delegation to inspect the western lands. They returned with ecstatic descriptions of soil which had potential beyond their wildest dreams. When the first wave of settlers headed west in 1892, they were so poor that the railway had to mortgage their belongings in return for fares. Thereafter the depopulation of Magnetawan continued apace as disillusioned farmers sought to begin a new and more prosperous life on the Prairies.

The final blow came in 1885 when the Northern and Pacific Junction Railway was lured to Burk's Falls rather than to Magnetawan. Although the impact was minimal at first, Magnetawan was left far from the most efficient export route and continued its decline while Burk's Falls prospered. From 1881 onwards, when Magnetawan boasted four businesses to Burk's Falls' two, the rivalry continued. By 1891 Magnetawan businesses were down to 27 and Burk's Falls had increased to 29. By the turn of the century, both depopulation and the effect of the railway decision had made a major impact; Burk's Falls peaked with 42 business enterprises while Magnetawan declined to only twelve. Gone were the early signs of prosperity as settlers left, the forests were depleted and Magnetawan was bypassed by both the railway and the main road north.

Today Magnetawan is a picturesque if sleepy community of 230 people. A plaque commemorates the Nipissing Road, and the tidy little marina seems to prosper. Three sleek, red and white cabin cruisers float beside the dock awaiting passengers who will trace the historic river route of the pioneers. Back towards the park, the river foams and churns, pushing and fighting its way through the narrow channel and over the falls. By noon, a hot sun bakes the main street lined by two small restaurants, a craft shop and a grocery store. Around the corner cars park haphazardly in front of the medical clinic staffed on Thursdays by physicians from Parry Sound. The "feel" is one of relaxed activity, waiting for a boom.

Even more than Kearney, Magnetawan is blessed by a site and situation which provide enormous potential. Very little would have to be done in order to transform it into a major resort. Ultimately, the precise factors that led to its decline could provide for rebirth.

Leaving Magnetawan we head once again north. The road to Port Loring ends ultimately at the "North Shore", a term used by the locals to describe the eastern side of Georgian Bay. Our route to this destination runs on endlessly, becoming a path of craters and cracks. On we drive through a land of treeless, rock-strewn hills shaped to perfectly rounded nudity by the ice where the glaciers scraped and scoured. Little in the way of deposition is now to be seen aside from the odd heap of sand and gravel. We travel past stunted growths of tangled tamarack, on beside boggy fields festooned with tiny flowers, finally to the Rye Road, a reminder of events and times long past.

In the early 1900s, there were rumours of gold in the rocks south of Golden Valley. The land was empty except for the occasional miner's shack and a few logging camps. By then, opportunities in the Walkerton, Mildmay and Neustadt areas of southern Ontario were few, as sons outnumbered the farms they were to work. The eldest and second son might remain on the 100-acre family farm, but others were forced to seek employment elsewhere. These second wave pioneers headed west or took to lumbering in the near north. One popular destination was around Rye, now abandoned and found only on old maps or by following rutted tracks in the forest beyond Mikisew Provincial Park. The road to Rye once joined Highway 522 near Commanda; we decide to follow it south as far as possible.

Long ago when camping in the area on a memorable, soggy day, my family and I left the car and trudged through dripping pines and brambles of blackberries. Soon narrow ruts widened to confront a small white church, paint peeling and windows boarded over. We came upon the remnants of a ruined store and garage. They stood, sagging and forlorn like sad messengers from the past. Windows had long since been broken, doors fell askew from their hinges, and cobwebs festooned the rafters. The children insisted that we explore the "haunted house" so we entered with trepidation and began to look about. Soon we discovered tattered accounts and papers in a drawer. Some were made out to a relative, dated 1938. We seemed to step back in time as we contemplated these artifacts from our own family history. Apparently the settlers had suddenly departed, leaving many of their personal effects. The children were thrilled with this latter-day "archeological dig".

Unfortunately, the episode is not to be repeated on our attempted trip to Rye from the north. A "No Trespassing" sign puts an abrupt halt to our journey. Progress! The road has been closed and ends ignominiously in a farmer's field. So much for our second historical adventure! Not to worry. On the road to Rye we pass two pieces of evidence that add to our tale of changing settlements and lifestyles. The first is the Commanda General Store; a three-storey Victorian marvel, ornately festooned with carved verge boards and wooden lace. It is considerably larger than the run-of-the-mill general store and contains the original fittings. Wooden counters, ladders for climbing to the shelves, churns, petticoats, implements, rows of tools and farm supplies are all there. When we peer in the window it is obvious that all are authentic artifacts. Unfortunately, it is now a museum that doesn't open till the 24th of May, that magic date when summer is officially started in Ontario.

Our other bit of settlement evidence is the yuppie house in the woods on the road to Rye. A neat complex of cedar buildings includes a house and pool beside a greenhouse filled with early garden vegetables and flowers. Children's toys and a playhouse are scattered about the back yard; a BMW sits in the garage. Who would live here so far from civilization? Possibly retirees, except for the young woman and evidence of small children. We speculate on a doctor or lawyer who commutes to Parry Sound or North Bay, but this seems to be a long trip, especially in the winter. Oh well, possibly it's an architect or engineer who keeps in touch with the office by modem and computer. The isolation of such a modern and comfortable dwelling convinces us even more of the new approach to country living that is sweeping the countryside. This house is particularly interesting since it lies almost beside a derelict farmhouse from the 1890s. The technological changes that destroyed the farming have made possible the country retreat!

The sun slowly slumps down the western sky as we speed on towards Port Loring. Fortunately,

Our other bit of evidence is the Yuppie house in the woods on the way to Rye. Who would live here so far from civilization?

The Yuppie estate near Rye is all the more interesting, since it lies almost beside a derelict farmhouse from the 1890s. The technological changes that destroyed the farming made possible the country retreat.

the road now runs smooth and even, slashing through the underbrush like a black snake. The community clings to the gentle slopes around the northern edge of Duck Lake. From the size of the homes and the verdant green expanses of lawn, it appears to be the remnant of a genteel summer retreat for the wealthy. Now the old hotel is peeling, its wide screened porch sagging sadly towards the lake and lawn below. The outfitting businesses look prosperous enough, but the new motel on the edge of town is for sale, and the hotel is still closed for the winter.

Our impression of faded importance along with potential is reinforced by some statistics. The settlement peaked in population at 200 in 1908 and obtained a post office in 1922. By 1976 the population had declined to 162, but it increased again to 222 in 1987. Even this far from the city, a few retirees and some new permanent settlers have chosen to live in an isolated but extremely tranquil and scenic environment. Port Loring may never be a boom town, but it certainly has the capacity for slow residential growth and modest tourism.

The road towards the setting sun and Georgian Bay takes us past Loring. Originally known as McConkey corners, the settlement became Loring when its post office was opened in 1884. At that time, Colonel W.E. O'Brian, the Member of Parliament for Parry Sound, petitioned for a post office and gave it his wife's maiden name. Like comparable service centres in the south, Loring grew quickly in the early days. In 1880, its population swelled when a group of German settlers arrived. By 1885 it boasted a blacksmith, a general store and a carpenter. The new road to Trout Creek was opened in 1887, making the hamlet considerably more accessible. By 1903 its population was 100 and its two general stores, sawmill, blacksmith and hotel served the numerous loggers who worked nearby.

The prosperity of Loring continued when a road to Salines (now Drocourt) was opened in 1908 and was reinforced after Arthur Walton and Sons began boat service to Lost Channel in 1913. Then the Schroeder Mills and Timber Company laid down the Key Valley railway from Pakesley, on the Canadian Pacific line, to Lost Channel. By 1922 the road to Trout Creek was graveled and became the main route from Loring. These events conspired to make the settlement an important

A typical northern scene at Trout Creek.

timber depot and service centre, but it too suffered as a result of poor farming and the depletion of timber supplies. From a population of 200 in 1922, it declined to 162 in 1976 and now stands at 140. Little remains to attract population, and it appears that most new development will occur down the road at Port Loring with its delightful waterfront location.

Now Loring has little to offer, so we continue west along the road that finally terminates at the intersection of Highway 69. Here the campers' store offers supplies for those staying at Grundy Lake Provincial Park. Stacks of green fiberglass canoes share space with the gleaming wooden Northland craft awaiting the swarms of summer woodsmen from the cities. Fond memories flood back, recalling swift sailing in stiff breezes and tranquil days of tenting or canoeing on the lake. What with contemporary crowded conditions, requirements for reservations and bureaucratic site selection procedures, we aren't so sure we wish to stay at the park again. At least not on a weekend during July and August.

Pushing north on Highway 69 we pass lakes, trees; trees, lakes; and finally the French River. Granite knolls guard the bogs and swamps which are studded with stumps of swallowed forests. Long narrow clefts in the cliffs intersect the highway at right angles, having posed innumerable challenges for the road engineers who produced today's smooth curves and easy gradients. From a tortured, twisting trail, creeping up, over, and around every obstacle, Sixty-nine slowly became a gently sweeping ribbon through the solid shield.

Soon we approach Sudbury with its belching white Inco stack, spewing dust and sulphur dioxide in a white plume across the sky. Now the chimney is the highest in the land, spreading pollution far and wide rather than dropping it locally. When the breeze carries the cloud down and towards the car, our throats begin to tickle. But things could be worse. They have improved considerably with the taller chimney. Green grass and trees have replaced the barren dark moonscape that once characterized Sudbury. Within the city, healthy green lawns have replaced patches of mud or rock, and trees are almost everywhere.

What a transformation has occurred in the nickel capital of the world. We pass the lake in the centre of town and view the modernistic buildings of the Science North complex. In a few short years, Sudbury has metamorphosed from a grimy mining town in the midst of desolation into a thriving modern metropolis with good restaurants and a university. But at what cost? Will the pollution now spreading for thousands of kilometers acidify and destroy the life in lakes all over eastern Canada, just as its predecessors devastated the Sudbury basin? Or will the government and Inco arrive at a solution satisfactory to the company and the Ministry of the Environment; one that will preserve jobs and save the environment at a reasonable cost? Only time and the wisdom of Solomon will extricate us from this recurring dilemma.

After Sudbury, the road skirts to the north of Georgian Bay, then dips south to follow the water near Spanish. At the Serpent River Indian Reservation we pass the Serpent River Trading Post with its three white tepees and stands of birches. A two-storey log building in the style of the French settlers, it stands well back from the road. It looks interesting and friendly, so we backtrack and enter.

What a delight! No "Canadian" (read Japanese, Hong Kong Taiwanese) souvenirs here. The floors are of varnished pine and open beams support the roof. Every wall is adorned by genuine and exquisite oil and watercolour paintings or prints by Indian artists. The shelves abound in superb native carvings of wood or stone. Leather goods, crafts from beads or skins and woven grass baskets are everywhere. Snowshoes and moccasins share space with pottery and glassware, all authentic and all reasonably priced. We learn that this is a band project employing three people, encouraging the resurgence of local handicrafts and stocking only the genuine article. What a relief and change from the run-of-the-mill "tourist trap" found in resort areas. This is an excellent example of entrepreneurial skill and native craftsmanship combining to produce a successful northern enterprise.

A few miles farther along we stop for lunch in a roadside park. We satisfy our hunger and are pleased that the park's washrooms are open and reasonably clean. Oh why, oh why, doesn't the Ministry of Transportation place small parks with facilities at decent intervals along our major highways? How much suffering has been endured by travellers with full bladders and empty stomachs on the highways of Ontario? If you've travelled with children on 401, especially near Toronto, you know the problem. For most of the route, the choice seems to be a grotty truck stop or the ditch. And the ditch is an unpleasant alternative in the dark or at 20 below.

Of course there are a few service centres on the main street of Ontario, Highway 401, but they are relentlessly being converted to plastic hamburger havens. This is fine for kids, but what about those who crave a soup and a sandwich? And their spacing may be adequate for camels, but for children and other human beings, intervals are far too great. Poor Nova Scotia seems capable of providing picnic parks on even the minor roads, as does Quebec. Someone in Ontario should run for Provincial Parliament on a platform of toilets for travellers! They would win in a landslide!

Highway 69 is the major land link between southern Ontario and the west. In the summer, tourists predominate, but at all other times, twenty-wheelers sustain the local restaurants and garages. They roar past, far above the legal limit, leaving us as if we were powered by a pair of gerbils. At the major truck stop west of Sudbury, row upon row of Mack trucks, Fords, gleaming tractor trailers, semis and pick-ups -- pause, idle and snort. They spread diesel fumes across the land while their drivers stop for a coffee or a nap. Logging trucks, fuel trucks, refrigerator trucks, moving trucks and chemical trucks share the lot with a few cars and trailers. For the equivalent of two city blocks they stretch, waiting to continue the life-line from the industrial heartland to the breadbasket in the west.

In this part of the "near north", truck stops often substitute for the rural service centres of the south. In many areas the only viable economic function among a group of houses along the highway is the service station/restaurant supported by passing traffic. Here the social interaction is mostly between truckers and staff; but these stopping places do support a surprising number of local employees, especially if they are open twenty-four hours a day, and many are. They provide a place where locals can purchase a meal or a few necessities such as bread or milk, thus avoiding a long trip to a proper grocery store.

Many northern truck stops qualify as bona fide outsized functions, doing a volume of business infinitely greater than the amount that could be generated by local customers. This example is near Sudbury.

Many northern truck stops qualify as bona fide outsize functions, doing a volume of business infinitely greater than the amount that could be generated by local customers. What a contrast to the outsized functions in the south, most of which rely for business on persons living within 50 kilometers and coming for meals, shopping or entertainment. Along the major highways of the north, the sale of gasoline, food and supplies is big business. But the social function is also important, especially for those who supply the bulk of the business. In a way, it is comparable to the function of the post office/general store of the 1880s.

Like a gathering of the clan, the drivers meet. Some are lean and fit, swaggering in their faded jeans and cowboy boots, keys dangling from their hips. But more suffer from bad backs and paunches from years behind the wheel. They relax, kid the waitress and exchange stories with their CB buddies. This radio link breaks the monotony in the night and is essential for emergencies. It has kept many a trucker awake long after the coffee and no-nod pills have lost their effect. The long-haul trucker is a nomad. He leads a hard and lonesome life on the highways of the land, linking scattered settlements to civilization in much the same manner as the stage-coach driver of the past. The isolation of the north is directly analogous to the seclusion of the early settler in the bush, both bonded by a slender thread of road to civilization.

Having experienced this local cultural and economic phenomenon, we manoeuver past the expanse of trucks and press on, hoping to reach Iron Bridge at dusk, when the sun's slanting rays produce optimum conditions for photography. Iron Bridge -- it conjures up images of an ancient rusting iron structure carrying modern traffic across the Mississagi River. Knowing that numerous tourist establishments and fishing camps have met their end here during the last twenty years, we speculate on its original attractions. Upon arrival, our romantic images are shattered.

No more Iron Bridge; only the foundations a few hundred yards

In Iron Bridge there is a wooden building labelled "Cold Storage; Fish and Game Froze and Packed; Blocks, Cubes, Worms". Down the street stands a general store beside the skeletal remains of a burnt out business.

off the highway and a new concrete structure. Instead of quaint fishing shacks, modern sprawling motels on the outskirts have replaced the earlier cabins and camps. There is a wooden building labelled "Cold Storage; Fish and Game Froze & Packed; Blocks, Cubes, Worms". Down the street stands a general store beside the skeletal remains of a burnt-out business. At the corner we pass a tacky "Souvenir Shop" in the worst Ontario tradition. The bleached, faded green carcass of a long abandoned motel hides as if ashamed behind the equally sad souvenir post. The stream and woods remain, but the reality is considerably different from the Iron Bridge we imagined. It is a stopping place for travellers and a service centre for locals, but not the charming and exotic settlement we hoped to find!

Once again we have encountered a settlement whose glory days are past, despite the fact that some new economic functions are being developed. Originally known as Tally-Ho, the name was changed to Iron Bridge when a steel structure replaced the wooden bridge that had served until 1884. In the past the settlement was a gateway to the interior of the rugged shield with its rich mineral and lumber resources. For many years it functioned as a supply depot for hunters, fishermen or explorers looking for minerals. Now they seek abandoned mine shafts which abound in the area. Its population has declined somewhat from almost 900 in 1971 to 814 today, and motels have replaced most of the outfitters and hotels of the early days.

Most of the homes are white frame bungalows, and someone's optimism for the future is reflected by roads (without houses) laid out into the bush on the northern side of town. The 24 businesses in town include several large and modern motels along the highway (one with camping), restaurants, a grocery and hardware store, a Lion's Clubhouse and a trucking company. The old centre of town is now overshadowed by strip development along the highway. This includes a large chicken farm called Mighty Fresh Eggs which seems a little out of place so far north but has access to a large market thanks to Highway 17. In fact the continued existence of Iron Bridge as a service centre and tourist town owes much to its location on this busy artery.

Iron Bridge offers little of interest to us, so we head back to Blind River, first looping north from Thessalon to Little Rapids and back to Iron Bridge. This route takes us through endless expanses of woods -- filmy, light green tamarack, tall ragged jack pine, scruffy cedar in the swamps. Here we encounter the boreal forest where pulp wood is king. Several hydro power projects are left far behind as we gather speed on these deserted roads. The immensity of the land becomes increasingly apparent where wilderness stretches to the horizon and beyond. Only a few kilometers off the main route west we encounter virtually no human habitation. Rabbit, deer, bear, blackbirds, beaver, coons, muskrat and hawks seem to have the monopoly on this expanse of blue water and green foliage. Keeping a watch out for moose we spot an owl instead.

We pass only one, tiny, neat settlement, nestled beside a dam. In Little Rapids, an ornate, carefully maintained gothic house catches our eye. It stands by the road, half hidden by its shelter belt of towering white pines. Freshly painted white clapboard narrows to form a sharp gothic peak at the front gable. A wide rambling porch provided ample space for "just setting" on a Sunday afternoon. Half a minute down the road, the lily-fringed pond escapes noisily through the gates of a dam. Here too once stood a thriving saw mill, long since made obsolete by its larger steam driven successors.

Little Rapids is a totally captivating scene in the early afternoon sun, but after it, nothing but bush and more bush confronts us. A delightful site such as this existing anywhere near to centre of population would long since have been overrun by commuters, retirees or others seeking rural tranquillity. Being in an area of sparse population and vast natural beauty, it will be spared all but a small amount of locally generated growth. With a small sense of relief we rejoin "civilization" again at Iron Bridge, and turn once more east, our brief encounter with real wilderness behind. But even more is soon to come.

Blind River is the last stop before heading farther into the northern wilderness. It is one of the most historic settlements on the North Shore, being known to Samuel de Champlain from his explorations as early as 1632. Then it was a gathering place for the native people who congregated in the sheltered mouth of the river which the Voyageurs named for its hidden entrance to the bay. A post office was established in the town in 1847, delivering mail that came across the ice by dog sled from Parry Sound in the winter. The McFadden Lumber Company, Daigle's Power House, along with Provencher's and Solomon's general stores, were prominent among early businesses.

Blind River has continued to thrive despite a disastrous forest fire in 1948 that burned virtually all the white pine in the area. Miles to the south and east, the skies were darkened as smoke from the raging inferno was carried far and wide by the wind. Until then, the lumber mills that lined the waterfront were among the largest in North America, processing vast amounts of wood for far flung markets.

Today the settlement boasts six churches, several plywood plants, and French and English schools which reflect its early establishment by French explorers. The main street runs at right angles to the waterfront and has been rejuvenated with interlocking paving blocks and new paint on the prosperous looking shops. The wide, calm river is corralled behind a dam before it froths and rushes down the incline to the bay. A number of large and modern motels are situated near the water, one along side the turbulent dashing water from the dam. The town is passed by the railway which parallels the main highway, reminding us of its early reliance on the iron horse as the only transportation to the south. Given its delightful site on the river and highway, along with important service functions for the uranium fields of the Algoma area, Blind River's future seems assured. Its tourist attractions, shops and industry supply a solid economic base, supporting a population of some 3,564.

The trip to the east will complete our loop across Ontario. In Canadian terms, we haven't really been near the frontier -- merely in the "near north" as it is called. This may be the case if you are a local, but the perception of this area from south of Sudbury is of emptiness, devoid of people and development. In that sense we're on the frontier as soon as we leave the Trans-Canada Highway.

Soon after striking out to the north and east, fire warning signs remind us of the hazard. Overhead, swirling plumes of dense black smoke from a distant conflagration drift and dissipate. They vividly recall tales of pioneers on the Bruce Peninsula and the problems of those in the wilderness nearby. On numerous occasions, raging infernos ravaged their land, destroying timber and farms alike. Fishing, forestry and mining are all subject to depletion, be it by man or nature. The economy and the country here are fragile; this, then, is to us a frontier.

We continue to drive north and the real isolation begins. So far we have followed the southern route to the west, but now we head towards the northernmost road across Ontario. Numerous roads thrust eagerly into the wilderness, eking their narrow paths between lakes and through the trees. But most are stunted, beginning at the Trans-Canada, only to end abruptly or be replaced by private trails for mines or logging.

On our trip towards Timmins we truly penetrate the Boreal Forest. The vegetation seems to shrink in size, as white spruce, black spruce, balsam and lodgepole pine replace the white and red pine of the south. Mile after mile pass on the road north and east. Tires sing on the endless blacktop pavement while we dash between timeless granite knolls. Little remains to see save an occasional mine head; and trees, more trees, smaller trees, swamp and more trees. The Sudbury Basin is still the heart of nickel, silver and lead mining in Canada, but minerals abound in these remoter regions, with gold heading the list. Certainly something bright and expensive is needed to lure anyone permanently into this vast and lonely wilderness.

We press on towards our destination in the Ottawa Valley. This brief encounter with the "near north" and even briefer experience with the southern edges of the frontier has given us a taste of an economy based on forestry, minerals and tourism. Now we shall explore "The Valley" of the mighty Ottawa River. A loop back to North Bay and Mattawa takes us to that historic route of voyageurs and explorers.

The Ottawa River was one of the first major pathways into the western and northern interior of this land. It rises almost 250 kilometers straight north of the City of Ottawa in Lake Capimichigama, after which it begins a turbulent and sinuous route by way of Lake Timiskaming, finally joining the St. Lawrence at Montreal. Our itinerary follows it south and east on Highway 17 from Mattawa, paralleling the river and the historic route of the early explorers.

Here as early as 1613, Champlain travelled on his futile quest for La Mer de la Nord. For years thereafter, great flotillas of Indians, coureurs de bois and traders for the Hudson's Bay and North West Company paddled up and down watery avenue into the interior. Missionaries, settlers and others also travelled this way, but the heaviest use was a result of insatiable European demand for beaver pelts and hair from which to make felt hats. As in the Maritimes many years earlier, trade preceded permanent settlement and the cultivation of the soil.

The Ottawa River consists of a series of tumbling rapids punctuated by large expanses of wide slow stretches forming lakes. The area known locally as the "Valley" lies in a graben, or block of land which has dropped well below its previous elevation. This depression was the result of a series of faults running roughly parallel to the river from north of Pembroke past Ottawa to the Quebec border. Long ago in the distant geological past, a slab of bedrock about 56 kilometers wide slipped down along the faults to form the relatively level valley that extends south from the river. To the north, the precambrian shield rises almost 400 metres, making a sharp delineation between the upland granites and the sedimentary rocks in the valley.

Much more recently, at the end of the Wisconsin glaciation, meltwater from the receding ice was ponded in the graben and merged with the Champlain Sea, a shallow extension of the Atlantic extending up the St. Lawrence Valley. At that time, ice up to two miles thick had depressed the land, making it possible for the ocean to flood the valleys of the St. Lawrence and Ottawa Rivers. When the ice began to melt and withdraw, drainage from the Lake Huron Basin spilled through the Ottawa Valley into the Champlain Sea, depositing vast deltas in the Deep River-Petawawa-Pembroke region.

While the isostatic recovery (or rebound from the glacially induced depression) continued, the land rose slowly, ultimately draining the Champlain Sea and leaving the Ottawa and St. Lawrence Valleys as they are today. A legacy of sand, silt, sediment and marine shells remains to remind us of this era of glacial history. This explains the sharp contrast between rich agriculture in much of the valley and the forest or barren rock on the approaches from either direction. Within the graben, excellent soils alternate with some poorer land and low scarp faces, resulting in a mixture of rich farmland with rough land in scrub or forest.

Remembering this fascinating geological history, we travel south and east to pass former logging towns which stand as a legacy to the cutting of wood, floating of logs and brawling of years gone by. We also recall the strong Irish heritage which imparts a distinctive character to the valley akin to that found in Newfoundland. Along the Ottawa and its tributaries, Irish lore and logging tales continue to be popular in places such as Calabogie, Barry's Bay, Sand Point, Shawville Quebec, and even Ottawa. Of all the lore, that surrounding the logging industry is the most colourful.

After the American Revolution, which greatly depleted timber supplies to Britain, enormous rafts of logs were floated down the rivers, eventually to reach their ultimate fate in the British ship-building industry. An average Ottawa River raft was like an enormous houseboat, with quarters for the crew and up to eight cribs of 2,000 to 2,400 timbers. According to local tales, the cooking on some of these enormous timber rafts was legendary. It probably had to be to keep the fractious, high-spirited crews full and contented. The total volume of wood in some rafts would have been as high as 120,000 cubic feet of first class white pine, often mixed with smaller amounts of red pine. By the turn of the century, the value of such a raft was over $100,000, and thousands were floated out. Estimates suggest that 85 million pieces of pine were taken from the valley between 1826 and 1894. Little wonder that settlements such as Bytown (Ottawa), Arnprior and Eganville, to name but a few, depended upon sawmilling as a mainstay of their early economies.

Given the rich diversity of Ottawa Valley settlements, it is difficult to decide upon a stopping place, but the decision is made easy for me by a long-standing passion. Years ago I had explored much of the subterranean United States as a spelunker (speologist in more scientific language), and the lure of the underground has never subsided. When we see the sign for the Bonnechere Caves near Eganville I can't resist. The prospect of seeing again stalactites, stalagmites and flowstone on a cavern wall brings us to an abrupt halt. These spectacular formations are all the result of water seeping through limestone, dissolving calcium carbonate, and then depositing it over thousands of years of dripping and evaporation.

On the land around the caverns, the Bonnechere River dashes madly through falls and rapids until it reaches the Fourth Chute. There in 1840, Alexander Murray of the Geological Survey of Canada noticed that a portion of the water turned off abruptly at right angles and disappeared into a subterranean limestone cavern. This portion of the cavern was dry during all but the spring freshets, so the local miller, Mr. Charles Merrick dammed the river, diverting the water permanently through the cave to his mill where, at the end of the tunnel, it ran the wheel located at the falls. Although this portion of cave has been known since the 1840s, it was not opened to the public until 1956 when lights and walks were installed.

Cavern formation is a fascinating process; one that has produced an environment for man for millennia, and material for numerous novels, including that classic *Tom Sawyer*. Conditions have to be just right to produce true solution caverns, and in this small area of the Ottawa Valley, they were. Millions of years ago, warm inland seas deposited soluble limestone in the Bonnechere Valley. Time passed, marine organisms lived and died, the deposits thickened, and faults occurred, dropping the sedimentary rocks to a point where they were protected from erosion. For thousands of years, water from rain and glacial melts alternately seeped through these strata or covered them entirely.

Since it contains oxygen and nitrogen, rainwater forms a weak acidic solution that dissolves limestone by a process known as solution erosion. Wherever it finds a weakness along a fault or fissure, it slowly eats away at the rock, ultimately forming long sinuous caverns. Elsewhere in fractured or more soluble strata, ground water dissolves enormous chambers and deep pits; sometimes hundreds of metres deep. Eventually a series of passages, tunnels, enormous ballroom-like openings and tiny fissures are left within the earth.

This is the erosional phase of cavern formation.

The depositional phase begins after the water table has lowered to uncover the subterranean channels and chambers. Little by little, tiny amounts of limestone solution run down rocks and across walls, depositing minuscule amounts of calcium carbonate as they go. After thousands and thousands of years they leave brightly coloured stalactites (which resemble icicles), stalagmites (which rise from the floor), columns, and flowstone (on walls). Red colours may be from iron in the water and blue from magnesium. The stark white formations are generally relatively pure calcium carbonate. The final result is an eerie fairyland of grotesque shapes, twists and turns, yawning chasms and water rippling through hidden underground channels. Little wonder that caverns have always held fascination for child and adult alike.

We enter the cool, dark recesses of the Bonnechere Cavern with great anticipation. From a hot sultry May day to a world where moisture and 10 degree celsius temperatures grip us like fingers, we snake down the wooden stairs into the underground world. The guide keeps up a constant patter, explaining the discovery and exploration of this natural wonder, and entertaining the visitors by pointing out faces and forms with his flashlight beam. Here the madonna and child, there a lion or a horse. With a little imagination, the variety of figures in the flowstone, stalactites and clusters of calcite crystals is endless.

Since the Bonnechere caves follow major fractures in the limestone, they are long and sinuous, tracing the ancient watercourses that scoured and dissolved the channels we follow. Ahead stretch long narrow tunnels, for all the world like a natural subway system. Since we entered at an upper level, below us we can always hear the distant roar of running water, glimpsing it occasionally at the bottom of a dark and yawning pit. At several lower stops we come upon branches of the Bonnechere River where it plunges through its underground passageway.

In many places the walls are fluted, curved and gracefully sculpted, revealing the work of running water in the past. Pits drop to seemingly bottomless depths, reminding us of the period when the whole system was submerged, and the weak acidic solutions dissolved the limestone in all directions. Now at the bottom of the cavern at the level of the present water table we encounter the river, where erosion still occurs. Through most of the cavern, the slow and relentless process of deposition continues at a rate estimated to be only a cubic inch in 150 years. Here and there in the walls we detect fossils of coral and other sea creatures that remind us of

In many places, the cavern walls are fluted, curved and gracefully sculpted, revealing the work of running water in the past. This is a typical scene in a limestone cavern.

the origin of these strata at the bottom of warm seas some 500 million years ago. Colourful lights play upon the walls and formations, illuminating and enhancing the already fascinating scene before us.

Exploring the Bonnechere Caverns causes us to reflect upon the crucial role played by such natural phenomena in the early history of man. Near to the edges of the receding ice he was subject to cold blasts in the winter and needed shelter from the rain in summer. Fortunately, limestone caverns provided secure havens where food could be stored, where safety from animals could be obtained, and with the addition of fire, where warmth could be preserved. Across much of Europe and North America at the end of the last glacial period, caverns just like these harboured and nurtured our ancestors, making survival just a bit more comfortable in an era when man was little more advanced than the animals. Today many European caverns contain magnificent paintings and other artifacts of early man. In North America many exhibit traces of occupation by Amerinds and evidence of use by early white settlers.

The closest settlement to the caverns is Eganville, along with Renfrew one of the places that began its economic development because of the Bonnechere River nearby. The river follows a tumultuous course, dashing over falls and churning through rapids for much of its length. In 1825 Gregoire Belanger came to the Fifth Chute to erect a shanty at what ultimately became Eganville. This transpired when John Egan from Alymer Quebec purchased an area known as "The Farm" from James Wadsworth, who had cleared the land and began a lumbering business. As time went on, the property changed hands after Egan built a sawmill, but he bought it back and then built a gristmill as well. By the 1850s, Egan's enterprises employed two thousand men at a rate of $14 to $16 per month plus board. They were said to have consumed six thousand barrels of pork and ten thousand barrels of flour in a month. In the winter, 1600 horses and oxen were used to move the timber, creating tremendous demand for oats and hay from farmers in the valley. The timber trade became the mainstay of the economy, and was for years the major export of the Ottawa and its tributaries.

Immigrants flocked to this prosperous new settlement. Most in the middle Bonnechere area were Irish or German; downstream near Douglas they were mostly Scottish. The Poles settled later, upstream near Round Lake. These settlers came to satisfy the vast demand generated by the lumber industry. By 1857, Eganville had carriage makers, carpenters, blacksmiths, millers, hotel keepers, general merchants, butchers and tanners. Its population then stood at 175, rose to 400 by 1871, and then increased to 710 in 1891 when the village was incorporated. A disastrous fire swept the community in 1911, destroying many houses and churches, but these were soon rebuilt.

Eganville's population reached 1487 by 1966 but has since declined. No longer does it benefit from the enormous lumber drives along the Bonnechere Valley with their influx of hungry and relatively affluent workers. But it does retain a sawmill and a nearby pulp industry. It is now a quiet community of 1257, having been bypassed by the rapid growth of earlier years, but retaining substantial limestone buildings, a number of pleasant churches and tranquil residential settings. Its location near the river and caverns make it an excellent base from which to explore the history and scenic splendour of the surrounding countryside. It continues to function as a regional service centre for an area whose major economic potential diminished after the heyday of the local timber barons.

From Eganville one can visit Renfrew, Arnprior, and the nation's capital; all having histories like that of Eganville, inextricably tied to the lumber industry and the mighty rivers in the Valley. Instead we make a quick traverse to the east before heading south. On the journey along narrow back roads we first pass abandoned log farmsteads, relics of the age when the demand from loggers, horses and oxen was almost insatiable. Now they stand, gaunt and abandoned, their small stable and grain storage sheds surrounding a courtyard enclosed by logs. Here where pioneers came early, and thrived when local demand was high, agriculture is no longer important. The small plots that sufficed in the early days on indifferent soil have long since lost out to their larger and more fertile rivals. But what an area for those interested in our heritage of early settlement. We can still ob-

But what an area for those interested in our heritage of early settlement. In the Ottawa Valley they can still observe two bay log barns and groupings of farm buildings in a style imported directly from their British antecedents.

serve two-bay log barns and groupings of farm buildings in a style imported directly from their British antecedents. Time has almost stood still in the western part of the Ottawa-Bonnechere Valley.

Travelling east, the valley widens, flattens, and becomes more fertile. At the eastern end of the depression near Hawkesbury, rows of farms follow the rangs just as in Quebec, reflecting the French influence upon early settlement. The lines of farm houses and barns are punctuated by row upon row of tall white or silver silos filled with corn. We could be on the Prairies, or at least in Huron County, to judge from the lack of fences and vast open fields. But this is the eastern Ottawa Valley, transformed from its earlier linear pattern of individual farmsteads to the homogeneity of factory-farming and agribusiness. What a contrast to the rougher areas not far upstream, and an even greater contrast to the near north from which we have so recently departed.

Our drive through the eastern valley takes us to several out-of-the way, but unexpectedly fascinating small communities. First we stop at Crysler, one of the many agricultural hamlets on the tiny brown roads on the Ontario map. Close to Moose Creek, Morewood and St. Albert, it sparkles in the late afternoon sun. An egg-grading station dominates its one street, where two general stores, a gas station and a restaurant constitute most of its economy. The restaurant is a family affair with a residence at the back, behind a forest of potted plants. People drift in to chat with the proprietor; first in English; then in French, and then back again. We are close enough to the Quebec border to hear both languages without an accent. This is bilingualism so complete that it makes us green with envy. It sets an example for those of us who profess both tongues but live too far from Quebec to practise what we preach.

Crysler is now a typical rural service centre in the midst of a thoroughly agrarian area. Far from any major roads, it is not the sort of place you would seek out unless you are a settlement explorer. And yet it has character and charm, despite its lack of new residential development or yuppie redevelopment of older homes. Its site on the banks of the South Nation River is typical of that of innumerable rural service centres in the early years. Water power and local agriculture stimulated the development of mills; the sawmill processed the logs, the grist mill ground the grain and the carding mill utilized the wool from numerous sheep.

Crysler was named for John Crysler, a United Empire Loyalist and member of the Legislative Assembly from 1808 to 1824. One of his many properties was the farm on which the village now stands. Another, and much more famous, was his land on the shores of the St. Lawrence where the Battle of Crysler's farm was fought in 1813. The first settlers came to Crysler around 1802, mostly English and Scots, but many later pioneers were of French origin, leading to the fluent bilingualism that we observed.

For the first few years, Crysler thrived in its local service role. Given transportation by foot or horse and buggy, it suffered little from competition until the car and truck became widespread in the 1900s. By 1861, the community had a post office, two mills, a tinsmith, three blacksmith shops, a tannery, a carriage maker, three hotels and several general stores. But for the location, this might have been Brussels, or Blyth, or Wroxeter at the same period of development. But alas, the car and truck did come, major highways were built to the north and south, and farmers began to expand and consolidate. Soon people could easily drive to Casselman, Winchester or even Ottawa for major supplies. Today the feed mill continues to operate beside the dam built originally by John Crysler, three churches built in the late 1800s are still in use, and the restaurant seems to thrive. The general stores offer a wide selection of agricultural necessities, and the egg-grading station reflects the rural roots. At 540, the population is more or less stable. Crysler continues as a peaceful, traditional, somewhat diminished rural service centre and is likely to remain so.

We continue our journey to the south through this gentle and bucolic land. Back and forth, past the plowed fields, into the falling sun towards our destination at Athens. Progress is slow, impeded by tractors pulling harrows or manure spreaders moving slowly along the narrow bumpy roads. We press on into the late afternoon sun, heading for an intriguing-looking location on the map called Oxford Mills. We have discovered that places still retaining the "mill" designation often contain ruins of formerly grand industrial structures or glassy ponds behind substantial dams. This former mill town is literally in the middle of nowhere, so our curiosity is greatly aroused.

The road winds along a stream and turns abruptly at a splendid stone house with a sign proclaiming "Antiques for Sale". Across the street, another, even larger, offers "Country Accommodation". This is Oxford Mills. Just down the road, the dam remains intact, although all traces of the mills have vanished. Its post office which opened in 1852 is still operating and its population has reached 148. Although this is down considerably from the 300 it boasted in 1886 when the mill hummed, the general store was busy and the hotel was full, it surpasses the 135 who made this their home in 1976. Despite its location near to what was once the more prosperous Bishop's Mills a few kilometers away, Oxford Mills is now growing.

Despite the strong early competition from its rival, Oxford Mills retains considerable charm and appeal today. The restored general store is now a beautiful antique shop, and the large stone bed and breakfast establishment offers comfortable accommodation. Although the mills are gone, the dam remains. And what a dam, now ponding a glassy lake, and attracting what must be all the local children to fish from its parapet. Below the falls, others attempt (illegally, I suspect) to spear the fish vainly trying to fight the current and climb up the rushing water. Downstream, others fish while their friends paddle in the swirling stream. What a sight, reminiscent of the early days when the mill would have hummed along and the general store would have been brimming with local farmers.

Now Oxford Mills is no longer a rural service centre like Crysler. This function has long since disappeared, but the church remains and a public library operates from the old school. The settlement is now inhabited by the lucky ones who have discovered an inexpensive house and commute to nearby jobs, or by those few who make a living from antiques and accommodation for travellers. At least it remains tranquil and charming. Will it soon be discovered by the civil servants of Ottawa or the yuppies from Brockville? It certainly has the scenic and architectural potential, although one suspects that the narrow roads and winter snow would be a deterrent for daily commuters from the city. Retirement for local farmers or for those leaving the city for rural tranquillity seem a more likely prospect for addi-

Oxford Mills -- and what a dam, now ponding a glassy lake and attracting what must be all the local children to fish from its parapet.

tional population growth. We leave Oxford Mills to visit our next mill town, Bishop's Mills, a nearby rival that was more successful in the early days. We wind among woods of willows along the stream on a gravel, potholed road that threatenes to swallow the car. After a few minutes we come upon what turns out to be a bit of a disappointment. Little remains except the ruins of a dam, an abandoned school and a few houses. No pond, and little of the charm of Oxford Mills are to be found here in Bishop's Mills. But things were different in the past.

In 1840, N. McCallister was the first settler. Then Chauncey and Ira Bishop erected their mills on the middle branch of the Kemptville Creek. The post office was opened in 1853 and by the 1860s there were two general stores in addition to the mills. A cheese factory provided local employment along with several blacksmith shops, churches, a school and a doctor. What had happened to this optimistic hamlet that had registered an official village plan in 1885? Its post office closed in 1972, and the population which had been as high as 150 in 1893 had dropped to less than 100. The last surviving mill was powered by gasoline and was run by Franklin Bishop in the 1920s. Today the population of Bishop's Mills is only 89.

The answer to our question about the decline of this settlement becomes obvious after a few minutes of contemplation and exploration. Bishop's Mills is even more isolated than Oxford Mills. To reach it we have traversed several kilometers of muddy, potholed gravel roads which are almost a match for the cobbled roads of rural Portugal. There is no dam remaining, and the structures that still stand are not particularly attractive. The ruins of a small wooden mill stand by the remains of the broken dam. No picturesque pond beckons the jaded city dweller, and even if it did, the trip would hardly be worth the trouble. An abandoned schoolhouse completes the picture, which is pretty in the failing light, but the hamlet is just too far from larger places to become a rural retreat for city folk. This is truly a dying village; too close to its rival to thrive economically today, and too difficult to reach to attract much additional development.

We leave Bishop's Mills and race towards Athens on a steadily improving road. I remember the Peacock Restaurant where, on a previous trip, I had enjoyed one of the best Chinese meals outside the Peoples' Republic, and had marvelled at the murals on the walls along Main Street. Orange rays shoot through the clouds, silhouetting the village and farmsteads against the washed-out sky. We enter town and head to the white clap-board houses we wish to photograph. This

done, we discover that several additional murals have been painted since our last visit, one in particular depicting a turkey harvest by the pioneers. Others adorn the sides of shops along the highway, adding a bright touch of colour to the scene.

The impressive town hall, clock tower stretching to the sky, stands beside the equally impressive library, both catching the setting sun against their ruddy bricks. What a monument to those with high hopes for the rural service centres of nineteenth century Ontario. Then civic structures were a symbol of the aspirations and enthusiasm for prosperity that few actually enjoyed. So too, the block-long buildings, two and three stories high, that once housed both people and shops, but now more often than not are half empty.

Athens was once known as Dixon's corner, and then quite appropriately as Farmsville, but the name was changed to Athens in 1888. In that year, a prosperous merchant by the name of Arza Parish proposed the name of the Greek capital because the village was a centre of learning just like Athens in its golden Age. The Ontario town then boasted a grammar school, a high school and a model school for teacher training. And so it became the Athens of Ontario.

The community was settled predominantly by United Empire Loyalists who came in the 1870s. A grist mill and store were erected and then a sawmill and carding mill. The prosperous local agriculture stimulated development, attracting Scottish, Irish and English

Back in Athens we discover that several additional murals have been painted on the walls of buildings since our earlier visit.
Here we see a mural in the background with some local children in the foreground. It is difficult to distinguish painting from people.

immigrants. Many large and impressive churches were built in the late 1800s and by the turn of the century, the population had reached approximately 1000. An impressive legacy of splendid residences, three-storey business blocks and municipal buildings remain to reflect this prosperous past.

In Athens, even recently, things have worked out reasonably well. Just too far from major cities to be a dormitory suburb, and in the midst of prosperous farmland, it has survived intact. If the take-out orders on a Saturday night and the crowds in the Chinese restaurant are any indication, Athens continues to thrive in its former role. On this issue, the statistics are somewhat contradictory, since its population dropped by 123, or almost 12 percent from 1971 to 1981. More current, and probably more accurate are the counts of businesses, which show an increase from 32 to 53 from 1971 to 1986. Today the population is 931, down slightly from its total in 1900, and a bit lower than in 1981, but signs of prosperity seem to bode well for the future. A large seniors' home on the outskirts seems to be a harbinger of things to come. Other signs of economic renewal and civic pride are everywhere. Even late on a weekday evening, the main street bustles with people from the country round about.

Leaving Athens, we head towards our next destintion, Gananoque. Gloom gatheres along the route which now takes us between glacial lakes and knolls of gneiss or granite. Here the farms are few and far between. Scrub has displaced cultivation and cottages now substitute for farm houses.

Gananoque is one of those communities that had all the advantages in the early days. Situated on the major route to the interior on the St.Lawrence, blessed with water power from the Gananoque River and settled by ambitious men, it was founded in 1792 by the Loyalist Joel Stone who came from Connecticut. Its future seemed assured when the road that became Highway 2 eventually linked it to Upper and Lower Canada by land. By the 1850s, Gananoque was known as the Birmingham of Canada. By then, the river was lined with industry from its mouth to the upper falls. In 1889, the Thousand Island Railway joined the town to the Grand Trunk, just over six miles to the north.

The lure of the Thousand Islands dotting the St.Lawrence drew tourists and permanent residents alike while the community grew and prospered. Although it

Athens displays an impressive legacy of splendid residences, three storey business blocks and municipal buildings which remain to reflect its prosperous past.

could never really compete against Kingston with its military presence, status as capital and excellent harbour, Gananoque remained a viable trade and industrial centre for many years.

Ironically, a transportation innovation threatened it in the 1950s, at least in the minds of some of its leaders. When highway 401 was proposed, consternation reigned in Gananoque. Having become heavily dependent on tourism, it relied on traffic from the main route joining Toronto and Montreal (Highway 2) for its passing trade. If the new controlled access road were to bypass the town, disaster was predicted. Cars packed with potential tourists would speed past, ignoring the once popular stopping place beside the lake.

Fortunately for Gananoque, another characteristic of highway bypasses was overlooked by the pessimists. The removal of through traffic transformed its main street from a frustrating bottleneck into a pleasant people place. Gone were the lines of cars, honking horns and choking exhaust. Suddenly, more parking was available. Soon locals, farmers and tourists rediscovered the pleasures of downtown without the trucks and noise. Furthermore, Gananoque was only a minute or two off 401, and remained a convenient stopping place for those travelling from western Ontario to Quebec.

The 401 bypass was ultimately of benefit to the town, rather than leaving it stranded, an orphan of modern transportation. This lesson has now been learned by those in many places supposedly "doomed" by being off a new highway. Just as the coming of the railway failed to destroy many of the settlements that it had bypassed, so the coming of the superhighway failed to weaken many of the communities that it had avoided in its quest for speed and efficiency.

Today Gananoque offers most of its earlier attractions and many that are new. Gone are the factories on the river, which now affords excellent views over the settlement. The best vantage point is from the bridge near its mouth before ten in the morning. Then light from the sun catches churches, boats and water in a magical spell, low and ruddy. Historic limestone churches stand on the banks, and nearby, a former carriage factory built around 1886 has become a waterfront hotel. The Thousand Island railway has long since ceased to operate, but its former terminal and associated hotel remain, restored as emporiums for the sale of food, trinkets and antiques. A reconditioned railway engine stands a few blocks inland, and from the dock the ferries continue to ply the water to

The Thousand Island railway has long since ceased to operate in Gananoque, but its former terminal and associated hotel remain, restored as emporiums for the sale of food, trinkets and antiques.

the islands.
Throughout Gananoque, relics of a gracious past remain. The stunning neo-classical town hall was originally the residence of John and Henrietta MacDonald, leading citizens in the 1830s. It stands as a monument to the vision and industry of the family considered to have given the town its earliest economic stimulus. John MacDonald was a legislative councillor when Kingston was the capital of the United Canadas, when the gracious ballroom that now serves as council chambers hosted numerous civic affairs and visiting dignitaries. The edifice, constructed in 1831 or 1832, stands at the western end of town, almost across from the Gananoque Light and Power Company, a reminder of an industrial past.

Despite the rows of motels, fast food outlets and a population that is now almost 5000, Gananoque retains a rustic small-town Ontario charm. On King Street, the former Albion Hotel has been restored as a museum, and on the side streets, mansions from the early days remain. The clock tower, Rogers' House, churches of several denominations and many other residences from the Victorian era make a stroll through its tree-lined streets a pleasure to remember. And for those interested in industrial archeology, the railway, power plant, dam and former factories provide adequate intellectual satisfaction. Water, shore, islands and accommodation may attract many of the tourists, but it is the built environment that holds Gananoque's real charm.

Farther west, past Kingston and the Catarauqi River we encounter another historic village. Bath, just across the North Reach from Amherst Island, may be known to some as the site of a correctional institution, but it also harbours the Captain Jeptha Hawley House, built in 1785 and reputed to be the oldest continually occupied residence in Ontario. This quiet community was founded by United Empire loyalists when one John Davy drew Lot 10 in Ernestown Township in 1784, the site of Bath today.

Still housing barely over a thousand people, Bath has capitalized upon its heritage to increase both business and population during the last ten years. In doing so, it has also generated local controversy about becoming "touristy" like Gananoque, or "bedroomy" because of its proximity to Kingston. To date it has escaped the worst symptoms of both these afflictions, but potential trouble may lie ahead if trends continue.

Why would anyone want to live in Bath? At first sight it is not particularly impressive, especially along the main street. About the only thing that catches the eye is the old town hall with its four white pillars, built in 1859 and restored in 1959. Like so many similar towns, the real attractions are found along the back streets, and in the tangible "feel" of the place. On Easter Sunday morning with the church bells pealing their call to worship and pink-frocked little girls on the grass outside, the atmosphere is captivating. Among the mature maples, between the white clapboard homes in the gentle sun-drenched breeze, this could be several centuries earlier.

The Bath Academy, built in 1811, stands across the road from St. John's Anglican church, built by the first missionary to the Quinte district in 1793 but not reconstructed till 1925. Down the street, the restored "Layer Cake Hall", constructed in 1866 to house Presbyterians downstairs while the Anglicans worshipped above, now serves as a museum and meeting place for seniors. Everywhere we feel the past and experience the pride of residents who have devoted time, effort and considerable sums of money to recreate the past.

Despite the attraction of the Yacht Club and Bath's historic architecture, the village will probably escape the fate of the Niagara-on-the-Lakes which have become major tourist attractions in themselves. But its residential function is another matter. Even now the desire of others to join the inhabitants of this sleepy settlement has pushed property prices steadily up. Between 1971 and 1981, its population increased from 810 to 1071, a 32 percent change. The number of business establishments rose from 22 to 33; a 50 percent increase in the same period. A few well-financed entrepreneurs or residential developers could transform Bath into a much larger commuter suburb or retirement centre in a few short years. The same could be said for someone who really capitalizes upon the potential of the marina and waterfront for a retail complex. The pity is that, if this happens, much of the enchantment

Everywhere in Bath we feel the past and experience the pride of residents who have devoted time, effort and considerable sums of money to recreate the past. This is the Peter Davy House, built in 1813.

that brought people here in the first place will be destroyed by "progress".

Will "progress, tourism, economic development" and many more residents change Bath forever, or will it remain a charming eighteenth-century backwater in the midst of progress? Only time and the resolve of the present inhabitants will tell. Like so many similar places, it is on the brink of change; a chronicle of the past and a possible portent for the future. We add it to our catalogue of interesting Ontario towns to visit again; another five years may transform it entirely.

Our visit to the near north, the frontier fringe and eastern Ontario has come to an end. We have experienced dying former service centres like Loring, those on the brink of change like Bath, those with outstanding natural attractions like Eganville or Magnetawan, and those such as Gananoque which were bypassed but continue to grow. Farther north we visited one of the many truck stops that are so vital to the local economy. We stopped at Iron Bridge which has lost some of its former importance and Blind River which continues to thrive. We explored Cecebe where little remains, and Little Rapids which would be a flourishing retirement community if it weren't so isolated.

In their own way, all the places we have visited depended upon the resources and attractions of their hinterlands, be they roaring rivers, fish-filled lakes, underground caverns or rich stands of trees and deposits of minerals. The success of each is tied ultimately to their links with the outside world and to the enterprise of their citizens. Some such as Oxford Mills will thrive and others like Bishop's Mills have all but disappeared simply because of minor variations in local physical attractions and transportation.

Even today, the story in the north is similar to that of the pioneer fringe a hundred years ago. Isolation is the enemy, the land is vast and largely untamed, and local resources are crucial to success. But today, local resources are often defined in terms of a lake or waterfall or a scenic setting instead of in terms of minerals or wood. Success may result from historic architecture, from an entrepreneur promoting a motel and hunting lodge, or from the traffic passing on the highway. When the original resources disappear, so does the original raison d'être. Substitutes must then be found if a place is to survive.

As we have seen, the possible substitutes for former resources are many, sometimes depending only upon the skill and enterprise of an individual who attempts to exploit the new resources. Sometimes he is successful, sometimes he fails and sometimes the settlement fails with him. On the other hand, success may occur in what seem to be the most unlikely locales. This is why we find diversity, complexity and change in the north, rather than a vast array of dying villages. This diversity and complexity is what makes our settlements interesting, both in the north and in the south. Continued diversity and complexity, fostered by a bit of local initiative, will be the key to sustained economic success and potential population growth in many of our towns and villages.

CHAPTER SEVEN

Rural Quebec- Rangs, Ruins And Resource Towns

Having spent considerable time in Ontario, we will now explore that distinctive and fascinating society to the east -- La Belle Province. This will give us the opportunity to see first-hand the effects of the seigneurial system upon settlement. In Quebec, initial development of farming occurred along the rivers, with farms extending back along the rangs about ten times as long as they were wide. Initially, the road ran behind the first rang, with the first houses on the water. The second rang with its farms began behind the first, along the parallel road. The resulting pattern produced a linear settlement system with less clustering of homes and shops than in Ontario.

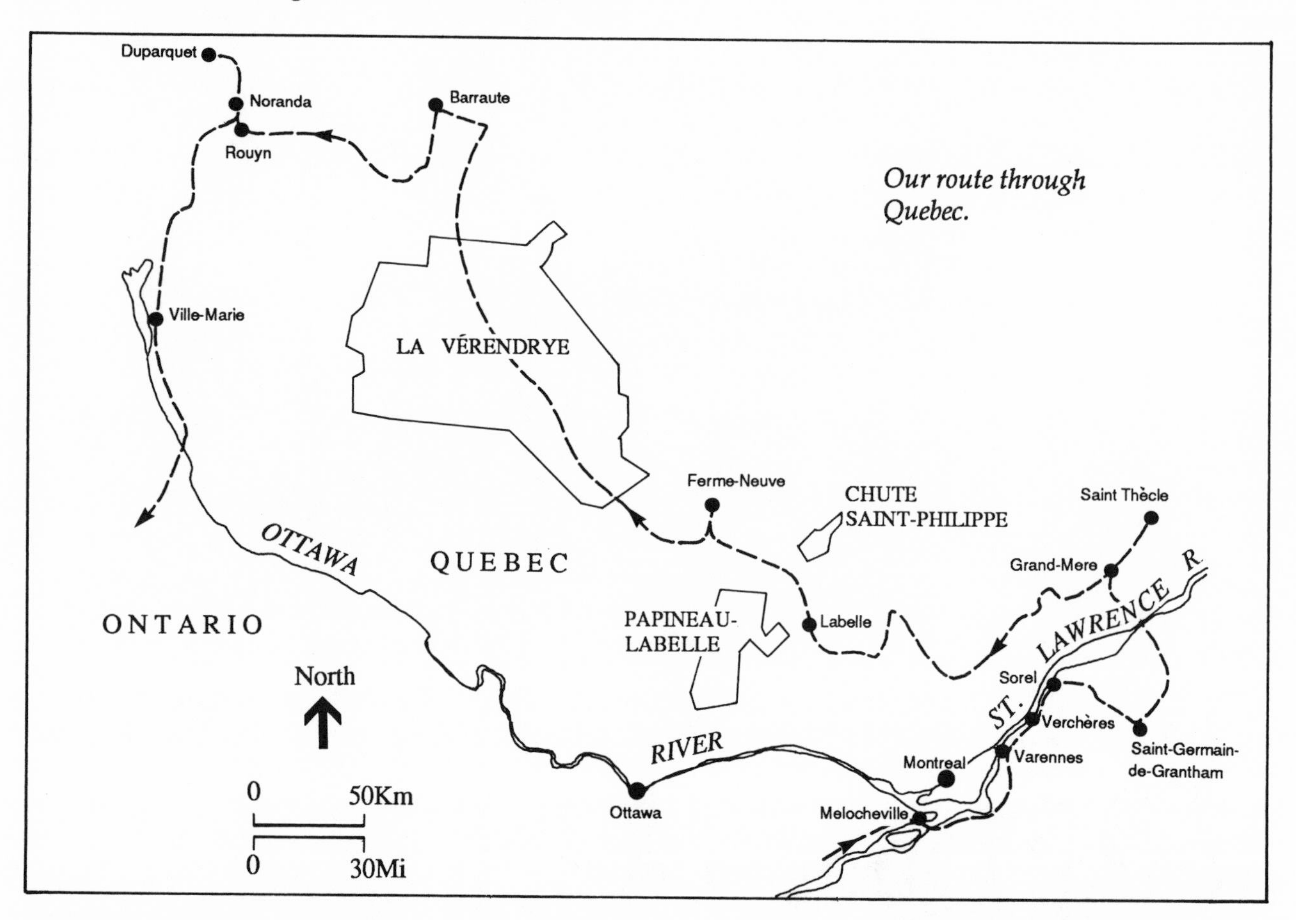

Our route through Quebec.

In Quebec, a country drive often consists of following roads lined by houses and barns, punctuated by the occasional thickening where a former manor house stood, or by a group of homes and businesses around a parish church. In these clusters we find shops and groups of houses more akin to the pattern which we have seen in Ontario. Of course, Quebec does have its nucleated settlements just as in Ontario. These are often found around mines, in areas of forest exploitation and where service centres for agriculture developed late or far from navigable waterways. But even there, the architecture and ambience are distinctively French. Graceful curved roof lines on newer homes, metal clad mansard roofs on commercial buildings, tall silver spires on statuesque churches, the pâtisserie or boulangerie -- all are distinct and different from their Ontario counterparts. And yet the functions are often similar. In both Ontario and Quebec we find retirement communities, commuter dormitories, dirty industrial suburbs and placid lakeside resorts. On this short excursion we will sample some of each, search for the factors of growth or decline and savour the distinctive culture of the Québecois.

The drive from Toronto to Quebec is quick and boring when you follow Highway 401, or "Main Street Ontario" as it is often called. The boredom is a direct result of the highway's raison d'être -- the rapid and unimpeded movement of vehicles from one place to another. It achieves this end on most days, but at the expense of the real joy of travelling -- the experience of our towns and villages. These are all summarily dismissed with a road sign at an exit, or not mentioned at all. From the highway we see the vast suburban sprawl around Toronto, and later Montreal, but the secrets of small town Canada are never revealed.

On the other hand, the sinuous black snake of a highway seduces most travelers with its speed, keeping them and their noise, pollution and exhaust fumes out of many towns and villages. For this we can be thankful, for the mere fact of being bypassed has al-

Initially, the road ran behind the first rang, with the first houses on the water. The second rang with its farms began behind the first, along the parallel road. The resulting pattern produced a linear settlement system.

lowed many a quaint country town to remain just that; peaceful and protected from trucks, traffic and turmoil. In many respects, the throughway had the same effect on settlements in the late 1900s as the railway had in the late 1800s. It stimulated those directly on its route, but left others little changed and thus preserved the past. Only today are we discovering the charm of so many of these bypassed and forgotten places.

Like everyone else, we speed along Highway 401, joining its Quebec continuation, Highway 20 at the border. Things begin smoothly as we head south from the highway to approach our first Quebec destination at Melocheville on Highway 132, a few miles south-west of Montreal. The day is sunny and clear, the temperature around 20, and our spirits high. We cross the St.Lawrence to Grande Isle and follow the rapids on the river to Saint Timothée. Things look a little less optimistic where the road widens and we pass between rows of casse croûtes (fast food outlets), and then by an enormous quarry operation producing heaps of black crushed stone. From the bypass highway, Melocheville does not look promising.

Just before the highway crosses to the mainland we discover the Rue Principale and follow it back to the west. Now we drive between small clapboard homes in the traditional Québecois style, punctuated by the épicerie, boulangerie, or boucherie. This is more like it. After about two blocks we come upon a charming hotel by the river, called Au Manoir. Its long wooden porch and lacy curtains draws us in to a cozy, old world dining room called Chez Mémé.

During lunch, we learn that the hotel was built in 1838 to accommodate those traversing the Beauharnois Canal. We also learn that Melocheville was the site of an important archeological park at Pointe Buisson. At the same time we sip our excellent white wine, slowly savour our garbure, and trade bites of rabbit and veal, both prepared and presented to perfection. Crème caramel (homemade), and dark roasted French coffee top off one of the most delightful meals we have had on this trip, in one of the most unlikely locations.

Well fortified, if somewhat sleepy, we continued to explore Melocheville, finding both Le Château Tonhata, a striking Italianate manor from an earlier

In Melocheville we come upon a charming hotel by the river, called Au Manoir. It was built in 1883 to accommodate travellers traversing the Beauharnois Canal.

era, and elegant new residences along the river. We also stop to view the massive dam and hydro power installations, passing along the way the enormous Alcan plant that provides employment for hundreds. The archeological site was formerly a camp for Amerinds for some 5000 years when they fished for sturgeon and hunted for beaver. Now, a well staffed, modern interpretive centre displays the hunting and cooking utensils used for so many years before the coming of the whites.

From a sleepy canal stop and native gathering place in the 1800s, Melocheville has been transformed into a bustling industrial giant. And the same physical factors that attracted native peoples and then the canal traffic are still at work today. Here the mighty St. Lawrence tumbles and cascades over rocks and rapids, increasing in velocity, necessitating canals or portages for safe passage, and producing vast amounts of potential power as a useful byproduct. For years and years, the rapids were a nuisance to be avoided or feared. Amerinds camped nearby and regrouped before travelling on. In the years that followed, missionaries, fur traders, explorers, and eventually settlers stopped here as well. By the 19th century, Pointe du Buisson at the end of the rapids had become a preferred location for rural festivities; ultimately it became a summer resort for people from nearby cities.

Now a well-equipped archeological park commemorates the history of the point; just upstream the Barrage Pointe de Buisson, and downstream, the Barrage Cascades, channel and divert the water through the massive Hydro Quebec installation. The foaming water is tamed and directed into turbines where it powers generators that produce vast amounts of hydro electricity. As a result, this once quiet resort town and canal port has spawned massive industry depending upon the electricity generated by the river. Hydro Quebec employs many, but with the addition of the modern, sprawling Alcan plant, the settlement has become a major industrial centre.

The effects of economies of agglomeration and interdependence have led to the development of other industries here as well. Metallurgy and chemical manufacturers are interrelated and all require vast quantities of electricity. As a result, in addition to Alcan and its aluminum fabrication, Chromasco, Elkem Metal and several other modern manufacturers provide employment for hundreds in the local industrial park.

Melocheville's aquatic heritage has not been forgotten either. The prettiest new residential areas front along the river and a modern marina has been developed at the end of the canal beside the locks. A waterfront park and bird sanctuary continue to preserve the local heritage. And of course we must not forget that venerable hotel, Au Manoir, former stopping place for river travelers; now a gourmet restaurant straight out of the 1800s.

As expected, the commercial and population growth of Melocheville have been affected by the development of local industry and by its proximity to Montreal. Between 1971 and 1981, its population increased from 1601 to 1899 for a 19 percent gain. The number of local businesses listed by the directories climbed from 22 in 1971 to 29 in 1986; a 31 percent increase. But these statistics don't really tell the complete story. When we conduct a field survey by traversing all the streets and counting every business, we discover 34 local enterprises, some small like the hairdressers, but others growing rapidly and likely to prosper further. If we add the major industries not listed because their head offices are elsewhere, Melocheville has grown substantially during the last twenty years.

In Melocheville we did experience the worst of modern industrial development with its blackened scars from quarrying and congested local highway. Neither were the new industries particularly attractive, unless you like industrial architecture. On the other hand, just off the highway, along the Rue Principal, and by the river, Melocheville exhibits all the qualities that make Quebec towns attractive. Tiny bustling shops selling all manner of exotic foods, the parish church and school and the archeological park all contribute to its ambience. The town will no doubt continue to grow. This is almost inevitable given its location and potential for additional river-front development. So far, the industry is far enough removed from residential developments to retain some semblance of tranquility. Let us hope that the situation continues.

After such a satisfying culinary experience and an interesting afternoon of exploration in Melocheville, we prepare to journey to Varennes, our next destination. It is situated on the south shore of the St. Lawrence, not far downstream from Montreal. We eventually reach Varennes, only to discover that it has been almost totally overrun by industrial spillover from Montreal. Only the river prevents it from becoming

In Melocheville, we experience the worst of modern industrial development with its blackened scars from quarrying and congested local highway.

Soon we reach the outskirts of Verchères to confront two gracious stone mansions between us and the river. Their sweeping curved roofs and wooden shutters remind us of another era.

physically a southern appendage of the city's eastern industrial suburbs. We drive slowly along and pass through a wasteland of the most unpleasant, bleak, polluted industrial landscape imaginable, eventually coming across the sign for Varennes. It stands in the midst of the tall white towers of liquid air manufacturers, oil refineries belching black smoke and flame, and massive quarries overshadowing small shops strung along the highway.

At least we have discovered the reason for what on paper seemed to be phenomenal economic growth in Varennes from 1971 to 1981. In that period, the population skyrocketed from 2382 to 8764, a change of 268 percent in ten years. It was easy to see why when we survey the massive industrial development, much of it very new and most of it noxious. Seas of split level houses and tiny bungalows stretch as far as the eye can see, punctuated at frequent intervals by strips of commercial development. If this has been planned, it is not readily apparent.

Varennes is an industrial ghetto, festooned with twisted cracking towers seemingly smothered in tentacles of white spaghetti. We cannot even find the old town centre around which this monstrosity had grown. How could anyone live here, we wonder aloud, all the while looking desperately for a faster way out. What was recently open fields is now littered with diminutive and unimaginative bungalows, inhabited no doubt, by those who can afford neither Montreal real estate nor the cost of commuting a hundred kilometers a day. Unfortunately, the situation is the same around most of our major metropolitan centres. Either high costs, long commuting times or an unpleasant environment are the choices for local residents. Sometimes they have to endure all three. All the more reason for the continuation of our quest for small-town Canada. Varennes serves as our prime example of the obliteration of a formerly quaint and quiet settlement by untrammelled industrial growth and economic stimulation from a nearby metropolitan area.

To escape this despoiled community, we drive through the industrial debris on the south shore while the sun descends slowly over the skyline of Montreal on the north. Red and orange hues shimmer from the water, skipping and skittering off the wake of a passing tanker. Gold gleams and glints about windows of skyscrapers ornamented by the tint of the late afternoon sun. Despite the frustrations of the last few hours, the beauty of man's works and nature combine to soothe our souls. Soon the sun is low in the sky and the vast expanse of the St.Lawrence takes on a glassy, pink and blue mill pond sheen. Industry slowly gives way to quarries and then to a few farmhouses. Things are looking up on our trip north and east, leaving our ordeal behind.

Verchères is the next community ahead, but now we have to compete for space with buses packed with commuters on the narrow twisting road. Soon we reach the outskirts of the village, to confront two gracious stone mansions between us and the river. Both are fenced and one boasts a matching garage and stable. Their sweeping curved roofs and wooden shutters remind us of another era. They are obviously from the 18th century and both have been carefully restored. Clearly, the wealthy have an eye for the most spectacular sites in this community.

We drive slowly along the single street that once constituted the town, passing new suburbs spreading to our right away from the river. We soon come to a magnificent three-storey frame house that has become a florist's shop, and then arrive at "Centre Ville" where the traditional town square sets off a limestone church beside an equally impressive manse surrounded by a grassy park complete with a modernistic sculpture. At one side of the square, local teens sit on a park bench to observe the traffic and the sunset, while on the other, a supermarket bustles with business.

Just behind the square we find a house built in 1643, now somewhat dilapidated, but in the process of being restored. Streets barely wide enough for one car hold frame houses edging up to the pavement. Their curved iron stairs ascend to the second storey in that delightful French Canadian tradition. Children play everywhere, making sense of the "Gardez nos Enfants" signs and the maddening stops at every intersection. Mixed with the tiny houses are hairdressers, boutiques and a Sears order office. We count 52 businesses in the town, including a boat works, several restaurants, an antique shop, a large supermarket and a medical clinic under construction. Farther along, the homes increase in size and elegance while white paint gives way to green and pink. The Bourgeoisie have found sites away from the river as well as on the shore.

Down the hill by the water a statue raises its arms towards the setting sun. Beside it stands an ancient tower that might have been a fort or a windmill. Teenagers on all-terrain vehicles roar past through the riverside park, shattering the tranquillity with their noisy engines. The plaque on the statue informs us that Marie Madeleine Jarret de Verchères, with her two young brothers, two soldiers and an old man, held off the Iroquois for nine days in 1692. This heroic act occurred while her family was away from the seigniory and she occupied the fort alone. It earned her the distinction of having this delightful village named in her honour.

Verchères is far enough from Montreal to have avoided the industrial development that has overwhelmed Varennes, but it is clearly within easy commuting distance of both. The elegant mansions along the river attest to its attraction for the affluent while the large new subdivisions clearly cater to the middle class. The traffic that we encountered on our way in leaves no doubt about its role as a commuter dormitory, although there is considerable local employment as well. Its narrow streets and compact shape probably preclude major changes near the town centre without massive destruction of heritage buildings; a fact that should enable it to retain much of its attractiveness. On the other hand, we can visualize more and more suburbs creeping slowly upstream towards Montreal as the pressures for growth increase. Let us hope that local resistance to major change combined with an appreciation for the past will save it from the fate of Varennes.

Next morning dawns bright and cloudless, leaving the car covered with glistening dew and us in a mood for adventure. Today our destination is St. Germain-de-Grantham, a rural service centre of some 1400, just south of Drummondville. Although its population has increased by only 24 percent from 1971 to 1981, the number of businesses there has risen by a healthy two thirds from 1971 to 1986. We are curious about the reasons and are interested in what constitutes the major economic base of the village.

The highway winds along the river, north to Sorel, which we are forced to visit. There are no bridges across the Richelieu which lies between us and our destination. Birch trees, a few maples and poplar line the route between the summer camps, occasional houses and enormous quarries. Just before Sorel, we pass an oil-fueled thermal power plant, festooned with thousands of high voltage wires, and tethered to the loading docks by an umbilical cord of pipes. It looms above us, white and somehow threatening, urging us to make our rapid escape to the east.

Sorel is completely overshadowed by the harbour, loading facilities and grain elevators. The business section seems to be totally dominated by boutiques and womens' wear shops, as have so many of the places we visited in Quebec. A pattern of poorly marked one-way streets fools us completely, and we back ignominiously out of one that we have entered in error, to the derisive hoots of the horns of oncoming traffic. Enough of these towns and cities! Back to the countryside and to the communities under 5000, where we somehow feel welcome and comfortable.

The map shows no easy route south and east from Sorel to St. Germain, so we decide to explore the territory on the back roads. Given our luck yesterday, and the warning on our map that cautions about their condition, driving on "grey" roads looks to be an adventure. When we leave Highway 133, we are delighted to find that the "grey" roads are blacktop, and follow the old Seigneurial Rangs. Nowhere are we more than a few hundred yards from a farmhouse as we pass the long narrow lots following the original survey lines. Many farms have a barn and cattle beside a small white frame house, while others have only a shed, the barn being at the far end of the land holding. Here on the bucolic south shore, the production of Maple Syrup and beef cattle seem to be the main rural industries. We pass field after field of corn, punctuated at frequent intervals by maple woods, streams, cattle, barns, manure piles and farmhouses. It is almost like parts of rural

St.Germain-de-Grantham is situated on perfectly level land directly in the centre of a fertile agricultural area. Feed and seed storage elevators tower over the side street, proclaiming its service to the farm community.

France.

After seeing numerous signs indicating "Cabanes d'Érable" in the trees, we decide to stop and purchase some fresh Quebec maple syrup, we hope at a lower price than in Ontario. We leave the blacktop and follow a gravel road through the fields, and then into a sugar bush where every tree is adorned with a metal sap bucket. After considerable discussion, mixing French with English we buy some maple sugar, and learn that most such establishments give tours of the sugar bush, cater for meals, and sell maple sugar, but supply all their maple syrup to wholesalers. Nowhere do individual farmers sell their products from their homes. What little syrup they have goes immediately to market or to a retail outlet.

Almost a third of the maple trees have died or have been in poor health during the last ten years. This year the crop is far smaller than before, partially because of unfavourable weather, but also as a result of Ronald Reagan's "harmless" acid rain. Many small producers have already gone out of business as a consequence of this man-made scourge, while others have suffered because many trees are over a hundred years old and near the end of their natural lives. We ponder the problem of which is worst; the advent of acid rain or the end of a natural cycle of life and death. Somewhat sadly, we return to the ribbon of blacktop and make our way along the rangs towards St. Germain-de-Grantham.

By noon the sun is hot. We roll into St. Germain, a sleepy village situated on perfectly level land, directly in the centre of a fertile agricultural area. Two feed and seed storage elevators tower over the side street, and an agricultural supply depot proclaims its service to the farm community. The main street runs straight and narrow through rows of white frame houses, punctuated by duplexes and fourplexes with outside iron stairs. A pharmacy and medical centre combination seem to sell everything from toys to clothing, and two large general stores dominate the business section. A few smaller shops and a restaurant-garage complete the commercial area, and in its midst, the twin-spired, fieldstone parish church and administrative building face a grassy park across the street.

St. Germain-de-Grantham is a typical south shore rural service centre. Standing as it does in the midst of prime agricultural land, far from any major urban areas, it functions as it has for years. The main street is a focus for townspeople and those from the farms alike. The post office seems to be one of the busiest destinations, with its steady flow of people in and out, most stopping to socialize or to chat with the post master. Could this too be a victim of the "economy" measures of Canada Post and go the way of so many of its defunct predecessors? Or will it be allowed to continue as a unifying force; one that draws people to the town and therefore helps to sustain numerous businesses depending upon farmers for their trade? Let us hope that it will remain.

Today St. Germain has a population of 1373, up a healthy 269, or 24 percent from 1971. Its businesses have grown and prospered as well. Between 1971 and 1986, their numbers increased from 56 to 93; a spectacular 66 percent gain. Somewhat surprising, especially for those who believe that small towns are dying is the importance of manufacturing here. From only five manufacturing industries in 1971, the total has risen to 20 in 1986. And although one produces food products, the majority manufacture items such as clothing (4), wood and chemical products (3 each), as well as furniture, paper products and electrical machinery (2 each). This community is already a regional rural service centre, and is rapidly diversifying to become an important small-scale manufacturing community.

The situation here is akin to those of settlements in the 1800s when the horse was king. But in the 1980s, it attracts people by car to its numerous garages, implement sales outlets, mobile home manufacturers, feed and seed depots and agricultural supply outlets. Like places that prospered even more when they acquired the railway in the 1850s, St. Germain-de-Grantham now has the advantage of being just off the Autoroute which gives its products easy and rapid access to the large urban markets of Montreal and Quebec. Rather than killing this community, car and truck transportation have enabled it to serve a large rural hinterland and to export its products to the cities beyond. This situation is directly analogous to that of numerous communities in Ontario where small-scale manufacturing has been added to their traditional service functions. Unless recent trends in both provinces are transitory, its future seems bright.

ACROSS THE RIVER TO THE NORTH SHORE

After making an inventory of the businesses and photographing several houses in St. Germain, we head towards our next destination, Ste.Thècle, across the river on the precambrian shield. On leaving the St. Lawrence lowlands, farms and alluvial soils give way to vast expanses of granite and trees. Just past Trois-Rivières the road climbs onto the ancient rocks and follows the easiest route along the St. Maurice River to the interior. To the right, billowing smoke from the industrial stacks at Shawinigan plume into the sky, making artificial mares' tails. On the southbound lane, lines of growling lumber-laden trucks roll past, burdened by the products of the forest.

Where the St. Maurice is visible, its surface is punctuated by logs, bouncing and jumping like jitterbugs in its turbulent water. The forests have been cut and now pass in a parade down the river towards their ultimate fate. These logs hurtle over chutes and dance in the water until they are finally corralled by booms across the calm lagoons. Grand-Mère is one such stopping place, where Consolidated-Bathurst plucks the logs from the water and hurls them like match-sticks into enormous mounds to feed the pulping mill. Beside the river stands the auberge that once housed mill managers far from home in this former frontier town; but more of that later.

Past the woods and water we drive until the Autoroute gives out and is replaced by twisting Route 153. Progress becomes slow as we wind past small farms and dip over valleys and streams. Respectable new bungalows share the road with ancient farmhouses little better than shacks. A vast rusting landscape looms ahead where carcasses of abandoned cars threaten to spill out of a huge establishment selling "pièces d'auto". We hurry past, once again racing the sun to reach Ste.Thècle before the light falls.

At a point where the road plunges into a depression, houses proliferate and we enter St.Tite, a town sprawling across rolling hills and into several valleys. It too has its distinctive church and an extensive business area that boasts several brasseries, along with one offering " danseuses nues", for the entertainment of its patrons. A little further along, Ste.Thècle comes into view, with the tall silver spires of its church glinting in the rays of gold from the setting sun. A large sign proclaims this as a town where people come to relax and enjoy, while an even larger one advertises "Glissade de l'Eau" by the lake. We find the large pond at the edge of town, but its fences arrest our attempt to discover its secret. Undaunted, we circumnavigate the water along a road to the outskirts, where we discover a splendid vista of the town and church. And we solve the mystery of the signs. There, looping sinuously down the opposite hill to the water, are three long blue water slides, obviously a major attraction, at least in the summer. We investigate the town's business enterprises, being especially impressed by the extensive lumber mill by the railway. It takes some exploration and careful scrutiny to realize that there is one large lumber mill, surrounded by several woodworking shops and a contractor. The major industry in Ste.Thècle faithfully reflects the natural resources of its surroundings.

Back on the main street, the sheer variety of goods in each store is astounding: fast food, groceries, beer and wine; mens' clothing, shoes and farm supplies. Another store specializes in womens' lingerie and bathing suits. Others offer sporting goods, fishing and hunting supplies, along with newspapers and magazines. Can it be that all the businesses in town are general stores? A quick glance at our statistics dispels that notion. Ste. Thècle had a total of 71 different businesses in 1986, up by almost a quarter of its 1971 figure of 57. These include 14 manufacturing enterprises, most of which produce wood products. But this is natural in an area where vast forests stretch to the horizon and logging is an important industry. Ste. Thècle presents us with a bit of a dilemma. At the same time that its business sector is expanding and diversifying, its population declined by 22 people. At 1.3 percent from 1971 to 1981, this is not a large drop, but it does represent a decline. On the other hand, the business statistics are from 1986, by which date the population had probably caught up. The settlement certain-

In Ste. Thècle we record all the business enterprises, being especially impressed by the extensive lumber mill by the railway. This business faithfully reflects the natural resources of its local environment.

ly looks prosperous even though it has lost three general stores and two restaurants since 1971. On the other hand, the addition of three new automobile sales outlets and four small variety stores more than compensate for the other retail losses. On balance, St. Thècle is diversifying, losing some of its traditional retail functions, but more than compensating by the addition of industry related to nearby natural resources. This is in stark contrast to the next resource town we are to visit.

Sooner than expected, we arrive at Grand-Mère, pass the paper mill, and catch a glance of a large old limestone building with the appearance of a château. L'Auberge Grand-Mère is perched across the road from the mill beside a bubbling stream that plunges to the river below. It turns out to be quite inexpensive for a delightful room with lace curtains overlooking the waterfall.

The Auberge was built 90 years ago as a residence for managers from the mill. At that time, Grand Mère was a frontier outpost, with little more than woods, a waterfall and a mill. The large stone structure across the street (now a theatre) had once been a hall for the entertainment of male workers. It was not till the advent of television that members of the fairer sex were allowed to visit this male preserve. The women's' liberation movement had undoubtedly given impetus to the desegregation.

The next day, we are captivated by the mist swirling off the icy waters of the river below, rising to form a delicate halo of moisture around the weak morning sun. We explore the dashing falls behind our hotel and marvel at the sea of logs behind the boom. Even on Saturday, the mill continues to function. Logs are plucked continuously from the water and heaved unceremoniously onto the heap from which they are to meet their fate in the shredder. They churn like the match sticks that some will soon become. Froth, first white, then turning yellow where it meets the river, foams around the rapids where the creek and main stream join. It flows relentlessly on, dragging the minor water in its wake. We dally and finally tear ourselves away to explore the seemingly endless main street of Grand Mère. Shop after shop, stately limestone church, bars and more shops stretch out before us. It seems like the longest main street in Quebec, but since the settlement is much larger than our

In Grand Mère, logs are plucked from the water and heaved unceremoniously onto the heap from which they are to meet their fate in the shredder.

population limit of 5000, we press on to the smaller towns and villages.

While we speed through the forest and granite, hunger pangs begin to materialize and the need for coffee becomes acute. In the middle of nowhere, a pine-clad casse crôute appears beside the road. We feast on what are the best eggs we have tasted for years. When we leave it becomes evident from the elongated metal outbuildings and feed bins that we are in the centre of a chicken farming area. This explains both the excellent quality and ridiculously low cost of our breakfast.

Our next destination is a settlement with a promising name -- Labelle, or "the beautiful" in translation. It is situated almost directly north of Montreal past the end of the Autoroute where it becomes Highway 117. This is a land of granite knolls, long curves sweeping through the wooded forest, lakes, and white water. Fortunately, the Quebec Government had the foresight to preserve much of the wilderness for posterity in a series of magnificent provincial parks which almost surround Labelle. Closest to it we find Papineau-Labelle and Mont Tremblant. A little farther away lie Rouge-Matawan and Chûte Saint Philippe. To the north-west, one encounters the vast expanse of La Vérendrye. All offer tent sites, hiking paths, innumerable lakes, rapids, falls and hills. Cross-country ski trails and downhill runs are available for winter sports enthusiasts. Little wonder that a settlement in the midst of such an environment would be named Labelle.

The town itself is situated along the Rivière Rouge at a roaring falls tumbling across a rugged granite outcrop. Given the local timber resources and handy water power, saw mills were constructed in the 1800s to capitalize upon the lumber industry. When the railway came, it supplanted the river as a transportation route and facilitated the shipping of wood products to the south. Today, the road has displaced the railway and the former station stands empty and abandoned. About all that remains of the early economic base is a large lumber yard and building supply outlet near the old station. But new functions have arrived to replace those that have declined. This is clearly indicated by the tremendous increase in population here during the last ten years.

Of all the towns we will visit in Quebec, Labelle has experienced the most population growth.

From a total of 1492 in 1971, the population jumped to 2112 in 1981; a remarkable 42 per cent increase. The number of businesses rose from 46 to 67 from 1981 to 1986; at 46 percent a very respectable change which reflects the economic growth that we observe along the streets. When one examines the business statistics in detail, the effect of the nearby tourist attractions and nearby provincial parks upon Labelle becomes immediately apparent.

While many towns this size lost retail outlets in the same period, Labelle added 10 for a 37 percent increase. Building supply outlets, restaurants, food stores, furniture stores and variety stores made the largest gains. Although the directories listed five restaurants in 1986, our field count turns up 11, including motel dining rooms. Clearly the tourist trade has greatly increased the demand for restaurants and fast food outlets. This is reflected also by the three motels and the campsite beside the river.

The main street exudes prosperity, with traditional businesses near the centre and a sprawling motel strip at the northern extremity. The site straddles rolling hills, providing excellent views from residential areas old and new. Just behind the main street, venerable homes provide sites for boutiques, antique shops and the ubiquitous Quebec lingerie store. An old fire station, its tall hose drying tower still intact, dominates the main intersection.

Down the hill, across the falls and towards the tracks lies the old town, still oriented to the river and railway, even though both have ceased to be important to the economy. Here we are away from the tourist-oriented businesses and discover an épicerie, a boucherie, a fabric shop and several variety stores. They are considerably older and more picturesque than the modern establishments across the river. This area preserves the historical legacy of the settlement and reminds us of its past as a lumber town on the river.

Given its superb rolling setting on a major route to Montreal and a location so close to the provincial parks, Labelle will undoubtedly continue to grow. Additional accommodation and restaurants will be built and more people will come to live and work there. This is only one of its functions, for today it is also an extremely attractive retirement destination for those enjoying the hunting, fishing and camping nearby. With its fast access to Montreal, it is easy for retired people to drive into the city for a night at the symphony or the ballet. The large senior citizens' home on the hill is evidence of an aging population, and if Ontario amenity com-

La Belle is situated along the Rivière Rouge at a roaring falls tumbling across a rugged granite outcrop.

munities are any indication, this is just the beginning. Like Bayfield, which began as a port and local service centre to be transformed into a tourist, retirement and amenity community, Labelle is also evolving. Its combination of physical setting and access have almost guaranteed future growth and success.

Our next destination, 20 kilometers north of Mont Laurier, also has an intriguing name: Ferme Neuve, or new farm in English. Is it some sort of frontier agricultural outpost, or is it just named after the first farm in the area? Our data indicate that its population has increased by almost 300 since 1971, a percentage change of 14. Even more impressive is the upsurge in businesses by two-thirds between 1971 and 1986, from 45 to 75. Ferme Neuve has prospered mightily over the last 15 years, and we decide to find out why. Maybe it is to be another concrete example of the economic impact of the parks, or maybe it is still an important local service centre.

Our first clue to the local economy comes from the name Sporti which seems to adorn half the businesses in town. Not only are sporting goods stores given this title, but also grocery stores, variety stores and several restaurants. We realize that sports are big in this area, an idea that is reinforced by the signs to lakes and camps on the outskirts. When we conduct our field survey, we count seven businesses that sell sporting goods and trophies, two very large hotels, and a motel. The hotels and motel have restaurants which supplement the nine other restaurants and fast food outlets. A sprawling motel drapes itself over a hill near one of the lakes, and there are a number of fishing outfitters along the adjacent roadways.

The town follows the Rivière du Lièvre, with one main street parallel the water and the other at right angles. A substantial Roman Catholic church with a single silver spire soaring above a crucifix stands beside the river. It is surrounded by the school and rectory which dominate the view of the main approach to centre ville. The disproportionate number of clothing stores seemed to overshadow the business district. At the next corner we discover L'Hôtel Château Laurentides, a delightful throwback to a more leisurely era, with its wooden veranda, square profile and crowning cupola. The structure rises splendidly to a third storey, suggesting an Italian villa. Its red-brick facade surrounds inviting small windows, each framed by multicoloured curtains.

We try to imagine the scene at L'Hotel in the past. A load of gentry arriving from Montreal, tired and thirsty, stopping to rest their horses; all enjoying a respite from the bumps and jogs of their carriage. Wine flowing, candles being lit and the table groaning with food. Song and the sounds of merriment float across the street until the dawn breaks the far horizon -- or so we imagine. Our inquiries reveal that this historic hotel, and the motel are now often booked with fishermen in the summer and skiers in the winter. After all, we are on the edge of the rugged Canadian Shield, a few short kilometres from some major winter resorts. Ferme Neuve is attractive in itself, but it also derives benefit from the overflow.

The main streets are all intriguing. The tourist function must explain the proliferation of sporting goods stores and clothing shops. Quaint clapboard commercial buildings with two-storey verandas are reminiscent of the American South. Several, with wide overhangs and colorful coats of paint, could be in Nadi or Pago Pago. Somehow, the flamboyant hues and distinctive architecture of the South Pacific have been transplanted to this community in Quebec. The street is crowded with people and cars. Prosperity is in the air. We stroll past the wooden two-storey duplexes with their curving outside iron staircases and frilly lace-curtained windows. We soak up the local colour and distinctive atmosphere in this neat, tidy and attractive town. New suburbs seem to sprout on the outskirts and a few apartment buildings line the major roads.

On the road out of Ferme Neuve, we pass supermarkets, a large dance hall and several building supply depots. We discover several variety stores, liquor outlets and another large hotel on the outskirts. Ferme Neuve has all the required services for its own residents, adequate facilities for the surrounding region and many oriented primarily to tourists. Blessed with a good agricultural hinterland, proximity to areas for winter sports and interesting local architecture, its future seems assured. This time the statistics didn't lie!

Our meanderings through northern Quebec have taken us to two former service centres, both prospering; one now important for tourism and retirement, the other thriving and diversified. But there is much more to this region and province than tourism, forestry and farming. At our next two destinations, we will sample some of this diversity and its varying effect upon Quebec communities. We continue north through La Vérendrye Provincial Park, a superb and scenic drive past unspoiled lakes and forests.
Although it may not be apparent to the casual observer, it is the scenic grandeur and attractions of areas such as this magnificent park that now attract the mainstay of many local towns. The tourist becomes king where nothing other than nature is available to provide an economic base. La Vérendrye is but one example of the way in which we may exploit nature without ruining the very qualities that attracted people in the first place.

The road through the park crosses shallow open valleys, deep narrow clefts in the rock, and grassy granite knolls. Lakes and rivers are everywhere in this land covered by conifers. We experience repetition and sharply contrasted landscapes. Great gashes stripped bare of soil alternate with carpets of forest and skeins of streams. This is a region of empty spaces and sparse settlement, set aside for the enjoyment of all by the Province of Quebec. Every few kilometers, tasteful signs announce a campsite or boat launching ramp, luring us momentarily into the mosquito infested interior. But the pain is worth the pleasure when we pass a pond planned and executed by the beaver, that workaholic rodent of the north. Sharp ends of severed logs stand sentinel to the tireless efforts of the animal which creates its own custom-made environment. And on the water, lilies float, delicately suspended in their private circles of leaves, hiding the singing frogs and sheltering the skittering newts.

This vast preserve embraces wilderness canoe routes and uncharted forests, but no commercial development. Fast-food dispensers, camping outfitters and service stations are restricted to a few infrequent locations along the highway. But mercifully, at frequent intervals, we discover picnic tables strategically placed at settings of scenic splendour. Without exception, these handsome havens supply facilities for the washing of hands and the relief of bladders; a major contrast and great improvement over the parallel situation in Ontario. Once again we ruminate on puritan politicians with bloated bladders, and an unforgivable disregard for the pleasure (not to mention comfort) of the public.

The fiery noonday sun speeds us on our way to Barraute. Heading west from Highway 113, we enter somewhat more fertile country, noting the occasional prosperous beef or dairy farm beside the road. Straight rows of recently planted pines shared space with fields of rough pasture and a few cultivated plots. We pass Senneterre and turn towards Barraute. Unlike the settlements that we had just left, it has declined, but not so dramatically as Duparquet which we will visit next. Barraute has lost about one percent of its population since 1971, declining to 1273 in 1981, but the number of businesses doubled from 34 to 68 in the same period. This is puzzling, since Barraute is considerably farther from Montreal than either Ferme Neuve or Labelle. However, Barraute is just a few miles off the main road through La Vérendrye Park and could derive considerable business from tourists.

Closer to Barraute it becomes obvious that the farm industry is far healthier here than farther south towards the park. It also has the advantage of being on the railway. A large new Roman Catholic church dominates one end of town, its twin silver spires stretching heavenward above all else. Just on the outskirts, two major saw mills provide insight into its economic base. In centre ville, a forestry management office reinforces the clue provided by acres of logs, lumber and mountains of sawdust at the edge of town. Here, in contrast to the situation in Labelle, the lumber industry is alive and well.

Two gigantic wood processing operations completely overwhelm the other enterprises that we have observed. Heaps of golden sawdust fall beneath the spewing conduits leading from the whirring saws. Acres and acres of land are covered by large and small logs, their piney resin perfuming the still noon air. The forest industry thrives, as does local farming, if the major implement dealer and hardware stores are any indication. Since 1971, five new industries associated with forest products have opened, along with four new food stores. An extensive subdivision of pre-fabricated houses on the outskirts convinces us that the next census will indicate population growth to match the increased business activity.

Our statistics show that transportation has become an increasingly important function here during the last ten years. By 1986, there were ten more such enterprises than there had been in 1976. These consisted of several school bus operators and eight freight transporters, most of which haul logs and lumber. We notice that three of the trucking companies have depots taking up several acres covered by large fleets of trucks. Almost certainly they and the saw mills are outsized functions.

In the centre of town we come upon an advertisement for a farm festival, and find the local office of the Farm Circle. The main streets are busy with pedestrians and traffic; parking is at a premium. Four restaurants promise food for all, and a number of grocery stores sell beer and wine. A major clue to Barraute's regional importance lies in the presence of a large primary school and a district secondary school. The mere presence of a district school attracts parents to evening events, making available gymnasia as well as auditoriums for social, cultural and athletic events.

In the Prairies, the presence of a secondary school defines a regional service centre, just as it does in northern Quebec. The loss of such a school has often induced economic decline in formerly important communities. Clearly this is not to be the case in Barraute, which seems to have increased its regional economic importance of late. The large size, recent construction and excellent condition of the churches in Barraute graphically underline this point. Here again we can reasonably expect moderate future growth, this time based on local service functions, strong industry founded on wood, and some tourism.

When we head north and then jog back to the west, population gives way once again to trees, interspersed occasionally with a small farm or shack. Near to Duparquet, our next stop, wilderness replaces farmed fields. Somehow, the terrain takes on a beaten look. In the mid-day heat, our spirits sag at the prospect of a dying village. The indications from both statistics and surrounding country are less than optimistic. Between 1971 and 1981, Duparquet lost over 200 people, or over a quarter of its population to fall to only 581 in 1981, so we expect to see the symptoms of decline. The number of businesses in the village remained relatively steady at 13 in this same period, in marked contrast with increases in nearby settlements.

We enter the town, driving along unkempt streets, past sagging wooden buildings speaking eloquently of economic decline. A tall faded stack stands like a giant impotent phallic symbol above the scene. No smoke or fumes here as evidence of a mine or a mill. Along the main street, grass thrusts between sidewalk cracks, attempting to reclaim its rightful place. Weeds infest the tiny central square. Streets are lined by shops, their windows boarded over. This is not yet a ghost town, but symptoms of decline are painfully obvious everywhere.

Farther on we discover the Radio Hotel, which advertises a bar with band, and Saturday night dancing. Above, apartments fill the rooms long ago vacated by travellers. A number of houses sport large "For Sale" signs planted firmly in their weed-covered lawns. These rows of frame structures all seem similar, reminiscent of a company town. Indeed, this might be the answer to the population decline. The mine was obviously once the major local employer, but now appears to be closed. We decide to explore.

A "No Trespassing" sign greets us when we approach the mountains of jagged black and brown tailings surrounding the mine and smelter. An eight storey building hovers unhappily over the debris, its broken windows peering like blinded eyes at the desolation below. Twisted, rusting wire cables lie tangled with remnants of broken and crushed machinery. The entrance of what was once a prosperous and important enterprise is now a seedy shambles. Behind the building, spindly spider legs support a water tower high above the edifice, overshadowing the industrial litter of broken glass, metal barrels, oil patches and rubble on the ground. Two or

In Duparquet the mine is closed. Now an eight storey building hovers unhappily over the debris, its broken windows peering like blinded eyes at the desolation below.

three lonely cars are parked in a lot designed to hold hundreds, looking lost and forlorn in the shadow of the smelter. A desolate sight indeed, exaggerated by the contrast of a stately frame house in the shadow of the stack.

Another drive around town turns up the large offices of a mining corporation, still occupied but seeming somewhat the worse for wear. Across the street, weeds push through the grass, while paint peels, curls, and finally flakes off building after building. The heat, which has been increasing quickly since our last stop probably makes it seem worse, but this is a depressing picture. The general store, video outlet and even the bar with the go-go girls look sadly neglected. Apparently the mine boomed when ore prices were high, but now production has slowed or stopped. Little employment is offered while other more lucrative deposits are being sought.

Duparquet seems well on the way to becoming a dying community, with its isolated location and single resource base. Service to the few local farmers sustains some of the businesses, but it will certainly never become a tourist mecca. We have finally encountered a community with almost insurmountable problems (unless ore prices rise even higher, or other new minerals are found). The buildings used for accommodation and shops remain, but few people are replacing those who have left. In such a situation, even the availability of fixed capital in solid structures may not be able to stem the tide of decline. Eventually, wind and weather will take their toll as the built environment continues to decay. The outlook is not promising for Duparquet. Sadly, similar fates have befallen many an isolated single industry resource town in Canada's north.

Our last major stop on this trip is to be Ville Marie, the premier settlement on the ancient canoe route north along Lake Timiskaming. To reach it we cut south to Val d'Or, head west on Highway 117 through Rouyn-Noranda and then follow 101 south to Ville Marie. We just skirt Val d'Or, but decide to stop briefly to explore Rouyn-Noranda.

In many ways Rouyn-Noranda seems like Sudbury in earlier years. It is considerably above our size limit for detailed study, but worth a brief visit on the way through. It does catch the spirit of the near frontier where we have been for the last few days, but this time the mines have not

The Hotel de ville in Ville Marie was built in 1939 as an Agricultural College. With its limestone towers and crenellations, it could easily be a château on the Loire. Beside it stands the pioneer village.

yet been exhausted. The smelter stacks and slag heaps dominate the settlement from all directions. Choking, blue-grey fumes waft down when the wind swirls, and fine white dust seems to be pervasive.

Near one edge of town, rows of square, squat two-storey apartments stand like soldiers for inspection along wide asphalt boulevards. Their wrought-iron stairs loop delicately to the second level, lending the streets a look of spidery grace. New suburbs comprise a mix of small wooden bungalows covered in aluminum siding, and graceful new structures of stone and log. They are regimented into curvilinear order, appearing pleasant and prosperous. The older central town, huddled under the slag and stacks, seems tired and gritty. We pass through quickly, looking carefully for the road to Ville Marie some 150 kilometers farther south.

Ville Marie was founded in 1886 as Baie des Pères. This occurred after Le Frère Moffat, then known as "Le Maiskisis des Algonquins", arrived in 1872. He recognized the potential for excellent local agriculture and encouraged permanent settlement by the French. Soon the village boomed, stimulated by trade, commerce and agriculture combined. It is now a thriving centre with over 2600 souls and 127 different businesses.

In the morning we stroll along the lake to pass numerous three-storey homes of white clapboard. Tall, majestic and freshly painted, they must have belonged to the merchants and traders who became leaders of the community. They guard the harbour, lined up along the street with the best view and a location near to the centre of commerce. Nearby, provincial and local governments have established a hospital, offices and services in what has become a regional centre. The Hotel de Ville was built in 1939 as an agricultural college. With its limestone spires and battlements, it could easily have been a château on the Loire. Beside it stands the pioneer village. Here local tours begin where log houses from the 1880s display the past.

The central area of Ville Marie offers an excellent range of goods and services and an air of prosperity. This is apparent in our data which show an increase in businesses there of 56, or a 79 percent change from 1971 to 1986. The retail and service sectors have gained the most, with increases of 13 and 22 units respectively. Variety stores, furniture stores and automobile dealerships lead in the retail sector. Among finance and services, car repair, general repairs and insurance have had the greatest growth. Six additional manufacturing industries opened between 1971 and 1986, while the same number of trucking companies were established in that period.

Population growth in Ville Marie is the second largest of the Quebec settlements that we have visited. Between 1971 and 1981, the total rose from 1995 to 2651; an increase of 33 percent. As a result, several new suburbs have developed around the town, displaying some excellent contemporary French-Canadian architecture. Many of the older structures near the waterfront appear to have been renovated, some converted into apartments. Six local hotels and motels provide ample accommodation for visitors, many of whom are attracted to the local fishing, hunting and national park nearby.

But Ville Marie is not only a tourist town, even though it is situated on a beautiful lake. As demonstrated by the statistics, it is a diversified regional service centre in the midst of a prosperous area of farms. It provides all the goods and services necessary to its hinterland, and accommodation for those from surrounding farms who wish to retire there. Frère Moffat was correct in his early assessment of its prospects: it has grown, prospered and become the leading town of the region. On his firm foundation of fish, furs and agriculture it has built and developed. Today it is proud and confident -- its future bright.

Lake Timiskaming figured prominently in the early development of Ville Marie, just as it is now a major asset and attraction. On our trip south along its shores we receive a powerful demonstration of its potential and a lesson in local history. We drive into billowing powder-puff clouds which soon give way to black anvil turbulence of rapidly growing thunderheads. Then the rain begins. As we hurry through the increasing assault of dime-sized raindrops, they slash and claw at the car which is now hydroplaning across rapidly deepening puddles. Thunder claps and a fine, loud, fulminating, cracking, storm develops. The sun is reduced to a faint orange orb, and then obliterated entirely. Almost beside the car, sheets of bitterly cold water whirl across the lake, dashing against the surface to mix with the waves below. And such waves they are: short, high and vicious. They churn from side to side, breaking before the shore, splattering foam upon the rocky slopes as if to leap from the lake to the land. Strength and danger are personified in their rage.

Time and time again, Lake Timiskaming has precipitated tragedies, when unwary canoeists have been swamped by vicious gales swooping along the unobstructed water to take them to their icy graves. Despite such disasters, campers and canoe trippers continue to come, following faithfully along the path of the explorers and fur traders who preceded them. The lake's extreme depth ensures that it remains bitterly cold, while its orientation is ideal for violent storms. In spite of repeated warnings by experienced locals, many poorly prepared and badly led canoe trippers have come to grief in these waters.

Long before the white man, this lake was the path of trade and commerce, from the waters of the north to the Ottawa Valley and points south. Fur traders, explorers, missionaries and adventurers followed, opening the country to religion and commerce. During the period of French settlement, Fort Témiscamingue became the entrepôt of commerce for north-western Quebec. For much of the 1800s it controlled the trade in furs which the companies had negotiated with the Indians. Its strategic location at a narrowing of the lake enabled its owners to build the fort and regulate passage along this vital route. Yesterday the strategic location at a narrow passage gave Ville Marie an advantage, today the lake attracts tourists. Today the momentum of early settlement, the good local land and the enterprise of local businessmen have helped it to endure.

Wisps of fracto-stratus lick down towards the water as we finally reach historic Fort Témiscamingue. The sweet, blacktop smell of rain on steaming asphalt reminds us of the earlier heat. Now all is fresh and fecund. The violent convectional storm passes as quickly as it had come. Glistening droplets cling to bent blades of grass like tiny diamond bracelets. In the dripping woods above, the trees are heavy with water. As the grey damp clouds lift like a muslin blanket, we pause to survey the remains of a magnificent fortified settlement on the promontory. Here guns and soldiers regulated trade and passage, making certain that the French rulers received their due. Here also trade and commerce began a long tradition of business in Ville Marie and its hinterland. Explorers, traders and missionaries stopped for supplies, created local demand and gave commerce its beginnings.

Displays in the park graphically portray the lives of the early pioneers and defenders. The remains of the fort dominate the point and detailed descriptions explain their activities. Nearby, several tasteful buildings display artifacts of the past. Fluently bilingual guides make us welcome and elaborate on the labelled displays. Coins, canoes, furs and cooking pots remind us of another era when travel on the lake was a matter of survival rather than part of a pleasure outing on a weekend. We decide that we will not begrudge our tax money if it is spent on historical projects such as this. Then the temperature drops as the sun falls below the horizon, ending our reverie and urging us on to Toronto. When we leave the park, a dazzling display of heavenly colour transforms the land into a fairyland of mist, sun and a rainbow.

While we speed south, we contemplate our incursion into the towns and villages of Quebec. Memories flood back, along with our yearning for a stay of more than a day in one place. Each seemed to have more to offer than the last. We have experienced the dying mining town at Duparquet, the growth and prosperous industrial development of St. Germain-de-Grantham, the tourist attractions of Labelle and the service functions of Ferme Neuve. All were similar in some ways to what we saw in Ontario, but all were also distinctive.

The French language, the rangs with their rows of farmsteads, the squat 300-year-old stone cottages, the new gracefully curved roof lines -- all told us that we had been in a different and distinctive portion of the country. Here too, diversity, complexity and change had added interest and colour, affecting each settlement in a particular way. Architecture, language, heritage, hard work, luck, local beauty -- each contributed a special dimension to the settlements, and each now lures us to return. One day we shall, but first we must travel to the east to explore other settlements based upon fishing, forestry and the sea.

The French language, the rangs with their rows of farmsteads, the 300 year old stone cottages, the new gracefully curved roof lines -- all tell us that we have been in a different and distinctive portion of the country.

CHAPTER EIGHT

Maritimes, Mills and Forests

In southern Ontario and Quebec, most of the towns and villages we visited were rural service centres, retirement communities and commuter dormitories. In the north, some were mining towns, some were lumber towns and others had just disappeared. Away from the southern centres of population, a local natural resource often provided the original economic base for a settlement. The presence of that same resource today is frequently a contemporary attraction for tourists. In both the north and the south, the presence or absence of a main road today, or a railway in the past could make the difference between prosperity and decline. In the early days transportation was essential to initial prosperity and it remains so today, for without it tourism and residential growth are impossible.

In the Maritimes, the equation is somewhat different. There the sea was often both the resource base and the early transportation route. Water provided fish for the settlers and their communication to the outside world. Now it is often the attraction that induces development. As in other parts of Canada, rivers, forests and minerals were important to the original development of the Maritime Provinces, but the sea is the dominating factor. On this brief trip we will visit a diversity of Maritime communities, exploring each and drawing contrasts or parallels with the evolution of their counterparts in Ontario and Quebec. In these eastern settlements we will experience first-hand the climate, hardships and attractions that make them unique. We will also journey back into time, visiting some of the very first European outposts in North America and staying in some of the oldest remaining homes.

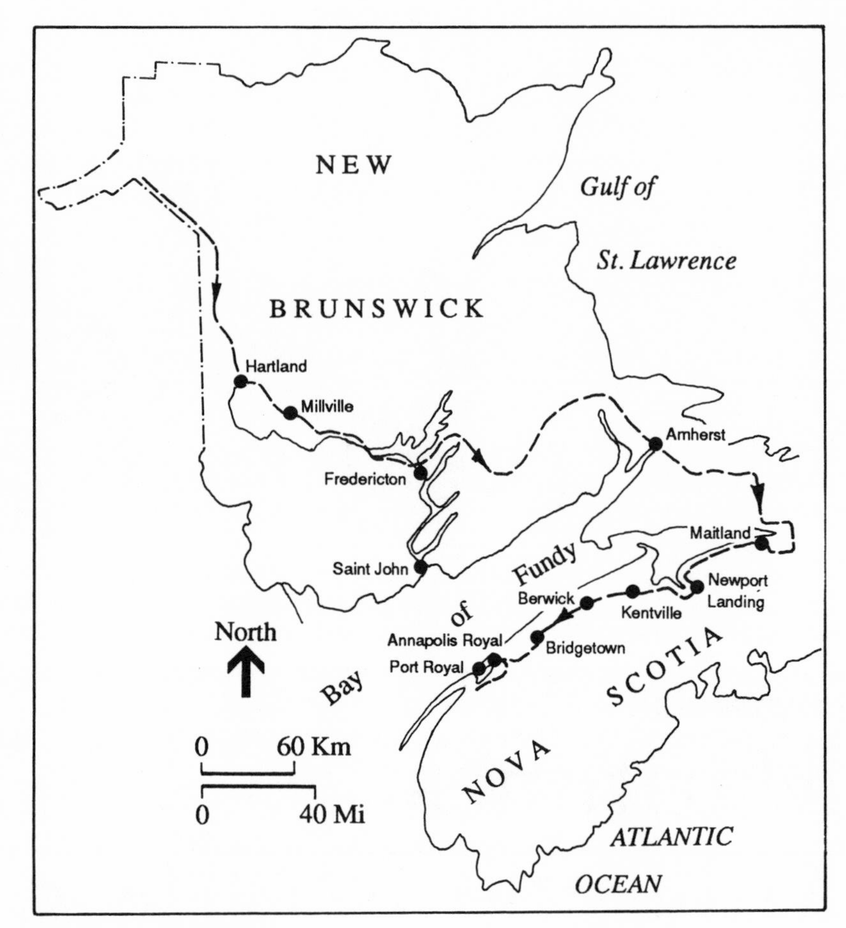

Our route through New Brunswick and Nova Scotia.

The sting of the sea, the taste of lobster and the scent of salt air have lured travellers to the east coast for decades. There they may explore remote little mill towns, seaside resorts, fishing villages, ports, outports, service centres and settlements rich in history and tradition. Around the coasts of New Brunswick, Nova Scotia and Prince Edward Island lie some of the prettiest and most intriguing villages in Canada. Just as in the rest of the country, some have declined and almost disappeared, some are thriving to the point of being congested and others are little changed from the past. We will visit a number, attempt to understand their evolution and make some prognosis for their future.

Today there are many tangible differences between the Maritimes and the provinces to the west. In the east, the pace of life is slower, the living more leisurely and the people more friendly. Maybe it's the maritime influence and maybe it's just the Celtic heritage, but we do notice a difference, especially in the smallest towns. We will begin our exploration along the St. Lawrence, downstream from Montreal, where it begins to widen and slow in its relentless journey to the sea. Then we will traverse New Brunswick, circle Nova Scotia and see a bit of Prince Edward Island.

On our trip to the east coast, we leave Toronto, pass through Montreal in a storm and stop for the night east of the city. Morning dawns misty and mild. Wisps of water vapour hang over the hills and the car is covered with tiny glistening droplets. To the east the sun struggles valiantly to pierce the humid blanket, thrusting faint and tentative shafts of pale yellow through the fog. But at least it isn't raining, and the motel proprietor assures us of a clear and sunny day by eleven.

"Always starts like this" he says. "Then the clouds break over the mountains, the mist rises and it's clear. No problems for today."

He is right. We drive through Mont-Saint-Hilaire to increasing brilliance from above. By the time we reach the Autoroute, the tops of the hills are clear, and by the time we pass Saint-Hyacinthe, there are distinct breaks in the high clouds above. The trip through Quebec is to be quick, simply because we have spent so much time here before. This time we join the throughway travellers for a while and bypass everything related to the smallest towns except their exit signs. But even this can be an education, especially for someone from Ontario.

It seems that we pass a thousand Saints between Montreal and Rivière-du-Loup. Sainte-Rosarie, Sainte-Hélène-de-Bagot, Saint-Germain-de-Grantham, Saint-Léonard-d'Aston, Saint-Ferdinand and Sainte-Croix all appear before Quebec City. What would the Québecois do without a Saint after whom to name a town or village? The one that is particularly amusing is St-Louis-de-Ha!-Ha! some 60 kilometers east of Rivière-du-Loup. We wonder whether he is a laughing Saint or whether the whole thing is really a joke. Nevertheless, the place exists, not far from Cabano near Lake Témiscouata on the main road to New Brunswick.

On our way past St. Germain, we recall our earlier visit. The view from Autoroute 20 emphasizes its service role in the midst of a rich agricultural hinterland. Its tall church spire stands like that of some medieval cathedral, dominating the hinterland. Fields of grain and pasture stretch to the horizon beyond. On we roll, coming ever closer to the mighty St. Lawrence which widens and slows on its inexorable journey to the sea. Across the flat expanse of glassy water looms the rugged shield of north-eastern Quebec, sparsely covered by stunted conifers. On the river, ocean going vessels steam by, carrying their cargoes of grain and ore to the east, passing others with machinery heading west. Ahead and to the right, outlines of low peaks rise to be silhouetted against the hazy sky.

We travel quickly now, following the wide, flat St. Lawrence and finally turning south at Rivière de Loup. From here we will soon be in New Brunswick. Highway 2 south along the St. John River seems to run endlessly through a carpet of spruce, tamarack, birch and soft maple. Kilometer after kilometer roll by while we hum along past trees, trees, trees and more trees. We understand a little of what the pioneers felt when they entered this land, and we realize why forestry, fishery and minerals are mainstays of the New Brunswick economy. In the 1800s, practically every community was a mill town where logs were assembled and floated down rivers or sawed for timber. Population increased along the St. John River valley, a depression virtually filled with small farms, pretty villages, cedar shag houses (and trees in the spaces between). On our way to our first stop at Millville, we encounter a bit of local history.

Turning off the Trans-Canada Highway we discover a delightful town, Hartland filled with structures of sandstone and clapboard. Its population rose from 847 in 1941 to 1025 in 1961. By the time we visit, the number of residents has dropped again to 846. It looks like another rural service centre that has suffered the ravages of rural depopulation and farm consolidation. Hartland claims, however, the world's longest covered bridge. This bridge was begun in 1899 as a private crossing of the Becaguimac (Salmon) River. In those days, the Toll Collector James Pearson demanded payment as follows: pedestrian 2¢; single team 5¢; double team 10¢ (horses). The structure was covered in 1922 to protect it from rain and snow, an act which created one unexpected problem. Snow then had to be hauled and spread over the roadway to allow sleds to cross. Fortunately, trucks soon replaced horses as the main movers of freight and eliminated the problem. The Hartland Covered Bridge is 1282 feet long and has been rebuilt several times since its construction.

Somehow we expect a busy, smoky, dusty town with a major lumber mill at Millville. What we find is a collection of white clapboard homes and a few square, commercial buildings strung along the side of a hill. An aban-

Given its pastoral setting on both sides of a sloping river valley, why has Millville's population decreased?

doned railway track runs through the settlement, but at first glance, we see neither river nor mill. We approach the friendly looking general store, and find that it is locked. Locked, at two in the afternoon? Of course, it is Wednesday afternoon; the time honoured closing day for small-town stores.

Millville housed 309 people in 1981, 43 fewer than ten years earlier. Its twelve businesses in 1986 were one more than its 1971 total. Today it boasts two service stations, a general store, post office with attached apartment, two churches, a key-cutting business, a New Brunswick telephone depot, a Jehovah's Witness hall and several three-storey apartment buildings. The settlement was established in 1784 to saw logs from the surrounding forest and supply the few farmers who made a living nearby. A small wood-working industry near the old tracks is all that remaines of its industrial legacy. Like so many early resource communities, it declined when the trees began to disappear, but had a brief resurgence when the railway came through.

Today, Millville is a tiny sleepy hamlet with few real attractions for visitors. On the other hand, the presence of a post office brings farmers to it from the surrounding countryside. Often they combine trips and do a bit of shopping at the general store as well. Aside from the stores that have been converted into residences, Millville does not display either signs of decline or that it was more important in the past. Given its pastoral setting on both sides of a sloping river valley, why has the population dropped so? It appears that it is too far from any major sources of employment to become a commuter dormitory. This conclusion is reinforced by the poor and narrow roads linking it to any major highway.

Despite its relative isolation, Millville is one of the prettiest pastoral settings that we have visited during our travels. As in all small towns, several houses are surrounded by old cars, tires, rubble and large barking dogs, but most others look like something out of Anne of Green Gables. Cattle graze in the fields and a brook bubbles happily under an old concrete bridge. Several gambrel-roofed barns stand right in the centre of town; most houses boast a large, neat wood pile, well kept flower beds and carefully manicured lawns. We detect the remains of a mill and dam just upstream from the

On several side roads we pass these peculiar half subterranean barns that make so much sense here. Most look like a gambrel roof central Ontario barn from one end, but recede into the side of a hill at the other. Many form a T, with a smaller entrance way leading to the half buried main barn.

bridge, and conclude that the grand Italianate villa under the spreading elm must have belonged to the miller. It stands near the mill site and is the largest home in the hamlet. The quality of the local residential environment remains high.

Our speculations and explorations are cut short at the top of the rise across the creek. First the blackflies discover our sun roof and mount a determined attack from the air. Then the gentle, billowing, fair-weather cumulus clouds begin to blacken and boil upward towards 40,000 feet. Then they become full-blown, cumulonimbus or thunderheads, filled with vicious down-drafts, rain and hail. The thunder cracks open the sky, shakes the trees and fuses with cold gusts of wind. This sudden summer storm disperses the blackflies, and sends us on our way south. Millville, we conclude, will continue to be a minor local service centre and will attract a few retirees from local farms. On the other hand, given its relative isolation and lack of any outstanding scenic attraction, it is difficult to see any major future growth. The local population is just too sparse and there does not seem to be any incentive for someone to develop an outsized function. There just isn't a large enough potential market nearby. We relegate Millville to the category of stagnant former mill towns.

The rain continues to dog us as we follow back roads into the interior of the province. We pass settlements with exotic Indian names such as Nackawic, Pokiok, Mactaquac and Oromocto as well as more familiar places like Marysville, Fredericton and Gagetown.

On several side roads we pass those peculiar, half subterranean barns that make so much sense here. Most look almost like a gambrel-roofed central Ontario barn from one end, but recede into the side of a hill at the other. Many form a T, with a smaller entrance way leading to the half buried main barn. This arrangement protects the contents (sometimes cattle, sometimes crops), from the elements and allows access to the loft from ground level at one end. In one sense, they are the Ontario bank barn turned the other way. In any event, they catch our fancy, adding interest and variety to the landscape.

After several small, rural diversions, the Trans-Canada Highway takes us back along the St. John River Valley, past Grand Lake, across Washademoak Lake, and eventually to Sussex. Between Sussex and Amherst we cross the magnificent marshes at the end of Cumberland Bay and admire the wild azaleas beside the road at the tourist office. Much to our chagrin, a small diversion through Amherst causes us to make several loops on and off the trans-Canada Highway. We finally find the correct highway, but a side benefit which we enjoy is a glimpse of the sturdy, red sandstone buildings that line the main street of the town. With its large trees, slow pace and delightful architecture, it could be in the south of England.

The road to Parrsboro takes us through a bit of New Zealand. Or so it seems. Gently sloping hills are covered with the greenest grass imaginable and dotted with hundreds of sheep. They look naked and cold, short wool barely covering their bodies, reminding them and us of their recent shearing. Small wooden bungalows and seascapes in the background complete a picture that could have been in Taranaki or somewhere along the Coromandel Peninsula.

Highway 132 from Amherst to Parrsboro passes through Chignecto, Athol, Southampton and Halfway River as it follows the Maccan River and skirts the Chignecto Game Sanctuary. Parrsboro was established in 1784, and with a population of 1799, is the largest town on the Minas Basin. The town and surrounding area are a geologist's paradise. Numerous gemstones are found in the metamorphic rocks nearby, and in 1985 an American geologist discovered a large number of important Dinosaur fossils from the Triassic and Jurassic Geological Periods, some 210 million years ago. The town attracts many rock hounds and persons interested in the time long before humans inhabited the earth.

Our interests are somewhat different, although we cannot resist a quick look around the local museum with its excellent collection of gems and mineral-working tools. It must be the twenty-foot-high statue of the God Glooskap that draws us into the building. Micmac legend has it that Glooskap created the Fundy tides, which are the highest in the world and reach their greatest magnitude in the Minas Basin. He was also responsible for the gemstones, which were his grandmother's jewellery, now scattered along the shore.

At the wharf, fishing boats and lumber freighters are left stranded high and dry at low tide. Mud flats stretch for what seems like miles before being covered by water. But when we return the next day, the salty froth laps right

In Parrsboro, a magnificent red brick post office with a clock tower dominates one end of the shopping area, but it is closed and boarded up. In it, we could visualise a theatre, meeting rooms, offices and shops. What a potential anchor for downtown renewal!

up to the wharf, floating the boats and adding a briny tang to the air. Only then do we fully appreciate the amazing rise and fall of the tides. Their greatest variation can be as much as 53 feet or 17 metres when the sun and moon exert their maximum pull. The amount of water discharged from the basin weighs about a hundred million tons; roughly 70 times the daily discharge of the Mississippi River. No wonder the Government of Nova Scotia has several pilot projects designed to harness this energy to produce hydro power.

Parrsboro is something of an enigma. It has lost population since 1971, dropping from 1807 to 1799 in 1981, but the number of businesses there increased by over 80 percent from 1971 to 1986. This increase of 34 businesses to the 75 we note today is spectacular. On the main street people go busily on their way and most stores are occupied. The fishing and lumbering tradition are still well in evidence, with a massive lumber mill working furiously and several fishing vessels being repaired and painted in a dry dock. A magnificent red-brick post office with a clock tower dominates one end of the shopping area. For some reason that is not apparent, this building has been abandoned and boarded up. Why doesn't someone inform Canada Post of the potential inherent in such splendid structures. We can visualize a theatre, meeting rooms, offices and shops. What an anchor for downtown renewal!

Why has the population of Parrsboro declined? Streets lined by stately maples overlook views that encompass tidal flats, surf, sea grass or marshes, depending on the time of day. White clapboard houses with tidy vegetable gardens are nestled on the slightly rolling streets. Just beyond town we cross burned fields which have been prepared for the local blueberry crop. Along the road we encounter several large storage and processing sheds being readied for the blueberry harvest. The area is somewhat reminiscent of the Canadian Shield north of Huntsville.

Parrsboro itself has clearly become increasingly dependent on tourism, with rock hounds, fishermen and geologists finding it attractive. The blueberry business is obviously thriving and many local farmers patronize stores in the town. We find an amazing variety of small industry in the settlement. Another change that is evident only from the statistics is the increase in the number of tradesmen there from three to eleven since 1971. Building supply outlets and wood product industries have also gained handsomely in that period. There was no blueberry industry in 1971 and now there are two processors. Despite general economic problems in the Province, Parrsboro seems to be healthy. No doubt the 1986 census will show a population increase to match the business boom that our directory data have uncovered.

One of the more pleasant aspects of settlement exploration in Nova Scotia is the scenery between the villages. It also turns out to be one of the major resources that provide economic stimulation to settlements that have (unlike Parrsboro) lost their traditional economic base of fishing or forestry. To reach our next destination at Maitland, we drive along the shores of the Minas Basin and Cobequid Bay. Here, woods seem to run into the ocean, streams cut deep channels into the soft red shale and glimpses of lapping water remind us that we are near the sea. On one long curve that sweeps around the shore in a graceful arc above the bay, we are particulary reminded of an earlier trip around East Cape in New Zealand. Maybe it is the coarsely graveled stretch of road that is so similar to the "metal" (read boulder) roads of East Cape, and maybe it is just the local lay of the land, but we can almost feel Waipiro Bay and Whareponga.

Driving on, we pass Lower Economy, Economy, and finally, Upper Economy, all quiet, wooded and quaint, stretching like German street villages through the forest along the shore. The last light is barely seeping over the horizon when we arrive in Maitland. First impressions are often lasting, and ours is excellent. A general store dominates the main intersection across from a splendid three-storey mansion with Gothic dormers that was once the hotel. The actual bed and breakfast that we are seeking is almost hidden in a grove of maples just around the corner. When we knock, a most delectable aroma of roasting pork dispels any reservations we might have about rural dining rooms. Before dinner we stroll through the immediate area and are astounded by the number and variety of spectacular residences in such a small village. Our accommodation for the night is called the Foley House Inn, and was built around 1830. Although it is large, some of the other houses simply dwarf it. There is more to Maitland than we first expected.

In the dining room we meet a delightful lady in her 80s from Arizona. She is a Canadian with roots in the area, and now that her husband has passed away, spends most summers here tracing down her family tree. A number of fiercely loyal Nova Scotians return to visit this area every year, and many more come back to retire after a spouse has died. The lure of tradition and maritime roots are strong, often explaining population increases in some otherwise unlikely places.

After dinner, we march briskly towards the water. Past the wharf we discern a long low ridge along the flats. It is topped by a path which we proceed to follow. This is one of the famous Acadian dikes that facilitated agriculture along the shore. Here they dammed the waters and produced hay for their cattle in the salt marshes that they had created. Their methods enabled them to augment the livelihood that they could wrest from the sea and sometimes inhospitable soils. What irony that the British chased the Acadians away, only to allow them back later because they couldn't cope with the cultivation of the tidal flats. Now the dikes had been restored in some areas and preserved for their historic value in others. Here they provided a handy pathway across the low lying flats and impounded water for a bird sanctuary.

The view across the bay from atop the reddish sandstone cliff is spectacular. Enough illumination remains to silhouette a spreading elm against the water; then lights from the far shore wink on with the darkening night. Gentle waves lap up to the flats of fine red clay, pausing, swirling; finally forming luminescent eddies as they slither back to the deep. Above, a canopy of black velvet sprinkled with hard white diamonds draws our eyes to the dipper and milky way. This is paradise: what was it like in the 1800s?

Next morning we find out, and in so doing discover the secret of Maitland. The setting that has so impressed us with its tranquillity the previous evening was once one of the busiest harbours along this coast. Here the mouth of the Shubenacadie River joins the upper reaches of Cobequid Bay, forming an excellent sheltered port. Vast forests covered the land in the nineteenth century and provided the raw material for what became a major centre of ship building. The mansions that

First impressions are often lasting, and ours of Maitland is excellent. A general store dominates the intersection across from a splendid three storey mansion.

we discover had once belonged to wealthy captains and ship owners who made their fortunes from the sea. Some were the retirement homes for former sailors, others were the centres of thriving ship yards.

The Lawrence House stands over the water at the eastern end of town and is typical of the grand homes of ship builders. It contains two large parlours, a number of bedrooms and an enormous working area at the rear. Here the servants and kitchen staff toiled while the master designed ships from a room at the very back. His workers could enter to collect their pay cheques without passing through the front of the house. He had a second-storey room at the front from which he could watch the ship building progressing on the shore.

Lawrence's crowning achievement was the ship, William D. Lawrence -- at 2459 tons, the largest built in Canada to that date. It was twice as big as its nearest rival, and drew a crowd of over 4000 people to see its launching on October 12, 1874. It was sold after eight profitable years of sailing the world for Captain Lawrence. We examine the architectural drawings and a scale model in the Lawrence House which is now a museum. The mystery of the marvelous mansions of Maitland has been solved. All that wealth and all those magnificent structures had their origins in the sea.

Maitland today is a minor local service centre with a population of 230. The former hotel is now just a rambling three-storey house but a large general store continues to operate as does a fast-food stand by the wharf. Farther along the road following the shore, a modern general store provides everything from groceries to fishing tackle. Only the mansions of the sea captains and ship builders remain to remind us that this was once a much larger and more prosperous community, employing and housing hundreds in the utilization of the rich timber resources nearby. Along the waterfront, the Acadian Dikes remain, but there is no trace of the extensive yards where the tall ships were constructed and launched.

Maitland is not dying, because an entrepreneur has capitalized upon its history and beauty to operate a small hotel while several stores continue to serve its residents. And the population is increasing slowly as a few expatriates return to retire, and several families from Halifax have taken over former mansions for country retreats. It is probably too isolated ever to become a dormitory community, but it will sustain a few more economic functions as long as tourists continue to travel the Glooskap trail and entrepreneurs are willing to risk their energy and capital in a picturesque remnant of a glorious past. Maitland's attributes seem to be almost the perfect model of the amenity and heritage factors that have breathed new life into once stagnant communities. We compare it to Alton in Ontario, where the struggle between those who desire additional growth and those who seek to preserve their heritage has already been joined.

Next day we continue to wind our way west towards the Annapolis Valley, the fruit basket of Nova Scotia, traversing more giant red scars where river and tide have scoured away the soft sandstone. Then we cross forests and farm, and finally arrive at Newport Landing hard by the Avon River. Here again we see evidence of early prosperity in the form of additional fine old mansions dating back to the age of sea and sail. After several days on back roads the highway from Kentville west is a surprisingly pleasant change. The charm of country villages is captivating, but not always, especially when you're in a hurry and farmer Brown ahead is not. At Kentville, we enter the historic Annapolis Valley and return for a day to an area where agriculture is king and the major settlements are inland. Here both the economy and the functions of the towns are closer to those of Ontario than the last few we have explored.

Our first stop, Berwick is a busy, thriving market town that was established in 1810 as Condon's Corners. It functioned originally as a service centre on the railway, shipping apples to the British market, but the station is now used for a very different purpose. Today, truck transport and its strategic location between two highways make it accessible to a wide area. Unlike many other towns in Nova Scotia, Berwick has grown recently in both population and industry. From a 1971 total of 1412, its population increased to 1699 for a 20 percent gain by 1981. Its earlier increase from only 960 in 1941 to 1300 in 1961 reflected the diversification in local agriculture which occurred when numerous old fruit trees were replaced with new stock or by crop and dairy farming.

The number of businesses in Berwick jumped a spectacular 126 percent to a total of 127 in 1986; far above its 1971 total of 56. The largest business gains were in agricultural processing. Fruit packing increased from one to nine businesses and hog processing went from none in 1971 to four in 1986. Other important growth industries are trucking, food stores, variety stores, and car sales; all traditional service centre functions. Berwick now supplies the Halifax market with food products as well as shipping agricultural produce abroad.

Even on a rainy Thursday afternoon, Berwick exudes prosperity. The local fish monger does a roaring business from the back of his truck while crowds throng in and out of the supermarket and variety stores. Busy traffic consisting primarily of farm trucks moves along the congested main street. The restaurants are busy and crowded. Hardware stores, both old and new mingle with real estate agents, hairdressers, laundromats and one of the largest beverage rooms ever seen. The very spacious railway station is now being used as a drinking place. In Ontario we saw many former railway stations turned into restaurants, but this is the first in our experience that has become an enormous pub. Like the general store-post office of old, this has become a major centre for socialization and meeting one's friends. Its central location which was once so convenient for rail passengers continues to be accessible to pub patrons. The built environment endures; only its function has changed.

Berwick reminds us of another thriving service centre in Ontario: Athens. Its tree-shaded side streets are lined by gracious two and three-storey homes and its many churches are solid and spacious. Here in Berwick the reasonable prices of real estate are astounding. One can purchase a huge old two-storey house for anywhere from $69,000 to $85,000. One which appears to have about 15 rooms is offered for $98,000 while small two bedroom bungalows go for $17,500. A new chalet is listed at $35,000, and a standard 1200-square-foot bungalow can be had for $52,000.

The local housing costs are a far cry from big city prices and explain some of the recent rapid population growth here. For anyone retiring or wishing to live in a small town, Berwick offers churches, schools, a wide range of shopping, small town atmosphere and employment. It is one of our best examples of a rural service centre that began that way and continues to thrive in its traditional role. But this is to be expected, given its location between two highways in the middle of the most fertile valley in Nova Scotia.

We leave Berwick and continue west along the lush Annapolis Valley to Bridgetown, one of the prettiest places we have encountered. And it isn't even on the water (unless you count the Annapolis River). Our first impression is of one long avenue, lined by mansions even more magnificent that those in Maitland. The street is covered by a canopy of maples slowly dripping heavy globules of rainwater to the grass below. We stop at a craft shop advertising the Tolmie Gallery and discover that the gallery is in the house next door. Even though it is past the posted closing time, the owner invites us to the house to see the watercolours of Ken Tolmie. Tolmie had spent ten years portraying the life and people of Bridgetown in sketches and watercolours. The home we visit is crammed with his work, now selling for thousands of dollars a painting. He successfully captured the streets, the buildings, the countryside and the people. Of all his accomplishments, his sensitivity for mood and facial features are outstanding. Our conversation turns to the striking portrait of a handsome elderly woman.

"Oh, that's Hilda FitzRandolph," says our host. "She was a great friend of Ken Tolmie. They had a love-hate relationship. Struck sparks and great debate every time they got together. But they were still very close. That's why he captured her so well."
"We really like the look of the setting behind her too," we reply. "Where is it?"
"Actually, it's just out of town on highway 201. Do you have a place to stay tonight?"
"No, we don't, but we'd like to remain in the area and photograph the town tomorrow."
"Well then, stay with Hilda. She runs a Bed and Breakfast now that she has retired. I'll call ahead for you."

And that is how we end up in a house on one of the oldest continually used highways north of Mexico. The structure itself was built for an American planter in the 1760s. The area was first settled by the Acadians in 1654. We are in the midst of history and are experiencing one of the longest traditions of settlement in British North America.

Hilda FitzRandolph was a high school teacher who must have taught everyone for miles around. The local merchants all know her, as does a waitress we met in Annapolis Royal. Her large, square colonial clapboard home is set at the front of a farm dating back to the original French survey. Its lot is ten times as long as it is wide. Down the road, ruined dikes can be found, and the pond from the painting in the Tolmie Gallery is indeed still there behind the house. Inside, the wooden floors are pine boards of variable width. Watercolours, antique furniture and family photographs are everywhere. If our visit to the Mennonite farm in Waterloo Region is reminiscent of the 19th century, this is reminiscent of the 18th. Even Hilda and her husband have a delightful ancient air about them. They have adapted perfectly to their historic environment, firmly attached by roots from the 1790s.

In Bridgetown every style of wooden house imaginable greets us as we walk in the rain. They are eclectic -- a strange mix of Italianate, Regency and Gothic. Several are all curves, their eaves bending round richly ornamented bargeboards.

Our blue and white room is undoubtedly the most elegant we have encountered in hotel or lodging house. Two double beds stand side by side, joined by a frilly lace canopy with a blue edge. On them, enormous bolster pillows in matching colours of chintz form perfect reading chairs. The furnishings are from the 1800s. A towel-rack of wooden dowels reminds us of childhood visits to the family homestead farm. Above the dresser, a mirror of wavy glass gives back crazily distorted images. A steamer trunk, repainted in white and blue sits at the end of the bed. The image is completed by a collection of china dolls on a shelf outside our room, and by the white lace curtains surrounding the eight pane windows. We are indeed in the pioneer past; one that can be discovered only by getting away from the city, off the beaten track and into the small towns and villages or the countryside. In the city, it is unlikely that you can have the opportunity to savour such a residence; in the small towns of Nova Scotia, such an experience becomes commonplace.

Next morning, Hilda feeds us homemade porridge, freshly brewed coffee, homemade preserves and a lesson in local history. After the Acadians were chased away by the British, Americans from Massachusetts came to farm the area. They took over the former Acadian land and replaced the original small shanties with their elegant clapboard structures. This area ultimately came to be considered a fourteenth state, but the settlers never supported the revolution because the Bostonians had drawn their ire by raiding Liverpool. These "planters", as they are known locally, remained loyal to the Crown, and thus preceded the "Loyalist" settlers elsewhere by some years. The FitzRandolph family acquired this homestead in sad condition from descendants of the original owners. Years of effort and labour have transformed it into the living museum where we slept for the night.

After breakfast we head through the fog and drizzle to the centre of Bridgetown. Its actual business district is unexceptional, but the magnificence of the homes and churches catches our fancy. Even in the rain, everything is sparkling white. What a time paint salesmen must have in the Maritimes! This reminds us of that other wealthy retirement community of Maitland as it must have been in the 1700s when the captains came home from the sea, but here multiplied by ten. Every style of wooden home imaginable greets us as we walk in the rain. Some are reminiscent of the Acadians, with several tall, steep gables dominating the front. Others can only be called eclectic, a strange mix of Italianate, Regency and Gothic. Several are all curves, their eaves bending round richly ornamented bargeboards, fancy, carved spooling adorning the corners. Seldom have we seen such a collection of decorative woodwork in such a small area. And it seems that all the homes are designed for families of ten or more. Their spaciousness is matched only by their elegance.

After an hour or so of admiring Bridgetown's historic houses, the rain and fog have thoroughly seeped into our bones. We have observed the history in the houses, but the present is seen through the businesses. On our chilly tour, we observe a river boat to take tourists along the Annapolis River, a large motel, several eating places, several general stores, a museum, clothing stores, hardware stores and service stations. The distillery on the edge of town continues to utilize fruit products from the Annapolis Valley for its alcoholic beverages. A soft drink and textile factory are also found nearby.

Most of the businesses look prosperous and the buildings are well kept, especially along the street that has been made into a mall. Clearly a conscious attempt has been made to attract the tourist, and it is succeeding, since the town is now on a historic homes bus tour. Given its heritage going back to French settlement in 1654, Bridgetown has lots of history to display. Its population increased from a low of 1,020 in 1941 to 1,039 in 1971 and 1,047 in 1981. This upward trend will undoubtedly continue as its splendid legacy of elegant old houses is exploited for tourism and retirement. The town has a vast amount of potential for anyone interested in history, architecture, art, or just a delightful location in which to spend their final days.

Past Bridgetown, the drive along historic Highway 201 takes us through an almost endless succession of what appear to be continuous villages. At first it seems strange that most houses have barns, many of which are the Erie Shore variety, especially designed for fruit and vegetables. We know that this is a major fruit production area, and soon recall that we are travelling along an ancient Acadian "Rang", where farmsteads are purposely set close together and lots are long and narrow. For a moment, we have forgotten the local French roots. How could we forget the unceremonious way in which those earliest settlers who had built the dikes and drained and farmed the marshes were removed by the British? Despite their departure, they left their mark permanently on the land. Otherwise, the Annapolis Valley is reminiscent of southern Ontario, or even of areas in central Waikato in the North Island of New Zealand.

Our impression of a New Zealand landscape is reinforced by the mist lingering languorously over the tops of the nearby hills, to be broken only occasionally by glimmers from a weak white spring sun. Then, just into the next valley, the heavens open, sheets of rain swamp us for a moment and then all subsides into damp calm. If the hills, mist, and unpredictable precipitation are any indication, this could be September in Auckland Province. There a folding umbrella and nylon raincoat have pride of place in any briefcase. Maritime climates are the same everywhere. Mild, misty, chilly, clammy, penetrating, hot, muggy, torrential, sunny, changing from valley to valley, but never dull. The sea is always present, the wind direction usually wildly variable, and fronts can rarely be tracked accurately for any distance. No one believes the weatherman, even when he ventures only percentage possibilities of rain. One is invariably in that small area where none of his predictions come true! But then it is difficult to track the weather, when, often as not, it comes across ocean, mountain, bay or harbour into an area of infinitely variable micro-climates. We should be glad that the meteorologists do as well as they do in such difficult circumstances. For travellers to this varied landscape, the climate provides infinite variations of moods, scenes and opportunities to see things in a different light.

The road finally leads to the end of the valley where the Annapolis River pours into the sea, and where Annapolis Royal has stood for 382 years. This makes it the oldest English settlement in Canada. Unfortunately, the fog and drizzle stay with us and our big chill continues. There is a side benefit however. In this weather, the town is almost deserted, at least by tourists. Down by the water at one end of town we come upon the weekly market, craft sale and sidewalk sale. Everything from fruit, vegetables, home made dolls, clothes and leather goods to tickets for today's art auction and bean lunch is on sale. Mercifully, it isn't windy, and the sales stalls are sheltered from the rain. A stroll to the waterfront reveals a ship, now converted into a summer playhouse. But the walk also chills us to our bones. Raw, cutting, soggy Atlantic winds cut through our jackets, forcing a quick retreat from the water. We stop for lunch at one of the excellent local restaurants called Newman's.

After lunch, the sun actually begins to peer from behind the clouds. What was a clammy, chilly day suddenly becomes warm and muggy. We continue to explore, this time in considerably more comfort. We pass Farmer's Hotel, built in the 1730s and now being restored. It is reputed to be the oldest building in English Canada. Along St. George Street, lovingly restored homes from the 1700s mingle with trendy shops in historic settings. We enter one bookstore only to discover that it is now also an outlet for the Old Mill leather shop in Blyth. They continue to sell a large variety of first rate books, but the owners feel that diversification is the key to continued success. The shop keeper informs us that Nova Scotians are "always on the edge" economically, and have to be flexible to survive. We are the beneficiaries of this particular diversification, because we picke up several leather gloves for less than their price in Blyth. What ever happened to the effect of shipping costs and economies of scale? Maybe this is last year's stock. In any event, we get a bargain.

Fort Anne stands proud and solid, guarding Annapolis Royal from the enemy. Its earthworks and fortifications have been restored, once again facing the sea intact and challenging all invaders. On this site, four forts had stood during the long tug of war between English and French. First, in 1643, d'Aulnay de Charnisay fortified the site for the French. Many battles raged between then and 1713, when forts were built and destroyed, some occupied by English and others used by the French. The issue of who owned the fort was settled for good in 1710 when Col. Francis Nicholson and his New England regiment recaptured it permanently and rebuilt it for the English. They then changed the name of the settlement from Port Royal to Annapolis Royal. It remained a British garrison until 1854, becoming a National Park in 1917. We stroll along its grass-covered earth-works, duck into the ammunition stores and explore the former quarters of the British field officers, now a splendid museum.

A little farther along, on Upper St. George Street, we discover the Annapolis Royal Historic Gardens. In addition to presenting a glorious display of flowers and trees, this is near the site of North America's first grist mill on Allain's river. Here in the salt marshes the Acadian dike system has been rebuilt where the first wheat field is reputed to have stood. The pioneer cabin is especially intriguing, complete with herbs drying on the rafters, an enormous open fireplace with cooking utensils, and an assortment of wood-working tools. We stroll past it to discover a complete kitchen garden, just as it must have been three hundred years ago. Summer savoury, thyme, sweet basil, marjoram, mint, dill and sage all grow in profusion to supply the settler's needs for herbs and seasoning. Beside the water, long yellow stalks of sea grass wave in the sun, offering their fibrous leaves and stems for anyone who wishes to weave or thatch a roof. Here, beside the river and near the sea, we understand how the earliest settlers survived.

Today, Annapolis Royal is a thriving tourist resort and port. Its population actually declined from 758 to 631 between 1971 and

In Annapolis Royal, lovingly restored homes from the 1700s mingle with trendy shops in historic settings.

1981, but this is not symptomatic of its economic status. In contrast to the population statistics, the number of businesses there jumped from 38 in 1971 to 101 in 1986; a 166 percent increase. This is the largest growth in businesses of any place that we have visited in Nova Scotia, but a look at the detailed data shows why it is so great. Overall, retail activities are up by 45 percent from 1971, being led by new restaurants, food stores and variety stores. There were six motel or bed and breakfast establishments in 1986 where none had existed in 1971 according to the directories. Along the main street, delicatessens, fashionable clothing stores, galleries and gift shops faithfully reflect the town's increasing importance as a tourist destination.

Given the sea, the fort, the historic homes and the large, elegant hotels in old homes, Annapolis Royal has many advantages. These attractions are combined with the entrepreneurial talents of those promoting the local theatre, with the development of a new shopping complex on the main street and with the energy of amateur historians who oversee the restoration of important buildings. Site, situation, history and local enterprise have all combined to give Annapolis Royal an encouraging economic outlook for the future. Will it ultimately suffer the fate of Niagara-on-the-Lake and be spoiled by its own success? True, it is much farther from major concentrations of population than its Ontario counterpart, but it is on a major tourist route around Nova Scotia. What will happen if it is really "discovered" by Americans from the heavily populated Eastern Seaboard? This pleasant settlement might be just on the brink of major economic development from tourism.

We leave Annapolis Royal and drive over the wide causeway across the Annapolis River, now bathed in the warm rays of the sun, to the Nova Scotia government's Tidal Power Project. Here water from the immense Fundy tides is harnessed as it ebbs and flows through the specially designed generation station. It is hoped that this prototype will be a model for many economically viable tidal power plants which will take advantage of the highest tides in the world. The designers have created a display area for visitors, where the project is explained, and a fishway to allow striped bass to pass through and avoid the turbines. Some believe that the project, unfortunately, is ad-

There are six motel or bed and breakfast establishments in Annapolis Royal, each reflecting the town's increasing importance as a tourist destination.

versely affecting local shellfish production. Nevertheless it is a monument to modern technology, in striking contrast to the pioneer habitation at Port Royal a few kilometers down the road.

After a quick tour of the power project, we spend the afternoon at the magnificently restored fort and living quarters at Port Royal. It is a thrill to be greeted by bilingual guides wearing wooden shoes and authentic costumes from the 1600s. This settlement is in some ways the culmination of our trip, simply because it is the oldest permanent white settlement north of the Gulf of Mexico. We enter and prowl through bedrooms containing wooden bunk beds and rough wool blankets, clothes carefully hung for the night. In the kitchen, cooking pots, utensils and dishes are ready to be used. The main storeroom contains pelts of fox, beaver and wolf. But the real treat lies in the meeting room. Here in 1607, Marc Lescarbot wrote and produced the first play, *The Order of Neptune*, for the members of the new world's first social club, The Order of Good Cheer.

We survey the long table, carefully laid out with pewter plate, goblets and candelabra. One can imagine that cold night beside a roaring fire, snow swirling off the sea, winds licking eagerly at the windows, while Champlain, deMonts and their company laughed and sang. Then the play began, lit by oil lamp and candle. The players would strut and fret their hour upon the stage for their increasingly inebriated audience. When the performance was over, all joined in the merriment, the only solution to surviving a winter in this cold bleak land, thousands of kilometers away from friends and family. But what a night it was; everyone filled with food, drama, music and wine. That night the beds would not feel as cold and hard as they had last night,and would again the next.

Unfortunately, the merriment in this little outpost of civilization was short-lived. They had managed to endure with assistance from friendly local Indians, fish from the sea, their meagre supplies from home and a few crops. But all was in vain, in spite of the elaborate social organization and sturdy fort. Everything, including Champlain's garden and "Promenade" was destroyed utterly by a marauding expedition from Virginia. Once again, the old French-English rivalry put an end to a noble settlement experiment in the New World. After

1621, when all Acadia was granted to Sir William Alexander by King James 1, the country was renamed Nova Scotia. In 1625 the Scottish rebuilt the fort at Port Royal in an attempt to colonize the area. Somewhat ironically, the expedition failed miserably and the site was abandoned. The French may have had the last laugh! Today, what was truly a "dying village" stands proud and restored; a place where we all can experience our pioneer roots and appreciate the suffering of the earliest settlers of this land.

Thanks to Parks Canada and to its location just a bit off the beaten track, Port Royal has not yet been overrun by commercial development. True, there are some bed and breakfast establishments nearby, but no motel or fast food strip. Given its proximity to Annapolis Royal, it will probably increase its attraction for visitors, most of whom will choose to stay and eat across the river in the larger community. Geography and good management have conspired to preserve Port Royal just as it was in the past. Having enjoyed this legacy to the full, we leave, heading onwards towards Halifax and back again to the twentieth century.

Geography and good management have conspired to preserve Port Royal. This is a restoration of L'Habitation de Port Royal as it was in 1605.

CHAPTER NINE

Around The Atlantic Coast: History, Tradition And Tourism

We leave the oldest permanent white settlement north of the Gulf of Mexico with a profound sense of history. At Port Royal it almost seemed possible to relive the ordeals of the Acadians in this cold and hostile land. The experience has left us with a renewed desire to discover our history and heritage. Down the road, we are to encounter even more of this heritage, but in a very different setting and in an entirely different manner. We press on, eager to reach our next destination. It is late afternoon, but the June sun is still high, so we head south, or is it west? In this part of Nova Scotia it's hard to tell. In any event, we take Highway 1 towards Yarmouth, hoping to find a scenic spot where we can eat a seafood dinner and have a room with a view. The road winds through that combination of woods and water that is so characteristic of Nova Scotia.

We drive through a few miles of dense pine forest, over a rise, catch a glimpse of sun on sea, cross a stream, skirt an inlet, pass three docks, fishing boats and a tiny settlement hugging the shore. Then we are back into the woods, creeping around more bends, up and down hills, only to discover the former scene in another variation; this time with a sandy beach and cottages instead of a rocky shore. Each tiny settlement has a small dock, a few houses and little prospect of growth. Here tradition lingers. The legacy of the built environment and local physical beauty keeps these places alive, but surrounded as they are by sea and forest, most have little prospect of change. Only those that are more accessible to a large population will be altered to any great degree. The others will no doubt remain as they have been for years; quiet, beautiful and isolated – inhabited by a few active or retired fishermen and the occasional tradesman.

We drive on and the country opens up. Here near New Edinburgh and St. Bernard, the land has long ago been cleared and people are farming. Warm slanting rays of the sun skitter off the water, outlining the increasingly frequent harbours and luring us on. Now we pass lines of homes on both sides of the road. Neat, colourful, white, green, red and blue clapboard, some with steep front gables, others square and boxy. The stone church on our right reaches heavenward, calling its faithful to worship on a Saturday night. It seems big enough to be in a major city, somehow out of place on this sleepy shore.

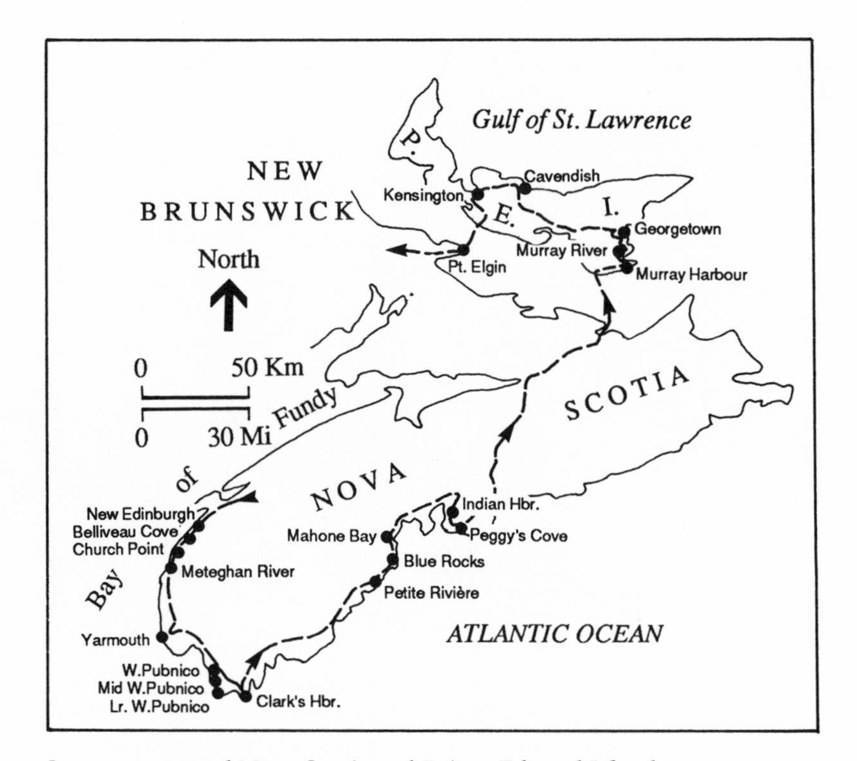

Our route around Nova Scotia and Prince Edward Island.

We coast down a long hill towards a general store/marina. Beside the road, a sign for a clambake causes us to stop abruptly. The enterprising proprietor of the general store and marina has set up a huge pot of boiling water and is cooking clams to order. Round tables with sun umbrellas beside the sea immediately recall a similar scene in Sesimbra, Portugal. This is too good to be true. The tang of sea air and anticipation of a feast of succulent bivalves is enough to bring the memories vividly back.

We sit under the umbrella and a young man proceeds to take heap after heap of steaming clams and pile them into a pyramid on large paper plates. He is very friendly, so we quiz him about this delightful spot. His name is Guy McCauley and he is 19 years old. He was working for Michael Belliveau, the owner of the store/marina when they decided that a continuous clam bake would attract considerable business, especially during the tourist season. Today Guy has boiled up many dozen, and trade is brisk in the warm sun. Yesterday, they were rained out. We inquire about the huge church in the background and Guy tells us that it is Roman Catholic, giving spiritual guidance to the many Acadians along this stretch of coast.

Soon a young woman joins us and enters into the discussion. She has

We sit under an umbrella eating clams and learning about the history of Belliveau Cove from Guy McCauley and his mother.

lived here for years and is also Acadian, despite her married surname, McCauley. We ask whether she is Guy's sister, but she smiles slyly and reveals that she is his mother. We can't believe it. She looks about twenty-five. They tell us that this is Belliveau Cove, an Acadian settlement going back to 1768. In that year, Joseph Dugas loaded all his possessions on a horse, and accompanied by his pregnant wife and small daughter followed Indian trails from Annapolis Royal to the site of the magnificent church which has already caught our attention. Their trip ended thirteen years of wandering, a result of the English expulsion of all Acadians from the Annapolis area.

In 1755, the British marched into the Acadian villages without warning, destroyed their homes and proclaimed orders for their deportation. Some were herded into boats and sent back to France, others were scattered along the Atlantic coast to New England, and others eked out a living on the uninhabited rocky shores of Nova Scotia. This was a sad fate for the pioneers who diked the tidal marshlands and successfully farmed the lands which they reclaimed. They were innocent victims of a senseless and seemingly endless conflict between England and France. Some who were not so lucky just starved in the forests or perished during the winter.

When peace was declared in 1768, some of the Acadians returned, only to find their fertile farms in the Annapolis Valley occupied by hostile English settlers. Like Joseph Dugas, they were forced to trek through the woods in order to find new sites to begin their lives again. When Dugas came to this area, he constructed a rough log shelter in which his wife gave birth twelve days after their arrival. Soon Jean Belliveau, Pierre LeBlanc and many others travelled the three hundred miles on foot from New England to try their luck in their old homeland. The first few years were tough. Dense woods grew right down to the shore and the settlers had neither axes nor farm implements. Long narrow tracts, fronting on the sea, enabled each family to have access to salt marshes where they could grow hay for cattle, to the ocean for clams or fish and to the forests for fuel and building material. Every family head was granted 80 acres, with an additional 20 for each member of the family.

Jean Belliveau established this part of the settlement where we now sit with Guy and his mother, proud descendants of these brave pioneers who endured so much. Although young, Guy has studied the local history and is determined to keep the culture alive. Both he and his mother are fluently bilingual. We sit and talk with them and eat clams. The sun is now sliding towards a cloudless horizon, but this is too interesting to cut short. Guy laments the fact that some English influence is diluting the Acadian traditions here, but he remains optimistic about the future.

"We are friendly and close in Belliveau Cove," he says with a smile. "If you have a car breakdown, you can knock on any door and they will help you out. In fact, most people here will offer you a meal and a ride to the nearest garage. Our difficult history has taught us that everyone benefits if we all cooperate. There is no room for rivalry or too much competition. We remember the past and how hard it was to get where we are now."

How difficult it must have been in those early days. Tools, farm implements, fishing gear, boats -- all had to be made by hand from the materials available. Fortunately, there was no shortage of wood or game in the forests. The settlers soon discovered the grosses coques, or bar clams, enormous and succulent, which abounded in the offshore bars revealed by the low tides. Fishing was done at first by traps, weirs and cages; later by boats and nets. With some arable upland for crops, salt marshes for hay, the sea,and hard work, the returned Acadians gradually moved from subsistence to reasonable comfort to prosperity.

By 1790 a solid line of settlements stretched from New Edinburgh to Meteghan. Sawmills lined the shore, exporting lumber far and wide. Small shipyards built fishing boats and vessels for voyages on the sea. Everywhere the people co-operated to create a new life from the ashes of the old. On this sunny Saturday afternoon, sitting with their descendants, we can almost hear the ring of the axe and rapid French speech of the original Acadians.

Today, Belliveau Cove is a straggle of houses and business enterprises along the shore of St. Mary's Bay. It is locally known for wood carving and is home to 404 people. The sea is still important, and harvesting grosses coques remains a part time occupation for many, and a full time business for others. Mussels are gathered from the rocks along the Meteghan River, while periwinkles are found almost everywhere that receding tides expose rocky shores. Further along at Meteghan harbour, scal-

The church at St. Bernard, like its medieval counterparts is a symbol of faith and early prosperity along this Acadian coast.

lop diggers, trawlers, herring seiners, cod and lobster fishermen continue their traditional ocean fishing. Given the linear development along this coast, it is difficult to determine where one place begins and another ends. The marina/general store and a garage are located in Belliveau Cove, while real estate agents, hairdressers, and a bakery are not far away. The residents of this area have now begun to promote tourism vigorously, offering local delicacies such as Pâté à la Râpure (Rappie Pie), a special potato dumpling stuffed with meat or seafood. Given the scenery and Acadian traditions, it appears that they will be successful.

Before visiting the Acadian cemetery at Major Point, we head back to check out the church, a symbol, like its medieval European counterparts, of faith and prosperity in times past. It was begun in 1910, but only finished in 1942. The massive fieldstone steeple towers over us and dominates the settlement of St. Bernard. We marvel that such a grand edifice can be supported by what seems like so few people, but it is obviously functioning and in good repair. It is similar to the larger and more elaborate churches that one finds in now almost deserted hamlets in rural France. Man's symbolism and faith endures, both in Europe and along this Nova Scotia coast. The difference here is that the local churches continue to be filled by the faithful, augmented in the summer by tourists and travellers.

We double back and follow the estuary beside the marina. The tide is out, stranding boats like beached whales on the slippery damp floor of the empty stream. They sit, all awkward and askew, impotent for now, but eagerly awaiting the inevitable coming of high tide. Beyond, on the flats, clam diggers lean and kneel in the sand, buckets in hand, collecting a meal or harvesting a crop to sell. Their outlines against black sand and distant water form a picture that burns indelibly into our memories. This is the real thing; man and the ocean co-operating to sustain a culture and an economy. Our reverie is broken by the nasty snarl of an all terrain vehicle roaring up the bank. It is driven by a grizzled Acadian lugging bushels of grosses coques. This is the modern way: noisy but efficient. At least the ATV is being used for a productive purpose. All too often it is the instrument of destruction of woods or dunes at the hands of some indolent teen with more money than brains.

The road to the cemetery follows a stream along its delta to the sea. A track might be a better name for the route we follow. Our progress is impeded, first by deep ruts, some filled with water. Then boulders the size of grapefruit become the surface of the road.

In the Acadian cemetery containing faded tombstones from 1771, a tiny white chapel, no larger than a broom closet stands to commemorate the courageous early pioneers who perished nearby.

Finally overhanging branches clutch like fingers at the car and screech along its sides. Between bushes and brambles we can still see the stream, now orange and pink in the setting sun. Across the fields, a log grouping of Acadian barns stands as it has for centuries. In this quiet corner of Nova Scotia, agribusiness had not yet come to eradicate all the rural artifacts of the past. Most remain intact, much to the delight of settlement explorers such as us.

Halfway to the end of the delta, a tiny white chapel, no larger than a broom closet, stands in the midst of a clearing, now partly overgrown. There, badly weathered and leaning on crazy angles we find four tombstones. Their inscriptions have long since been obliterated by years of exposure to the elements, except for the date 1771 remaining on one as a faint scratch. A plaque in the chapel carries an inscription informing us that this cemetery was established in 1769, and that Marie Doucet was buried here in 1771. The first mass at the chapel was conducted in 1888.

Even earlier in 1755, 120 Acadians who escaped from Major John Handfield at Port Royal spent the winter in this bleak, isolated spot. With that group was Pierre Belliveau, father of John who later founded Belliveau Cove, the site of our clam bake with Guy and his mother. Somehow we feel that we have discovered this little piece of history all by ourselves. We are pleased and satisfied.

Having experienced a bit of history first hand, we continue our trip along this fascinating Acadian shore. We cross another estuary and soon descend a long gentle grade. There ahead against the background of deep blue and green, we spot the graceful spire of St. Mary's Church, thrusting into the darkening sky. Once again we are tempted to stop and explore. How can such a grand edifice exist in such a rural locatio? And how can they build a church of cathedral-like proportions out of wood? We meet the kind old verger who is just leaving, but insists on giving us a tour of the church and its museum.

The first chapel on this site was built in 1786. The promontory which stretched out into St. Mary's Bay thereafter became known as Church Point. Several subsequent churches were built here and then destroyed by fire. From 1820 to 1829, the "Grande Église" was constructed, only to be replaced in 1903 by the even larger building that we now admire. It is 190 feet long and 135 feet wide. The steeple originally rose to 212 feet, but was struck by lightning in 1916, losing 30 feet before the rain put out the blaze. Divine intervention, some said. The details of its construction were supervised by a master carpenter, Leo Melanson, who could neither read nor write, but could follow plans. This magnificent, ornate church is listed in Ripley's *Believe it or Not* as the largest wooden building in North America. Much of the interior and the stained glass windows were brought from France. Beside it stands Université St. Anne, established by Eudist Fathers in 1890. It is now the centre of Acadian culture and the only French University in the province. Not bad for the 400 Acadian families in the Parish of St. Mary's, Municipality of Clare, Nova Scotia. Their determination and enterprise have endured in both cultural and physical manifestations.

We drop a suitable donation into the museum collection box, thank the verger for his tour and head back to the car. In a way, this church and our stop at Belliveau Cove personify the French Coast of Nova Scotia. Gentle people, history, tradition; settlements strung out along the shore like jewels on a necklace, thickening only at a church or estuary. The closest parallel which we have encountered was in Quebec along the St. Lawrence where a similar settlement pattern was developed by people from the same country.

What a surprise when we walk out of the church into the gloom of thick, damp, grey fog. The maritime climate has struck again; this time with almost impenetrable mist that rolls over the land, obscuring the church almost to the top of its tall steeple. We continue south along the shore, following a road that hugs the cliffs as if tacked on to their sides, and skirting bay after bay filled with enormous, succulent clams. Up from the water come even more silent grey fingers of fog. Now we are driving through an occluded green thickness that could have been split pea soup. It creeps up from the ocean as if on foot, filling a gully here and opening for a moment on a rise. Visibility continues to decrease.

We come to a small bridge crossing an estuary. The tide is out and here the fog has lifted slightly. There on the bank, stranded like

At the Meteghan River, soft light of a dim sun filters through the fog briefly to illuminate the forms of the boats huddled in upon the shore. There on the bank, stranded like ghost pirate ships are several steel fishing boats waiting for repairs.

ghost pirate ships from the past, are several steel fishing boats waiting for repairs. The soft light of a low sun filters through the fog briefly to illuminate the dim forms of the boats huddled in upon the shore. Behind, gaunt metal arms of cranes reach up and out towards the obscured sky, waiting for daylight and some useful work. Beneath the bridge, currents eddy and swirl, their luminescent froth pulling and pushing at the pylons holding the bridge. Rickety wooden buildings, corroded iron rails and peeling white paint can barely be seen in the shipyard beyond. Somehow this scene captures the very essence of the struggle between man and sea, man and climate, man and nature. Thoughts of French pioneers flood back. We linger and look until the creeping night forces us on to seek shelter and a bed.

About twenty minutes later we reach our destination for the night, tired but content. Now we have a real feel for the contribution of the Acadians to our heritage. We will never forget the McCauleys, the little chapel at Major Point, or St. Mary's Church on Church Point. It has been a memorable day. We settle into our comfortable bed, elated that we personally have experienced a bit of Canadian history without the benefit of a display by Parks Canada. Happy and contented, we curl up and sleep peacefully, snug and warm as snails in their shells.

Next morning we set off in the rain. Thunder rattles our windows which won't clear of mist, and the rain continues to assault the car. It bangs upon the roof, then pelts and pecks, finally subsiding to a steady soft patter that dampens our spirits and obscures the road. Well, today we will make time. No sense in exploring in this murky mess. We pass Salmon River, Hebron; Yarmouth (where we inspect the harbour in the rain) Tusket, Eel Brook, Central Argyle and Argyle. Then we notice a peninsula lined by Pubnico, West Pubnico, Middle West Pubnico and Lower West Pubnico. This is intriguing, so we deviate east to have a look. When the Red Cap Motel and Diner in Middle West (the locals refer to the Pubnicos as West, Middle West, Lower West) comes into view, we stop.

Across from us sit a group of young Acadians, obviously recounting stories of last night's party, laughing and slapping their thighs for emphasis. We listen closely and discover a new language. Is it Franglais, or

In the Pubnicos, the fishing fleets still ply the water, the processing plants pack and ship the catches, and the French language is alive and well.

Fracadian, or Encadian? We never do find out, but it is the most delightful blend of English, Classical French and Québecois that we have ever heard. The menu reflects this easy tri-lingualism, so it is simple to order clam chowder and lobster sandwiches. Never have we eaten such thick, creamy, clam-filled chowder and such sweet fresh lobster. How did they do it away out here? The waitress satisfies our curiosity by telling us that everything comes fresh from the fish plant across the road each morning. Our luck has held. Once again we have discovered a culinary gem in the middle of a road leading nowhere.

The Pubnicos still rely on fishing for their livelihood, but now a few tourists have come to augment the economy. A motel, restaurant, service station and numerous wharfs reflect both the old and the new economies. Between them, the Pubnicos now house about 700 residents in structures that date back to the Acadian settlement in 1653. Here in the oldest Acadian settlements in the province, culture, heritage and way of life have been preserved. The fishing fleets still ply the waters, the processing plants pack and ship the catches and the French language is alive and well, even if somewhat diluted by English.

The rain has diminished to a steady scotch mist by the time we leave and turn towards Clark's Harbour. This settlement was first established by the French in 1758 and then destroyed by the British. Now most of its people are descendants of pioneers from Nantucket and Cape Cod who came after 1760. In the drizzle, it turns out to be a typical sprawling fishing village; economically viable, unspoiled, but not particularly conducive to a long stay. This is a working community, not a tourist resort.

Docks, fish sheds, boat builders and lobster traps are everywhere, as are the homes of the fisherman. All the rocky, narrow roads seem to lead to clusters of houses near the water which are surrounded by boats and drying nets. Somehow, we just can't grasp this amorphous, scattered settlement, and there is certainly no place to stay. But then this is the quintessential Nova Scotia fishing village, and the statistics prove it, as does its built environment.

The number of businesses listed in the directories for this foggy stop is 65 in 1981; a 170 percent increase over the number in 1971.

By far the greatest gain was made in the fishing category, with the one enterprise noted in 1971 increasing to 16 by 1986. Next are fish-processing plants which increased from none in 1971 to seven in 1986. Of course, these statistics do not include the smallest independent fishermen or fish processors, neither of which were listed at either year. We count dozens of houses with fishing gear in their yards, and over 30 fishing boats at the three large docks. Today the importance of the fishery cannot be overestimated, for a number of the plants are very large and have their own docks. Along with the fisheries are the boat builders. The three that we observe range from a tiny one-man enterprise to a major business employing five or ten people. Everywhere we see evidence of the overwhelming importance of the sea and its rich bounty of fish in Clark's Harbour.

Despite an appearance of prosperity, with many new cars and well maintained homes, the population of Clark's Harbour declined by 23 to 1059 between 1971 and 1981. In years gone by, it fluctuated from 965 in 1921 to 887 in 1941 and then back down to 945 in 1961. Variations in the prosperity of the local fishery no doubt account for many of its population changes. Given the rather utilitarian, somewhat messy environment, where houses sprawl across rocks and nestle on the few level patches of land, we can see why people will probably live here only if they work here as well. Aside from the sea and rock, there are few attractions for retirees or tourists. In fact, one of the local grocery stores has closed and the motel lies deserted and in ruins. With the modern fishing and processing techniques that are obviously in use, a healthy fishing industry can function quite efficiently with fewer employees than before.

We take a few photos and leave, disappointed that our preconceived images have been shattered. On the other hand, we have experienced a true fishing village; one that provides the appropriate facilities for the local economy with no frills or concessions to tourists. This is the other side of the Nova Scotia economy. No mill, no railway, no fancy restaurant, no commuters, few retirees except for aging fisherman who frequent their local club -- here the sea is king and we feel like interlopers. And yet this is the essence of much of the province, both today and in the past. Safe harbours, ships, fishing, constant struggles with the weather, the riches and ravages of the sea -- all have combined to produce classic Nova Scotia fishing villages, changed little from 200 years ago. Yet this is the Nova Scotia of today; efficient, mechanized and

Blue Rocks. In its own way, this is as beautiful as the fog shrouded inlet of two nights ago.

carrying on the historic occupation, albeit with the most modern equipment that technology can provide.

Next day we drive on, passing tiny tree-ringed lagoons containing small wharfs and fishing sheds. The road winds and twists, following every indentation of the deeply incised coast, joining harbours and inlets like a chain of blue amethysts. What a change from a just few hours earlier -- that maritime climate is at work again. It is now almost hot under the relentless June sun that hangs above us like a giant orange orb. The green of trees fringing the sea sets off the choppy turquoise water capped by tiny peaks of white.

We reach Petite Rivière which was settled in the 1630s by the French. It now boasts a general store, service station, post office, a large new marine supply outlet and several artists' studios. Nearby is a sparkling white beach fringed by cottages and a few permanent residences. The friendly station attendant where we stop for gas serves us coffee with our fill-up and reminisces about her stint in Ontario.

Come to think of it, half the people we meet here seem to have lived in Ontario at one time or another, only to return to the tranquillity and slower pace of life in the Maritimes. A lady in Shelburne has also returned from Ontario and has no intention of going back. Friendliness, a sense of place and superb quality of life lured her back to her Atlantic roots. The other thing that strikes us in this area is what sounds like American accents. Every other person here sounds as if he or she is from Boston or at least from somewhere in Massachusetts. Of course it is the Loyalist influence. Even after several hundred years, the residents of these relatively isolated settlements have retained their original accents.

We head to La Have, hoping to catch the ferry without a half hour wait. We are in luck. Just as we arrive the gates close, we pay our 50 cents and are hauled by cable on a modern craft across the inlet between us and Mahone Bay. What good fortune; now we will arrive in the village in time to look carefully for accommodation and relax before dinner. But, once again, the spirit of adventure and exploration takes over. This time, a small but delightful diversion delays our arrival at our ultimate destination for the night.

On the way along the estuary to Mahone Bay we pass through Lunenburg, one of the true marine towns on this coast. It seems that every other shop sells maritime supplies, boats, fishing gear or navigation equipment. Driving up and down its hilly, narrow streets we pass historic homes and intriguing restaurants. This will be a stop on our next trip, but today we want to visit Blue Rocks before we reach Mahone Bay. The Nova Scotia guide book states that Blue Rocks is a mecca for painters and photographers. It is only a few miles, the light is warm and low, and we have to see it for ourselves.

Soon we have followed the coast to a point where trees and grass are replaced by banded, folded gneiss running right down to the water. Here, little tidal pools filled with orange seaweed shelter coyly behind weather-beaten boulders covered by lichens draped over them like green doilies. Water laps lazily against bleached cedar docks piled high with lobster traps and fishing gear. One solitary fishing shack, its rough-hewn boards warped and pulling away from rusty nails stands sentinel on a tiny rocky island in the cove. A few houses cling to the rough pre-cambrian rocks, guarding the harbour and adding colours of white, red, green and blue to the scene. We have discovered the picture-perfect fishing village, free of commercial development but redolent with the life and feel of the sea. Almost all its inhabitants are fishermen like their ancestors for decades before. The goods and services that they require can easily be obtained in nearby Lunenburg. But how soon is this secluded gem to be discovered by masses of yuppies, dinks and retirees? Already it is well known to artists and photographers. We linger, taking photographs and observing until the sun passes behind some clouds. In its own way, this is as beautiful as the fog-shrouded inlet of two nights ago.

Three churches greet us when we eventually enter Mahone Bay from the south. They stand in a row at the end of the bay, United, Lutheran and Anglican, competing for the faithful and for the best site in town. Along the road into the village, we pass several tourist homes and a fancy restaurant. The docks in the harbour are shared by fishing boats and pleasure craft. Main street has more than its share of antique and fabric shops. We have stumbled

Three churches greet us when we eventually enter Mahone Bay from the south. They stand in a row at the end of the bay; United, Lutheran and Anglican, competing for the faithful and the best site in town.

upon another Elora, this time catering to Halagonians instead of to Torontonians. The pace of life here seems more like that of Ontario than what we have experienced during the last few days. People throng the streets and the stores are packed with merchandise for tourists. We have returned from our historical sojourn with the Acadians to the reality of modern life in Nova Scotia. We can almost feel the difference, and we aren't entirely sure that we approve.

In the evening we explore the waterfront of what is obviously a town with enormous potential for growth. By the time we reach the dock, the sky is a pale orange canvas reflected by the flat glassy water of the bay. Not a wave stirs or laps on this perfectly still June evening. In the distance, three steeples reach toward the star-filled heavens, framing silhouettes of sailboats bobbing gently on the water. Darker and darker falls the night. Then a faint glimmer like the edge of mother of pearl appears on the horizon. It is the moon, rising to compete with the setting sun and sparkling stars for its rightful place in the sky. We linger and walk beside the ever-changing scene. Next day we speak at length with the proprietor of our bed and breakfast accommodation, Shirley McKenzie.

"I'm fairly typical" she says. "Here on the edge of the Canadian economy, we have to hedge our bets. When I moved back, I bought this house and the barn out back. Since I majored in history, I had a vast collection of books that I could no longer store, so I started the Book Barn as a used-book business. Then I decided that I may as well take in guests, so the bed and breakfast business evolved. I'm a trained accountant, and soon people were asking me to do their books. At tax time it's frantic, but for much of the year I manage all three jobs quite nicely."

"Are you really typical?" we ask. "I think so. We're close enough to Halifax to get lots of commuters, but even more who just want to get away from the city. There's a former professor across the way who now lives by doing custom woodwork. A number of people combine fishing in the summer with lumbering in the winter. Several others look after yuppie property or do odd jobs for commuters. A number of the proprietors of the craft shops practise other professions in the winter. And many of the local ladies do hand sewing all year

Since 1971, the number of local businesses in Mahone Bay had increased by a striking 182 percent. Many now cater to the affluent crowd from Halifax. Have we discovered the Bayfield of Nova Scotia?

round for Suttles and Seawinds, one of our largest local employers. They started as a cottage industry in New Germany, but moved to Mahone Bay a number of years ago. Now their handmade skirts, quilts, dresses and blouses are sold all over the country. Their country styles are beautiful and quite unique. Yes, we're a mixed and resourceful lot."

"But how well do people seem to do?" we ask.
"Well, if property prices or restaurant business are any criterion, I think very well. The demand for accommodation has increased lately. Some people want to retire here, others want to use it as a base for commuting and others want to make a living here. We're not yet as upscale as Chester, but take a look into the shops or at the restaurant menus. They certainly don't cater only to local people."

Of course she is right. Mahone Bay is becoming an important local community in its own right and a commuter dormitory. The bay, trees, quiet beauty and accessibility have conspired to improve its fortunes immensely. Recent widespread appreciation of amenities, small towns, friendly people and economic opportunity from unconventional sources have hit Mahone Bay with a bang. Fishermen in the summer become electricians in the winter; several "burned-out' professors are running organic farms; a writer and painter live and work in small but comfortable quarters. Since 1971, the number of local businesses has increased by 62, or a striking 182 percent. Population, now 1228, decreased slightly from 1971 to 1981, but is beginning to catch up to the businesses which have already derived much benefit from tourists and peripheral commuters. We notice advertisements for houses ranging from $76,500 for a modest structure on three acres, to $119,000 for a modern two-storey home on the ocean. This is a far cry from prices in Halifax, a hundred kilometers away, but lot prices of $40,000 to $60,000 for those with water access are a sign of things to come.

From Mahone Bay, Halifax is an easy drive, so we set out about noon after purchasing several varieties of smoked fish from a local fisherman's truck. We must at least stop at Peggy's Cove, that most photographed fishing village in Canada, and we do. It is pretty as advertised, but thronging with people, even in June. It is one of Nova Scotia's premier tourist attractions, now designated as a preservation area. Many of its inhabitants continue to fish from its rugged shores, but they have been overwhelmed by the tourist industry. The lighthouse which dominates the rocky granite coast no longer operates except as a subject for thousands of photographers each year.

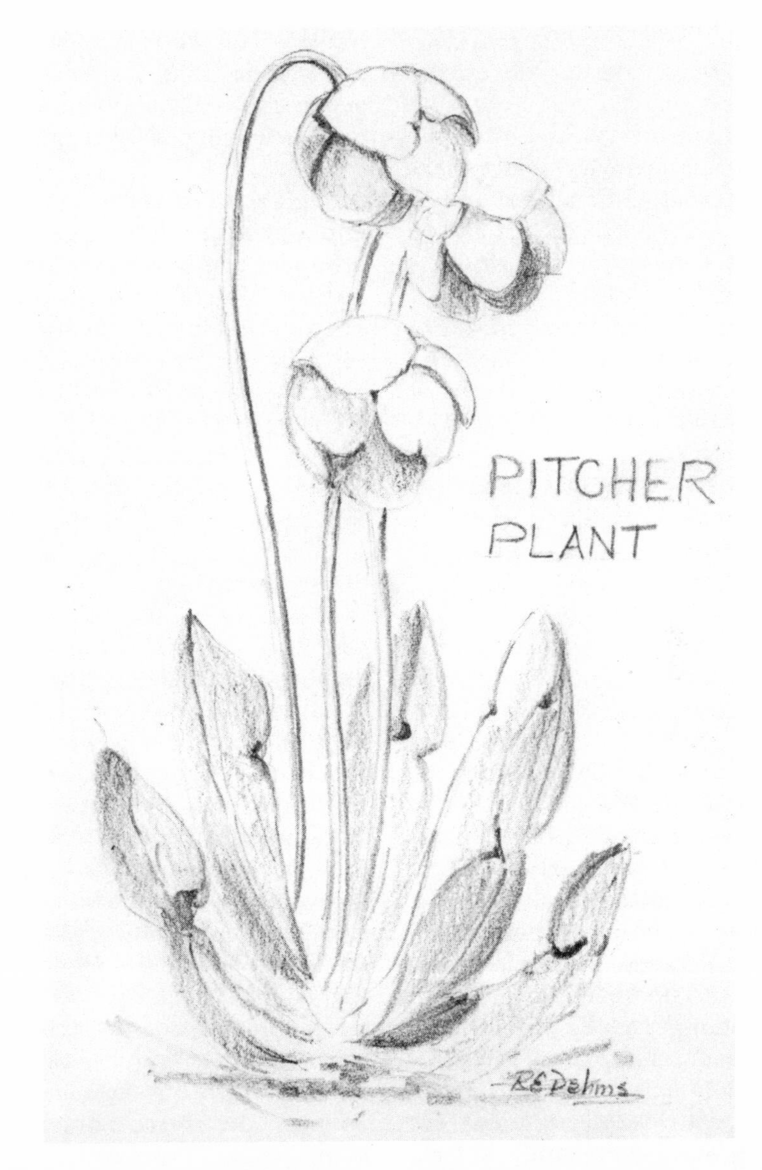

Restaurants, gift shops and guided tours have all taken advantage of the quaint architecture and spectacular physical setting of this once quiet and isolated hamlet. Today, only the population statistics and small jetties reflect its former status as a fishing port. The number of people who call it home increased to 90 in 1971 from 60 in 1966, only to decline again to 54 in 1981. The local fisherman remain, but they are outnumbered by those who cater to the tourist in the gift shop and restaurant. Now, throngs of visitors on day trips from Halifax along with others from all over the world almost overrun it on any day with reasonably pleasant weather. Despite its scenic grandeur and the fact that no new development has been allowed, Peggy's Cove has already been spoiled by overexposure and popularity. We compare Peggy's Cove to Niagara on the Lake; still extremely attractive in the off-season, but far too congested for our taste whenever the weather is pleasant. Success has almost spoiled another formerly "dying village". Will this too be the fate of Elora and Bayfield?

We pass some lovely white cottages on the road to Peggy's Cove and return on the off chance that they will have a vacancy so late in the day. Lover's Lane Cottages at Indian Harbour sit on a grassy knoll overlooking a tiny inlet with two fishing docks in the foreground and a lighthouse in the distance. To us this is perfection. The grounds are beautifully manicured, festooned with flowers and a vegetable garden. Roseville and Helen Hubley, the proprietors, take great pride in providing a warm welcome to their spotless housekeeping cottages. Here, just five minutes from Peggy's Cove is a scenic and unspoiled section of the Nova Scotia coast. Transportation again plays a key role, since we are beyond Peggy's Cove for those coming from Halifax, and the majority just never bother to drive this extra half kilometer. True, in this hamlet of 318, there are gift shops, an art gallery, a lobster pound, a motel and a restaurant, but the crowds are absent and the commercial enterprises are widely spaced. Here on the western side of the peninsula, the homes and lives of fishermen are predominant. Early every morning from a dock just below our window, a fishing dory putt putts out to sea to take its daily catch.

The igneous rocks along the peninsula are what really make this area interesting. Unlike much of the Nova Scotia coast, they roll down here to the sea, sparsely covered by scrub and lichens. Smooth granites and gneiss dip gently into the water in places and fall abruptly as cliffs at others. Crags and clefts form perfect shelters for fisherman at the cove itself and here at Indian Harbour. Proximity to Halifax makes this whole scenic area a premiere tourist attraction.

We sit on the rocks to watch the sunset, determined to explore next morning. It dawns cool and bright, just right for a stroll past the marshes beside the road to the rocky shore. We pick our way carefully across the boggy moss and brambles, passing pink lady slippers, pitcher plants and juniper bushes. In the air above, gulls and terns swoop and sail, using the updrafts like gliders to lift them gracefully towards the clouds. A song sparrow trills happily while two yellow finches rush past close to our heads. On the ground we examine black, orange and grey lichens, tiny boletus mushrooms, partridge berries and weathered gneiss. Nearer the water, tiny sea creatures swim and float in tidal pools which eddy to and fro. At the shore, sleek smooth swells swirl towards the rocks, pause, break with a roar and dash furiously against the granite. Time and time again the scene is repeated, each with a slightly different pattern, each with more beauty than the last. The infinite variety of the waves in this sea hypnotizes and transfixes us. We sit in the sun and gaze, too fascinated to move and save ourselves from the sunburns that we will inevitably acquire.

At night we look across the rocks and harbour, where the sun produces yet another stunning display to accompany our meal. This time it settles slowly through a thin haze of cirro-stratus clouds hugging the horizon. First the sun becomes a fiery red ball casting a narrow path of flaming red across the water. Then the light diffuses, softens and spreads to the filmy clouds. What a display; pink at the edges melting imperceptibly to shades of orange and yellow near the apex. Tips of waves catch the tints, transforming them into splashes of incandescence dancing on the ocean. Slowly the hues darken and change; deeper reds, scarlets; azure above and then a flagrant blaze of glory when the sun succumbs and finally falls below the water. Darker solid colours of night without shape or shadow spill over the scene. The sun is gone; a fitting and spectacular finish to our stay at Indian Harbour and a reminder that nature in the form of its scenic splendour is a powerful economic force in this part of Nova Scotia.

The last leg of this trip takes us to another island; this time to that low red slab named after Prince Edward. Unlike the other island province, Newfoundland, which is a folded puzzle containing some of the oldest rocks on the globe, P.E.I. is relatively young and straightforward. That is if you consider the Triassic period about 250 million years ago recent. Compared to much of Newfoundland, P.E.I. is both youthful and geologically simple. Its soft sedimentary sandstones have eroded into rich, deep, red soil which characterizes so much of the Island. Here, agriculture is easy, the climate is more benevolent than that in Newfoundland, and the sea is bountiful: nature's recipe for early prosperity and success.

Our luck continues to hold on the trip to P.E.I. When we arrive at Caribou, the Wood Island ferry is ready to leave and we drive on, the last car for the crossing. The low tree-lined shores of sandstone and shale on the island are visible from the ferry. Our first and lasting impression is of a totally manicured landscape, devoid of rocky outcrops except along the shore and covered from sea to sea by crops. Neat, white or cedar-covered barns stand in clusters beside pastures or fields of potatoes. The towns are equally ordered. It is as if someone mows the grass in the fields as well as on the lawns. This is like a tidy, miniature cross between parts of New Zealand and parts of England.

One jarring note is provided by the roads. Anywhere except between the largest places, they seem to be a continuous succession of asphalt patches. We jostle and jolt along, content (indeed forced) to drive at a leisurely 70 kilometers per hour and drink in the signs and scenery. Yes, again like England, everything is signed. Not just places, but bed and breakfast homes, resorts, fishing camps, toy stores, wharfs, gift shops, hotels, general stores and campsites. It would be almost impossible to get lost, even without a map. But if one does, no problem -- less than half a day will takes you almost anywhere on the island, a distinct advantage for the explorer and for the gasoline bill.

We head for the two Murrays; Murray Harbour and Murray River, both of which have experienced mini-business booms over the last ten years. We soon see why. Murray Harbour stretches out in a thin line along the banks of the inlet which shelters numerous modern fishing trawlers and lobster boats. It is completely delightful, with neat freshly painted clap-board houses, the usual general store and a number of craft and antique shops. There has been new residential growth on choice sites along the river and several modern commercial additions. The fishing boats and facilities are spanking clean and modern, exuding prosperity. The lobster season has been good this year and it shows. The population has increased by 20 percent since 1971, from 367 to 443. From 1971 to 1986, there was an increase in businesses from eight to ten. A major addition was commercial mussel production with the attendant processing and shipping. A new antique store and general store are well supplied for tourists and residents alike. Clearly there are a few yuppies and commuters here as in Mahone Bay, and retirement is becoming more important. The village offers numerous sites near the water and ample vacant land for considerable residential development.

Not far along the same road we arrive at Murray River, yet another of these perfect miniature P.E.I. settlements. Here we explore the back streets to find a beautifully restored working grist mill. Its setting is superb; a mill pond dotted with water lilies and fringed by cat tails. Birds swoop from the overhanging trees while a great blue heron stands stoically on one leg in the stream below, patiently awaiting some unsuspecting fish for its supper. The population here has dropped from 478 to 439 since 1971, but some businesses prospered. There were three new agricultural processing enterprises and the same number of recent additions to construction trades. Retail activities have declined slightly since 1971, but there are two new trucking companies in town by 1986. Overall there was a 71 percent increase in businesses listed by the directories from 1971 to 1986. Here, fishing and agricultural processing are providing local employment and saving the settlement from further decline.

Next morning we head to Georgetown, anxious to see whether it is as stagnant as suggested by population fluctuations from 769 in 1941 down to 744 in 1961, up to 767 in 1971 and finally back down to 737 in 1981. Today's population is lower than its total of 831 in 1861. Great plans for this community never quite bore fruit, mainly because of its isolated location. On the other hand, the picture isn't all negative. There had been an 88 percent increase in the number of businesses listed from 1971 to 1986 when the total was 15. Two new fishing businesses and three additional

In Prince Edward Island everything is signed -- not just places, but bed and breakfast homes, resorts, fishing camps, toy stores, gift shops, hotels, general stores and campsites.

In Murray Harbour, the fishing boats and facilities are spanking clean and modern, exuding recent prosperity. The lobster harvest has been good, and it shows.

general stores have begun. Georgetown commands an excellent deep water harbour, has a number of docks, but its main street doesn't appear to be very prosperous. In fact, it houses the tattered remains of what must have been a magnificent hotel and general store, now used for residences. On the waterfront a major industrial complex that was once a fish processing plant went bankrupt because the local fleet supplied insufficient catches. It is being renovated by private enterprise to become a farm to breed trout and Atlantic Salmon. The workmen who show us around are confident that their company will succeed where the government before them has failed. Salmon are both scarce and expensive; an excellent portent for economic success.

The local ship-building industry continues to take advantage of one of the finest deep water harbours on the east coast and is still building ships. There are fishing boats at the wharfs, but in total, Georgetown looks a bit run down. The King's Playhouse offers summer theatre, but the only accommodation is in cabins, in contrast to the numerous tourist homes in other smaller communities. Another look around turns up even more large old homes in need of repair and more derelict businesses. Georgetown obviously has been a victim of changing technology and transportation. In the early years it shipped large amounts of wood, food and agricultural produce, but this business declined with forest depletion and the motor vehicle. Its deep water harbour is no longer such a major asset, local fish stocks are somewhat depleted, and it is a bit off the beaten track. We add it to our list of ill, if not dying, villages. But who knows? Maybe the new fish farm will inject more life into the local economy, and some entrepreneur will really take advantage of its harbour and fishing. The potential is there; only capital, skill and initiative are needed to make it come to life.

On our trip around P.E.I. we must stop to see the Anne of Green Gables House and the enchanted forest. They are all that we expect, but we are warned about the town of Cavendish by the proprietor of the general store in New Glasgow.

"They've ruined that place in the last two years," she says. "Now it's a strip of fast-food outlets, motels, amusement parks and honkey-tonk trash. And the prices are the highest on the island. They're

Georgetown has obviously been a victim of changing technology and transportation. Another look around turns up even more large old homes in need of repair and more derelict businesses.

going to kill the goose that laid the golden egg."

When we arrive we agree with everything she said. The white clapboard home where Lucy Maud Montgomery set the Anne stories is impeccably furnished in period pieces. The grounds are immaculate and the enchanted woods take us right back to our youth. But Cavendish is another story. Not only are there the usual plastic food dispensaries, but also Fantasy Land, King Tut's Tombs, Matthew this and Blithe Spirit that, cottages, motels, ranches and almost anything else one can imagine.

We wonder about the proportion of local people who find employment in all the outsized functions that rely upon the attraction of Anne. In 1961, there were 156 residents, but by 1971, the total had fallen to 86, only to rebound to 93 in 1981. Clearly, this is more a place of employment and enjoyment for outsiders than a residential retreat for local people. On the other hand, there is no doubt that it is one of the major generators of economic activity on the island. The combination of a popular story and careful restoration of a home was the initial attraction. Entrepreneurial initiative has done the rest. Repelled by the blatant commercialism, we get out of the area fast. Only an hour away in Kensington we are to find peace and quiet in a tourist home for half the price of anything in this travellers' jungle. Private enterprise has gone mad in Cavendish, no doubt spurred considerably by the splendid Canadian television production of Anne. Oh well, at least the house and woods have been left alone, guarded forever by the National Park Service.

We drive through more of this bucolic island after our night in Kensington, remarkable mostly for its line of cedar sheds along the tracks, its many churches and its vast farm-implement dealership. This town is the epitome of the quiet rural service centre in Canada's smallest province. It housed 556 souls in 1921 and 884 by 1961, displaying slow but steady growth. While its population had risen from 1,086 to 1,143 between 1971 and 1981, the number of businesses there increased by 140 percent to a total of 108 in 1986. By far the greatest increases in business activity were in the agricultural sector, where the three enterprises in 1971 swelled to 24 in 1986. Field crops, beef, hogs, crop preparation and poultry are among the agribusiness industries that increased the total, but this is to be expected in an area that is primarily rural.

Other sectors of Kensington's economy have derived benefit as well. There are two new agricultural wholesaling businesses, eight additional construction companies and tradesman, four new manufacturing industries and eight additional retail stores. Financial and service businesses increased from none in 1971 to four in 1986. To accommodate travellers, a number of tourist homes offer inexpensive accommodation. This will make a good location from which to visit tourist attractions in almost any part of the island. We stay overnight and then head back towards the ferry at Borden. It is time to return to New Brunswick.

On our first stop on the mainland, we find what appears to be a real dying village at Port Elgin. Other than some of the outports of Newfoundland, this appears to be one of the least prosperous places we have encountered on the trip east. The village has lost population since 1941 and looks it. In that year it housed some 681 souls but declined to 553 by 1971. In 1981, its population stood at only 504, a 26 percent decrease from its 1941 total. The main street is lined by derelict buildings, some boarded up, others falling down. Only the facade of main street Wroxeter seems comparable to this example in the Maritimes. On a Sunday morning it looks like a real ghost town. On the strength of the visual evidence of decline and the population statistics, one might be prepared to write it off. But let's look at the recent business history.

In 1971, the directories listed only eight business enterprises for Port Elgin. These consisted of two general stores, two grocery stores, a car dealer, a repair shop, a variety store and a tradesman. By 1986, there were 26 businesses; an increase of 225 percent, despite the outward signs of decline. What has happened to cause this remarkable change? The first clues are in the local agricultural sector. By 1986, a dairy farm and three general farm operations specializing in livestock were listed, none of which appeared in the 1971 data. Three new tradesmen had set up business and two additional auto sales outlets opened. A building supply company, two new restaurants and two woodworking shops had also appeared. Add to this a Sear's order office, a tourist home, a pharmacy, a consolidated elementary school and a large retirement home in an old house and the picture doesn't look as bleak as it did. Maybe the large school is having the effect here that it had in Ferme Neuve. It certainly gives parents a focal point for activities and a reason to visit

In Port Elgin, the main street is lined by derelict buildings, some boarded up, some falling down. Only the facade of main street Wroxeter seems comparable to this example in the Maritimes.

Port Elgin.

We drive around again and decide that the settlement is not without charm. The river and harbour are picturesque, with a delightful old bridge spanning the water and a lovely vista along the main street. Beside the abandoned railway, the old steam powered mill stands sentinel, its tall chimney intact, and the cedar shag siding in remarkably good repair. Several large old homes along the tracks remind us of the prosperity brought by rail and steam a hundred years ago. Just a kilometer out of town by the sea we discover the ruins of French Fort Gaspareaux, built in 1751 to guard the entrance to the estuary and keep the hated English out.

Port Elgin truly has potential, reflected by a brand new retirement home on the outskirts and by the 1986 business statistics. It is an intriguing combination of past success, present pause and future possibilities. Given its site, situation and physical artifacts, Port Elgin is clearly poised to regain some of its former status. With its location not far from the ferry terminal at Cape Tormentine, there is considerable scope for tourism. All it needs is an ambitious entrepreneur with enough financial backing to open a hotel and restaurant in the old mill. Or someone can promote its picturesque harbour to the artistic crowd. The opportunities are there, and have been reflected by the recent gains in local business activities. A number of large buildings on the main street remain empty or under-utilized, but they can be restored to their former condition and put to good use. So far, the appropriate person has not yet appeared to exploit them.

Somehow it seems fitting that our travels have ended at a community which displays both the outward signs of decline and some recent potential for growth. This almost epitomizes our experiences in the provinces that we have visited. We have seen some real ghost towns in our travels, and a number that clearly declined since the 1800s, but most others combine signs of growth, decline, and most importantly, change. Even where cursory visual inspection and population statistics suggest a bleak future, we find some evidence of change and possible hope for tomorrow. Again and again, one is struck by the diversity and complexity apparent in even the smallest and most remote settlements in the Maritimes. This of course is a reflection of the rich historical legacy of Acadians, English, French and Loyalists, not to mention the Scottish and the Irish. In these seaside provinces, man and nature have combined to produce infinitely variable cultural and physical landscapes; all of which affect the life and economy of the towns and villages that we have visited.

We have found the stagnating Millvilles and Georgetowns, the booming tourist attractions like Peggy's Cove, and the prosperous fishing villages such as Clark's Harbour. We have also discovered commuter dormitories and tourist towns in Mahone Bay and Shelburne, along with places like the Pubnicos where the traditional way of life has been altered little by the passage of time. Where agriculture is supreme in the Annapolis Valley or in Prince Edward Island, rural service centres like Berwick and Kensington grow and prosper. In more isolated locations, tradition and history still reign supreme, and the sea continues to dominate local life. Elsewhere, especially near to cities or along busy highways, new economic functions are replacing the old. Everywhere our senses have been bombarded by variety, diversity, complexity and change. Here, as in Ontario and Quebec, the smallest settlements characterize all that makes our nation great. Enterprise, hospitality, honesty, and a sense of place -- we find them everywhere, but nowhere more convincingly than in the towns, the villages and the hamlets. They comprise the heart of our country, preserving the past and pointing the way to the future.

We drive around again and decide that Port Elgin is not without charm. The river and harbour are picturesque, with a delightful old bridge spanning the water and a lovely vista along the main street. Maybe we should not dismiss its economic potential so quickly.

CHAPTER TEN

The Past And The Future: Continuing Trends And New Horizons For Our Towns And Villages

From the "burnt-out academics" refinishing furniture in Mahone Bay, to the retirees in Lions Head, to the busy entrepreneurs of Annapolis Royal, we have met some of the new residents of our "dying villages". We have discovered that there is a place for the former Torontonian or Halagonian among the cows and silos of the countryside. There is opportunity for the entrepreneur from Montreal to start a business in La Belle, and there is a warm welcome in Bayfield for the retired executive from London. Along the roads between the villages we have encountered workers who commute to local warehouses, enormous factory farms operated by major corporations and elegant country retreats complete with pools and riding stables. Elsewhere we have found independent businessmen selling crafts and antiques to tourists, proprietors of truck stops serving modern diesel stagecoaches, and abandoned farmsteads sagging under the weight of age and neglect. The variety of people and structures has been enormous, but overall the trends have been clear.

We need no longer doubt that people are returning to the country. They have flocked to commuter dormitories like Belfountain or Bath, and they have swelled the populations of rejuvenated rural service centres such as Berwick and Kensington. Each of these communities has enjoyed indigenous population growth, but in many centres, retirees from the countryside or fugitives from the city have added to the total. For those who love the land and wish for a different lifestyle, our villages and countryside have offered haven as well as opportunity. But along with opportunity we have discovered risks: the risk of too much development; that of too few services for the elderly; the possible destruction of the physical environment. The very people who have rediscovered the heart of the country now must strive to retain those assets which attracted them in the first place. Sometimes they even attempt to exclude all who follow in their footsteps and work to keep the places to themselves. The balance between growth and change, preservation and exclusivity, or gentle stagnation and slow evolution is difficult to achieve. Before we end our journey, let us examine this delicate balance and make some prognostications for the future.

Now that we have travelled through eastern Canada, it is time to reflect and consider all that we have seen. What can we say about the future of the countryside, the impact of factory farming, the demise of the rural service centre and the future of the communities which cater primarily to retirement and tourism? How have history, location, natural endowment and the activities of entrepreneurs affected our rural settlements? And what have we learned from our observations? Can we detect any trends that we would like to arrest or reinforce? Are there any opportunities for planning to guide the future development of our communities? Has Canada Post made a grievous error in closing so many village post offices?

It is now clear that the picture in the real world is not nearly as simple as those who have spoken of "dying villages" would have us believe. Neither is it all rosy, for we have found some ghost towns and others greatly diminished from their peaks of prosperity. Some are indeed retirement communities, others have become major resorts or tourist attractions, while others have changed little in a hundred years. All the settlements which we have investigated contain much to remind us of their history, and many display portents for the future. It is clear that diversity, complexity and change are the primary characteristics of many communities and that no simple generalizations suffice to describe them all. And yet, there are some common characteristics, some general traits, some frequent processes at work. We will explore the most significant of these and attempt to combine them into a few recommendations. These will have implications for anyone who desires to live in rural Canada, for those who are already there, for planners, for politicians and for all who love our towns and villages.

When we look back over our travels, we are able to categorize the communities where we stopped in several ways. Some have depended primarily on their local physical environment and its resources for their early prosperity, and today they exploit this same environment to attract tourists. Shelburne, Annapolis Royal, Bayfield, Benmiller and Elora fall into this category. In each of these places, entrepreneurs have exploited their historic buildings to complement local physical attractions. Others which began as rural service centres have declined with the advent of motor transport, but are now important as residential settlements for retirees or for persons not tied to the city. Brussels, St. Jacobs, Kensington and Berwick are but a few from this group. Others are isolated and have changed little in form or function over the years. Little Rapids, Kearney, Duparquet and Georgetown are good examples. A few such as Niagara-on-the-Lake, Cavendish and Peggy's Cove are on the verge of being spoiled by their success. In these communities, opposition to further economic development is increasing, but such settlements are still in the minority. Some others such as Port Elgin, New Brunswick, and Alton stand at the crossroads, at the threshold of popularity and prosperity, waiting for the right business to come along and invest its money.

How can we generalize from all our impressions, from our brief visits to so many places, from the few statistics that have been available? Certainly it is not easy, but just the experience of seeing each community, of reviewing its history and of speaking to its people should point the way to a few plausible conclusions. The overwhelming first impression is that each place is unique, but this is really not so. We can distinguish between those places with origins as service centres, resource communities, ports or railway towns. Today evidence of their origins endures in every settlement, and in most, these origins have affected subsequent development.

Many of the former resource-based towns remain relatively far from major centres of population. They now attract development only if they are near rapid routes to major cities or if they have outstanding physical attractions. People have moved to rural service centres which have become commuter dormitories if they are accessible to employment, or have acquired outsized functions in the form of renovated mills or hotels. Settlements with historic forts or harbours have often been restored by new arrivals seeking profits, or by local historical associations with government help. Many have become tourist attractions. In other communities, expansive old homes, tree-lined streets and a rustic atmosphere have lured individuals who wish to retire in tranquillity. Elsewhere, those places with a ski hill, conservation authority, provincial park or sandy beach have become homes to retirees or are primarily residential neighbourhoods within the dispersed cities discussed in Chapter Four. In addition to becoming homes to migrants from other areas, some also provide amenities and attractions for day visitors.

Our explorations have given us some personal insights into the future of our towns and countryside, but we must now augment subjective impressions with objective facts. By examining a few statistics pertaining to the places that we have visited, we may make some rough conclusions about general trends in small towns. For this book we compiled data on population changes between 1971 and 1981 for 37 carefully selected settlements in the provinces which we visited. We also tabulated the number of businesses in 1971 and 1986 for these same places. Most of these communities, along with a few others have been described and discussed in the pages above. These visits have given us a "feel" for their character and function; something that is very important to the intelligent interpretation of statistics. Our data provide only generalized information on trends, but they are indicative of overall change in a representative group of communities across central and eastern Canada.

When we examine population trends between 1971 and 1981 for all places combined, the data support our impression that growth has occurred in many. The average change for all places was an increase of 104 while the largest loss was 286. In contrast, the biggest gain in any settlement was 871. Of all the communities considered, 15 lost population between 1971 and 1981, while 22 gained. The story of business change is somewhat different, partly because it is possible to obtain more recent statistics on businesses. For them we tabulated information from Business Directories for 1971 and 1986, and then checked our results by counting all the enterprises in the settlements that we visited. We saw numerous new enterprises in the most unlikely places, and these observations were clearly reflected by the data. Our findings were encouraging.

The largest business gain in any settlement between 1971 and 1986 was an increase of 108, whereas the greatest loss was a decrease of only nine in the same period. The average change in the number of businesses was an addition of 24. This is quite respectable for a group of settlements whose mean population in 1981 was 1408, and whose size ranged from 309 to 3901 in that year. The business prospect looks even brighter when we compare gainers with losers. Between 1971 and 1986, only one of our settlements lost businesses. New entrepreneurs from other locations have augmented the local economy in numerous small towns and villages. It is obvious that opportunities in many of these places have been recognized and exploited.

The only community to lose businesses was Brussels, a diminished service centre in the heart of the rich farm country of western Ontario. Of course, Wroxeter lost as well, but it was one of the few settlements that we visited which was not part of the statistical sample. Even when it is included, the data hardly point to a group of dying villages. Indeed, if we remember the residential attractions of both Wroxeter and Brussels, even they seem to have a reasonable chance for some future growth. We discovered new homes and small apartment buildings in both these "declining settlements". And in both, despite the business losses, the population has increased.

Our observations and the data that we have collected indicate that most of the towns, villages and hamlets surveyed do indeed have some potential for modest population growth. Their quiet, shady streets, small town ambience and access to nearby employment opportunities will continue to attract people from the city as well as from the surrounding countryside. Most have even greater possibilities for additional economic development, especially if discovered by an enterprising businessman willing to take a few risks. Even though the business statistics are encouraging, we cannot extrapolate these findings to all small towns. We must not forget those such as Peepabun or Cumnock where all traces of earlier settlement have long since vanished. There is little to suggest that settlements that have existed only in name for many years will ever grow again.

Of necessity, the majority of the communities which we visited were those that retain vestiges of their former functions, and a few buildings which have attracted residents or entrepreneurs. Our maps are covered with the names of former rural service centres that have vanished entirely, and there is little prospect that they will ever reappear. On the other hand, there are also numerous clusters of homes, businesses and people which are never recognized separately, simply because they are too small, or are contained within a larger statistical unit. Most of the information on "rural non-farm" population or about the people living in "unincorporated settlements over 25" is buried in census tabulations that are not easily accessible. Yet when we drive along country roads or visit the tiniest hamlets we see the new residents, their homes and their businesses. To truly appreciate the significance of what is happening beyond the city it is necessary to augment statistics with exploration and curiosity. Some of the smallest communities have the potential to grow and change, just as many that we visited have done in the last 20 years. Statistics seldom tell the whole story, and statistics can sometimes be misleading.

Having perused the data and visited the actual settlements to which they refer, we are now in a position to answer more of the questions posed in the Introduction. The first of these was the matter of who lives in our towns and villages today, and what do these people do? As we have seen, there is no simple answer. In the midst of the rich agricultural areas of southern Ontario or the Eastern Townships of Quebec, the answer is generally straightforward. Most of those in Blyth, Brussels or St. Germain-de-Grantham are local businessmen, or employees and their families. The difference between what we find today and the situation a hundred years ago is that not everyone in business continues to depend on the surrounding rural hinterland. Now some operate small manufacturing or wholesale enterprises which serve large areas by truck. If they have established a restaurant, hotel or clothing outlet in the form of an outsized function, a few may cater to day visitors from far afield. Others are retired farmers from nearby, while some are those "footloose" individuals who travel a wide territory, have their own local enterprise, or drive to work in a shop or factory a few kilometers away. These are the new inhabitants of the dispersed city. Communities such as these will probably continue to increase slowly in population and business activity as long as the car and the computer continue to be widely accessible at a reasonable price.

At the other end of the spectrum we find the Ville Maries, the Bayfields, the La Belles and the Shelburnes. These communities were once dependent primarily on the natural resources of the sea, the lake, the forests, the land, or the bedrock, but have found new economic stimuli from the very same sources. Their harbours, their hills, their rugged scenery and their accessible locations have enabled them to become amenity communities where tourism and retirement are now important. They continue to function as local service centres, but increasingly they provide accommodation for persons wishing to live out their days in a pleasant small-town environment. Often they have attracted growing numbers of tourists to swim, ski, explore or to shop at their sophisticated stores. If the local architecture is extraordinary, they may also have become tourist attractions in their own right. Depending on the enterprise of local businessmen, and on the proportion of tourist-oriented stores, they may now rely more on visitors than on inhabitants or local farmers for revenue.

Duparquet, Millville, Loring and a number of isolated former fishing villages probably have little prospect for additional growth and change simply because their original raison d'être has either disappeared or diminished. When the mine closes in a single industry resource town like Duparquet, the outlook is bleak, especially if it is situated in an area of little fertility. Remote fishing villages are no doubt scenic, but so are many that are more accessible, and they are the ones that benefit from tourism. Former lumber towns have declined, and if they lack historic architecture, easy access or outstanding scenery, they too will languish. In such places, there is little to attract the entrepreneur, the tourist or the retiree.

Now we can turn to that controversial question of the local post office. In almost every settlement in the late 1800s, the post office was combined with the general store and became a major magnet for people from miles around. Even after prohibition killed the pubs and the motor car enabled farmers to bypass their local service centre for the city, the general store/post office endured. If one general store in a community was to survive, it was inevitably the one that everyone visited daily or weekly to collect mail. It continued to be a meeting place, a social centre, a supplier of food and hardware just because people came to it with regularity. Its presence often contributed to the viability of other businesses which would be visited on one stop trips to "main street" for mail and shopping.

We need look no farther than the daily newspaper to appreciate the importance of village post offices even today. Loud and vigorous protests have greeted the call for their closure, and with good reason. In many of the smallest communities, those whose economic viability is the most precarious, the demise of the post office will be a disaster. With it gone, the general stores will lose business as will all other local enterprises. Without a reason to come regularly to the main street, shoppers will seek their necessities at larger places where they can find more variety and lower prices. A downward spiral will set in and we may see a repeat of the events after 1911 when rural mail delivery was introduced into Ontario. In that period, local service centres "dropped like flies in DDT", some never again to recover their former status; others to disappear entirely. The same could occur again today if we are not careful. Canada Post would be well advised to consider the totality of the social and economic implications of closing village post offices, rather than worrying only about the "efficiency" of their operation. Far more is at stake than profits or losses for Canada Post in the post office closing controversy.

The future is gloomy for the very smallest, isolated settlements that have lost their original economic function and have nothing with which to replace it. The closing of the post office will no doubt seal the fate of many. On the other hand, the value of fixed capital in homes or business blocks will sustain some villages as small residential communities. The settlements near to major employment will no doubt continue to attract commuters who wish to leave the city, just as country roads will continue to sprout their crops of bungalows and split-levels inhabited by non-farmers. This will be especially prevalent in areas of rolling moraine and woodlots where farming was never particularly prosperous. Vast areas in southern Ontario have already become almost saturated with these new country residents.

Farther from the city, diminished rural service centres will no doubt continue to feel the effects of farm consolidation, agribusiness and rural depopulation. But with the recent interest of many in small town living, the increasing diversification of industry in the countryside and the ageing of the population, many centres will continue to grow and prosper. Even though our best agricultural lands require fewer farmers than before, it is in these same areas where non-farm building is discouraged. Fortunately, there is plenty of room in our established communities to accommodate retirees or families desiring a small-town environment. Some of our readers may spend their final years in just such locations. The opportunity is there for those who wish to pursue it.

It is difficult to prognosticate for the future, especially if we are concerned with individual settlements, but a few generalizations are in order. First there is the solidly based matter of retirement in small towns with scenic amenities, accessible locations, or attractive architecture. Our research, and that of many others, has shown that this is already important to the growth of many places. Statistics Canada has provided data to reinforce this view. There are now over a million Canadians older than 75, and they are living longer than before. Current trends suggest that the number of Canadians over 65 will triple in the next 45 years. In settlement after settlement, the percentage of the population over 65 has increased, to the point where many small towns can classify a third or more of their citizens as seniors. Migration data from recent studies indicate increasing flows of elderly from major cities to retire in resort towns where they formerly had a cottage. This is already a major component of population growth in settlements as diverse as Kensington, Lion's Head, Bayfield, Brussels, Berwick and Elora. There seems to be no doubt that such trends will continue, especially as the proportion of the population over 60 increases and "lifestyle" considerations remain important to those choosing a retirement location.

Other contemporary studies indicate an expanding number and variety of employment opportunities in small towns or just in the "middle of nowhere". In the north, suppliers, outfitters, general stores, truck stops and craft shops proliferate in scenic locations. Farther south, feed and seed processing, fertilizer and pesticide dealers serve the farmer along with agribusiness consultants and wholesalers. Elsewhere, custom woodworkers, electrical and electronics fabricators or clothing and crafts manufacturers are locating in the countryside and in some of the smallest places. They provide a new variety of opportunities for anyone wishing to live in the country or in a small town and drive to work on tranquil, scenic roads. The new inhabitants of the dispersed city will continue to grow in number and importance until gasoline prices become prohibitive. Experience in countries with far higher energy prices than ours suggests that this will not occur for a long time to come.

Of course there are some problems lurking along with the new opportunities in our towns and villages. Some will be confronted with the decision of whether to continue to grow and therefore to install (at great cost), piped water and sewage treatment plants. Others will find that their local doctor cannot cope with an ageing population, and that the elderly have become isolated by the lack of public transport and mail delivery. Hospitals may become overextended when called on to care for those who might be better off in their own homes, but lack the necessary support services. The demand for retirement homes, nursing homes, medical care, services and transportation in our smaller settlements will create problems for some and economic opportunities for others.

Finally, we must consider the matter of our past and our future. A hundred years ago, Canada was a county of farms and forests, towns and villages. Today it is primarily an urban society, with farming employing only a fraction of its former numbers. And yet the countryside is not dead, and neither is the small town. With increasing affluence and mobility, many can indulge their desire to live in a woodlot or in a tiny village. These people have lovingly restored former schoolhouses, mills, blacksmith shops and farmhouses. Others have taken up residence in what was formerly a business on the main street of a rural service centre, while others have renovated the Victorian mansion that was so long inhabited by the elderly widow. Some have built new homes within the towns and villages or in the trees along the concession roads. Large-scale retirement communities have been developed from scratch beside a river or lake, complete with golf courses and fishing docks. In the hills, chalets and condominiums have been constructed as first or second homes. We have rediscovered the country, we have gained a new appreciation of the heritage of our past -- and in increasing numbers we have taken advantage of the opportunity to return to a slower, more rural way of life.

But the dangers to which we alluded above must not be overlooked. Many a quiet, rustic hamlet has been obliterated entirely by the flood of commuters from a nearby metropolis or has been overrun by industrial growth. Varennes is an example of the latter while Verchères could eventually exemplify the former. In the opinion of many,

Niagara-on-the-Lake is already too crowded. They say that pressures of commercial development have ruined it for summer visitors and local inhabitants alike. Much the same may be suggested about Peggy's Cove, while Bayfield, Elora and Annapolis Royal must guard against a similar fate. Around the fringes of Toronto, Halifax, Montreal, Charlottetown and Fredericton, some country roads are almost solidly lined with homes of rural non-farmers. In addition to creating traffic congestion and obliterating rural panoramas, these developments may compete for rich agricultural land or prevent the extraction of valuable aggregate resources. Even in the north we find strips of commercial buildings which despoil that natural environment which gave them birth.

In each of the situations described above we find conflict: quiet residential communities versus tourism and commercial growth; agriculture competing with the desire for rural residences; preservation of the natural environment against the ambition to exploit it for profit. One of the major conflicts is the desire of those who have found their ideal residential retreat to keep others out. The addition of more people will often destroy the very charm that made a village desirable in the first place, but who is to say that growth must stop soon after the place has been "discovered"?

Ironically, it is often the newcomers who wish to preserve historic architecture and the small-town atmosphere, while the "old timers" encourage population growth and economic development. Such conflicts are becoming more common and increasingly difficult to resolve. Of course, they will ultimately be resolved, but not without dissent and confrontation. In each conflict situation we find the seeds of successful resolution along with the potential for lasting harm to the human or physical environment. Our task for the future is to strike an appropriate balance between competing aspirations for the future of our towns, villages and countryside. Such a balance will be difficult to attain, but it must occur if the heart of the country is to remain attractive to those who desire to leave the city and rediscover rural delights.

This is not to say that urbanization and economic growth in the cites have ceased, because most continue to grow and thrive. But what we have seen in the towns and countryside may be a glimpse of the future. As the population ages, more and more of us will feel the desire to rediscover our roots and our heritage. And we can be sure that the entrepreneurs will assist by renovating buildings, constructing subdivisions and opening new enterprises which cater to our wishes. More than a desire to leave the city, it is the aspiration to discover the countryside and to live in a tranquil and sometimes less expensive setting that encourages so many to seek a small-town environment. The sentiment that "small is beautiful", the conservation ethic, and a renewed appreciation of beauty and quality of life are at work among a growing proportion of our citizens. We will never completely recreate the settlement fabric of the 1890s, but it seems safe to say that a rural and small town renaissance is likely to continue for the foreseeable future. The question is, will our children see the future in the same way, or will they leave the towns and villages for the city as did their ancestors before them?

If we look to the past for answers, we might conclude that our children will tire of rural and small town life and move as quickly as possible to seek excitement and enjoyment among the bright lights of the city. On the other hand, they may be somewhat less materialistic and more idealistic than were their parents at the same age. Maybe the concern for survival, the interest in the environment, the questioning of capitalist values and aspirations will take them in a different direction. It is just possible that they too will place quality of life ahead of materialistic gains, and will seek solace and contentment, or "self fulfillment" in the towns, villages and wilderness of this great land. Others may emulate their predecessors of the sixties who moved to farms or rural communes to escape from threats of war, or who left the mainstream of a society which they deplored. If the actions of some are any indication, this may occur, but trends, fads and ideals change with the times and with economic circumstances. We are reasonably certain that an increasing number of retirees and "footloose" workers are opting for the towns and villages in the heart of the country, but we will have to wait and see whether they have initiated a trend which will be followed by the young. The future of our towns and villages seems bright, but only time will tell!

References

BEAUMONT, RALPH, 1973. *Cataract and the Forks of the Credit: Pictorial History*, Cheltenham: The Boston Mills Press.

BEAUMONT, 1977. *Alton: A Pictorial History*, Cheltenham: The Boston Mills Press.

BLACKBURN, D.J. AND F.A. DAHMS, 1981. Eastern rural communities, *The Agrologist*, Vol. 10 pp. 8-10.

BROWN, R., 1979. *Ghost Towns of Ontario*, Langley, B.C.: Stagecoach Publishing.

BROWN, 1984. *Ghost Towns of Ontario*, Vol. 2, Toronto: Cannonbooks.

BROWN, 1984. *Backroads of Ontario*, Edmonton: Hurtig Publishing.

CARTER, F.E., 1984. *Place Names of Ontario*, London: Phelps Publishing Co.

CHAPMAN.L.J. and D.F. PUTNAM, 1966. *The Physiography of Southern Ontario*, 2nd ed. Toronto: Ontario Research Foundation.

CLARK, A.H., 1959. *Three Centuries on the Island: A Historical Geography of Settlement and Agriculture in Prince Edward Island Canada*, Toronto: University of Toronto Press.

CLARK, 1969. *Acadia: The Geography of Early Nova Scotia to 1760*, Madison: University of Wisconsin Press.

DAHMS, F.A., 1975. Some quantitative approaches to the study of central places in the Guelph area: 1851-1970, *Urban History Review*, No. 2-75 pp. 9-30.

DAHMS, 1976. Synthesis of major issues discussed at Guelph area Habitat seminar, in *Human Settlements Issues in Ontario*, Vol. 2, Toronto: Ontario Secretariat for Habitat, Ministry of the Environment, pp. 40-46.

DAHMS, 1977. How Ontario's Guelph district developed, *Canadian Geographical Journal*, Vol. 94 pp. 48-55.

DAHMS, 1977. Declining villages, *Second Annual Agricultural History of Ontario Proceedings*, Guelph: University of Guelph School of Part-Time studies and Continuing Education, pp. 50-65.

DAHMS, 1978. *Historical Background, Population Change and Agriculture, Wellington County, 1840-1977*, Guelph: University of Guelph Centre for Resources Development Publication No. 89; Dept. of Geography Studies in Rural Adjustment, No. 7, 75 pp. [2nd Printing, revised, 1984].

DAHMS, 1980. The changing functions of villages and hamlets in Wellington County, 1881-1971, *Urban History Review*, Vol. 8 pp. 3-19.

DAHMS, 1980. The evolving spatial organization of settlements in the countryside - an Ontario example, *Tijdschrift voor Econ. en Soc. Geografie*, Vol. 71 pp. 295-306.

DAHMS, 1980. Small town and village Ontario, *Ontario Geography*, Vol. 7/8 pp. 19-32.

DAHMS, 1980. The evolution of settlement systems: a Canadian example, 1851-1970, *Journal of Urban History*, Vol. 7 pp. 169-204.

DAHMS, 1981. *Changing Functions of Settlements in Wellington County, 1961-1977*, Guelph: University of Guelph Centre for Resources Development Report 106, 73 pp.

DAHMS, 1982. The role of the country town in Ontario, yesterday and today: the case of Wellington and Huron Counties, in A.A. Brookes (ed.) *The Country Town in Rural Ontario's Past*, Guelph: University of Guelph School of Part-Time Studies and Continuing Education, pp. 58-78.

DAHMS, 1982. Viable agriculture = a viable rural community?, in *Proceedings: Approaches to Rural Development*, Guelph: University of Guelph School of Part-Time Studies and Continuing Education, pp. 234-238.

DAHMS, 1982. *The Changing Functions of Rural Settlements in Huron and Southern Bruce Counties: Historical Background and Major Trends, 1951-1981*, Guelph: University of Guelph School of Rural Planning and Development Publication No.110, 66 pp.

DAHMS, 1983. *The Changing Functions of Settlements in Bruce County: Historical Background and Major Trends 1951-1981*, Guelph: University of Guelph School of Rural Planning and Development Report No. 116, 54 pp.

DAHMS, 1984. The process of urbanization in the countryside: a study of Bruce and Huron Counties, Ontario 1891-1981, *Urban History Review*, Vol. 12 pp. 1-18.

DAHMS, 1984. Demetropolitanization or the urbanization of the countryside? - the changing functions of small rural settlements in Ontario, *Ontario Geography*, Vol. 24 pp. 35-61.

DAHMS, 1984. Wroxeter, Ontario: the anatomy of a 'dying' village, *Small Town*, Vol. 14 pp. 17-23.

DAHMS, 1984. Small towns, in *Ontario at 2000*, Montreal: CBC Publications, pp. 38-39.

DAHMS, 1985. Siting Group Homes: The view from a Member of the Plan Advisory Committee, *Canadian Institute of Planners Forum*, No. 2 pp. 6-7.

DAHMS, 1985. Ontario's rural communities: changing - not dying, in A.M. Fuller (ed.) *Farming and the Farm Community in Ontario: An Introduction*, Toronto: Foundation for Rural Living, pp. 329-350.

DAHMS, 1986. Residential and commercial renaissance: another look at small town Ontario, *Small Town*, Vol. 17 pp. 10-15.

DAHMS, 1986. Diversity, complexity and change: characteristics of some Ontario towns and villages, *The Canadian Geographer*, Vol. 30 pp. 158-166.

DAHMS, 1987. Regional urban history: a statistical and cartographic survey of Huron and southern Bruce counties, 1864-1981, *Urban History Review*, Vol. 3 pp. 254-268.

DAHMS, 1987. *Population Migration and the Elderly: Ontario 1971-1981*, Guelph: Department of Geography University of Guelph Occasional Papers in Geography No. 9, 65 pp.

DAHMS and J.A. FORBES, 1971. Central places in the Golden Triangle: The Guelph System 1970, in A.G. McLellan (ed.) *The Waterloo County Area: Selected Geographical Essays,* Waterloo: University of Waterloo, pp. 113-127.

DAHMS and J. A. FORBES, 1976. A comparison of three central place systems: Guelph, Barrie and Owen Sound, *The Canadian Geographer,* Vol. 20 pp. 439-441.

DAHMS and CAROL HOOVER, 1979. The evolution of settlement functions in the southeastern Parry Sound district: 1871-1976, *The Canadian Geographer,* Vol. 23 pp. 353-360.

DAVIDSON, G., 1984. Current issues in rural planning policy, in M. Bunce and M. Troughton (eds.) *The Pressures of Change in Rural Canada,* Downsview: York Monographs in Geography, No. 14. pp. 328-348.

DUN AND BRADSTREET, 1861-1981. *Reference Books,* Toronto: Dun and Bradstreet of Canada Ltd.

ENCYCLOPEDIA OF ONTARIO, 1976. Vol. 1. *Historic Sites of Ontario,* Belleville: Mika Publishing.

ENCYCLOPEDIA OF ONTARIO, 1977. Vol. 2. *Places in Ontario,* Belleville: Mika Publishing.

FIELD, N.C., 1982. Migration through the rural-urban hierarchy: Canadian patterns. Unpublished paper. University of Toronto Department of Geography.

FILBY, J., 1974. *Credit Valley Railway: The Third Giant,* Cheltenham: The Boston Mills Press.

FISHER, J.S. and R.L. MITCHELSON, 1981. Extended and internal commuting in the transformation of the intermetropolitan periphery, *Economic Geography,* Vol. 57 pp. 189-207.

FOX, W.S., 1973. *The Bruce Beckons,* Toronto: University of Toronto Press.

FRIEDMANN, J., 1978. The urban field as human habitat, in L.S. Bourne and J.W. Simmons (eds.) *Systems of Cities,* New York: Oxford University Press, pp. 42-52.

FRIEDMANN, J. and J. MILLER, 1965. The urban field. *Journal of the American Institute of Planners,* Vol. 31 pp. 312-320.

HART, J.F., 1975. *The Look of the Land,* Englewood Cliffs: Prentice Hall.

HART, J.F., N.E. SALISBURY and E.G. SMITH, Jr., 1968. The dying village and some notions about urban growth. *Economic Geography,* Vol. 144 pp. 343-49.

HEAT, W.L.M., 1982. *Blue Highways: A Journey into America,* Boston: Little Brown & Co.

HODGE, G.D., 1974. The city in the periphery, in L.S. Bourne, R.D. MacKinnon, J.Siegel and J.W. Simmons (eds.) *Urban Futures for Central Canada,* Toronto: University of Toronto Press, pp. 281-301.

HODGE, G.D. and M.A. QADEER, 1983. *Towns and Villages in Canada: The Importance of Being Unimportant,* Toronto: Butterworths.

HOOVER. C.L., 1977. A Study of Rural Settlements of South-East Parry Sound District 1871-1976. Unpublished B.A. Thesis, Dept. of Geography, University of Guelph.

JOSEPH, A.E., P.D. KEDDIE and B. SMIT, 1988. Unravelling the population turnaround in rural Canada, *The Canadian Geographer*, in press.

KENNEDY, C.C. 1970. *The Upper Ottawa Valley*, Pembroke: Renfrew County Council.

KONTULY, T. and R. VOGELSANG, 1988. Explanations for the intensification of counterurbanization in the Federal Republic of Germany, *The Professional Geographer*, Vol. 40 pp. 42-54.

LAW, C. and A. WARNES, 1981. Retirement migration, *Town and Country Planning*, Vol. 50 pp. 44-46.

LAW, C. and A. WARNES, 1982. The destination decision in retirement migration, in A.M. Warnes (ed.) *Geographical Perspectives on the Elderly*, New York: John Wiley, pp. 53-81.

LEGGET, R.F., 1975. *Ottawa Waterway: Gateway to a Continent*, Toronto: University of Toronto Press.

LONGINO, C.F. Jr., 1982. American retirement communities and residential relocation, in A. M. Warnes (ed.) *Geographical Perspectives on the Elderly*, New York: John Wiley, pp. 234-262.

McCANN, L.D. (ed.) 1982. *A Geography of Canada: Heartland and Hinterland*, Scarborough: Prentice-Hall.

McMILLAN, C.J., 1974. *Early History of the Township of Erin*, Cheltenham: The Boston Mills Press.

MIKA, N. and H. MIKA, 1972. *Railways of Canada: A Pictorial History*, Toronto: McGraw-Hill Ryerson.

PUTNAM, D.F. (ed.) 1965. *Canadian Regions: A Geography of Canada*, Toronto: J.M. Dent.

ROBINSON, J.L., 1983. *Concepts and Themes in the Regional Geography of Canada*, Vancouver: Talonbooks.

RUSSWURM, L.H. and C.R. BRYANT, 1982. *The City's Countryside: Land and its Management in the Rural-Urban Fringe*, London: Longmans.

RUSSWURM, L.H. and C.R. BRYANT, 1984. Changing population distribution and rural-urban relationships in Canadian urban fields, 1941-1976, in M.F. Bunce and M.J. Troughton (eds.) *The Pressures of Change in Rural Canada*, Downsview: York-Atkinson Geographical Monograph No. 14.

SCOTT, J., 1966. *The Settlement of Huron County*, Toronto: Ryerson.

SCHULL, J., 1978. *Ontario Since 1867*, Toronto: McClelland and Stewart.

SPELT, J., 1983. *Urban Development in South Central Ontario*, New Edition, Ottawa: Carleton University Press.

STATISTICS CANADA, 1981. *Census of Population.*

STATISTICS CANADA, 1984. Special Tabulation: Population 15 years and over in the employed labour force by place of work (145) for the census divisions of Bruce, Huron, Waterloo and Wellington, 1981 census.

STATISTICS CANADA, 1985. Special tabulation: migration by place of residence in 1976 (164) for the census divisions of Bruce, Huron, Waterloo and Wellington by census subdivision,1981 census.

STATISTICS CANADA, 1986. *Population,* Various early releases.

STOKES, P.J., 1971. *Old Niagara on the Lake,* Toronto: University of Toronto Press.

TAAFFE, E.J., H.L. GAUTHIER and T. A. MARAFFA, 1980. Extended commuting and the intermetropolitan periphery, *Annals Assoc. of American Geographers,* Vol.70 pp. 313-329.

TROUGHTON M., 1985. Stresses on land in southwestern Ontario. *Ontario Geography,* Vol. 26 pp. 25-36.

WARKENTIN, J.(ed.) 1968. *Canada: A Geographical Interpretation,* Toronto: Methuen.

WOOD, J.D.(ed.) 1975. *Perspectives on Landscape and Settlement in Ninteenth Century Ontario,* Toronto: McClelland and Stewart, Carleton Library No. 91.

** Many other detailed references to specific places may be found in the publications by the author listed above.

Index